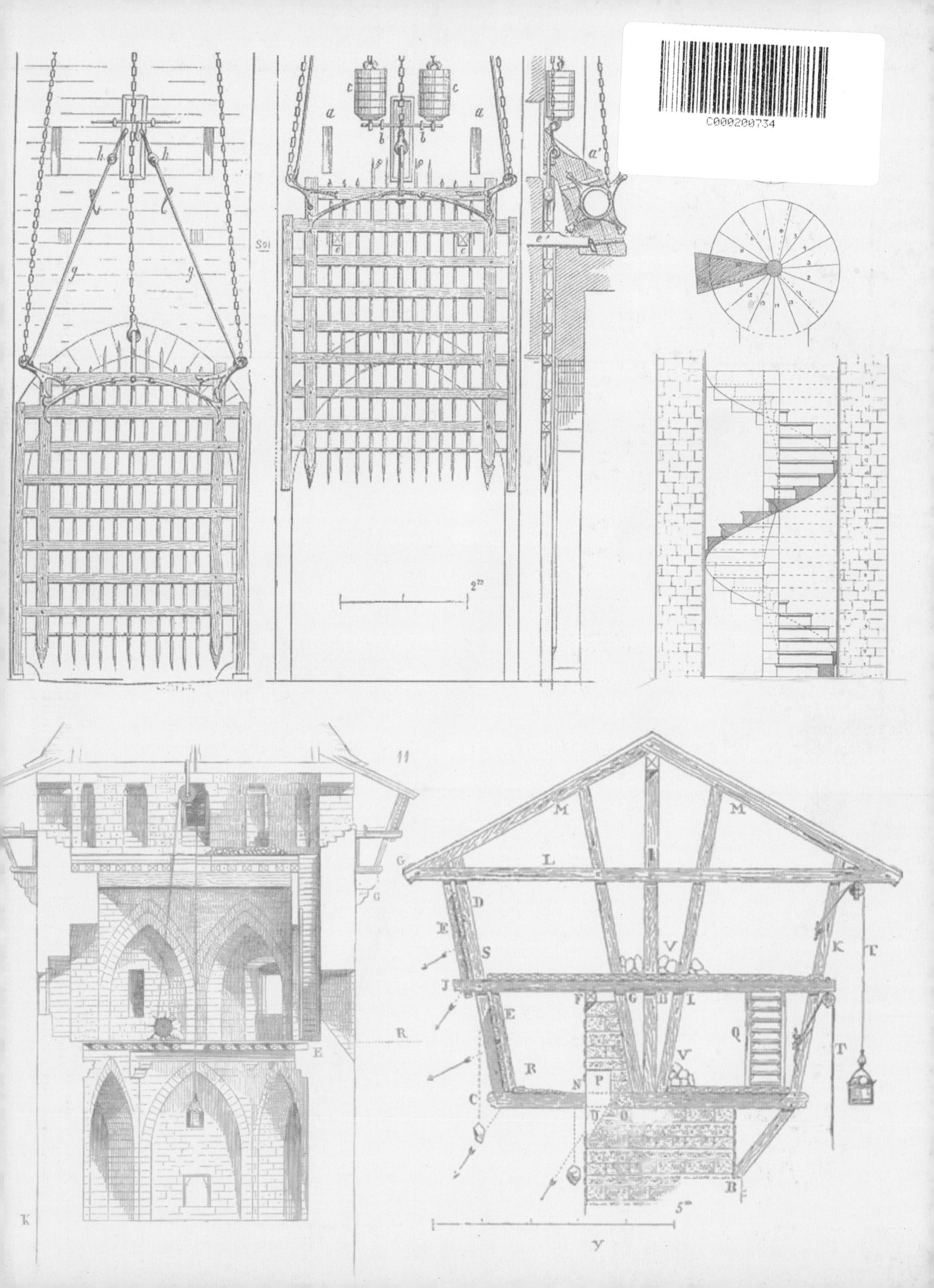

Soi
2m
11
M
M
L
G
D
E
S
V
K
T
J
F
G
H
I
Q
R
E
R
P
C
T
B
5m
K
Y

THE MEDIEVAL CASTLE

FOR ALISON

Enormous thanks to Sarah Preston at Guédelon for welcoming me warmly to the site early in the first rather chilly days of the 2017 building season, and for her untiring, always good-natured help with my myriad queries and picture requests. Huge thanks also to this book's peerless commissioning editor, Joanne Rippin.

THE MEDIEVAL CASTLE

DESIGN • CONSTRUCTION • DAILY LIFE

A FASCINATING BEHIND-THE-SCENES STUDY OF HOW THESE FORMIDABLE FORTRESSES WERE BUILT, MAINTAINED AND LIVED IN

CHARLES PHILLIPS

Haynes®

guédelon

CONTENTS

FOREWORD

In 1997, on the site of an old stone quarry, surrounded by trees and lakes, the first stones of Guédelon Castle were cut, dressed and laid. Twenty years later, what had once been an ambitious idea is now an almost completed structure, with defensive walls, towers, a courtyard, a Great Hall and a chapel. I had the privilege of spending a season working with the team at Guédelon, helping with, and sometimes hindering, the building process while filming the BBC series *Secrets of the Castle*. I have been involved with several experimental archaeology projects in the past, but Guédelon beats them all, hands down. Carving a stone with a chisel, cutting a mortise-and-tenon joint in a piece of wood, or intricately shaping a piece of iron gives valuable insight into the physical aspects of the different crafts, but doing all those things at the same time, and combining the processes to make a wooden door, strengthened with iron strapwork, or stone guttering lined with lead, gives an insight into tangible history that other scholars can only dream of. The scale of this project has created a community that works together, and is reliant on each other. The masons need the stone cutters and the carpenters need the wood cutters; the basket weavers provide baskets for transporting rubble and mortar, the carters moving materials around the site also convey messages, and if, for any reason, the blacksmiths stopped work, the whole site would grind to a halt because the tools would be too blunt to work with. Guédelon is a magical place, which has changed my life. There isn't a day that goes by when I don't think about it, and every time I visit a medieval building I have a much greater understanding of how it was designed and constructed. I also have an extraordinary insight into the community that would have created it, and the lives that were lived in and around it. This is the story of Guédelon but also about its 13th-century context, applying the knowledge to castles that were built in the same era and how they were used. I hope this book brings you, the reader, the same joy and sense of awe that Guédelon brought to me, as it brings to life this truly wonderful place.

PETER GINN

INTRODUCTION

POWER AND MONEY

In the summer of 1295, the construction of Beaumaris Castle on Anglesey, North Wales, was proceeding apace. On site were around 375 quarriers, 450 stonemasons and 1,800 workmen. King Edward I of England wanted the castle built as soon as possible because the previous winter a Welsh revolt against the king, led by Madog ap Llywelyn, had resulted in the killing of the sheriff of Anglesey.

Building work was under the direction of celebrated Savoyard engineer-architect Master James of St Georges, who had previously designed the castles of Conwy, Harlech and Caernarfon. Edward was pouring resources into the project – the wages for the huge castle-building team amounted to £270 a week – but nevertheless Master James ran out of funds and in spring 1296 had to write in justification of the vast expenditure:

'In case you should wonder where so much money could go in a week, we would have you know that we have needed – and shall continue to need 400 masons, both cutters and layers, together with 2,000 less skilled workmen, 100 carts, 60 wagons and 30 boats bringing stone and sea coal; 200 quarrymen; 30 smiths; and carpenters for putting in the joists and floor boards and other necessary jobs. All this takes no account of the garrison ... nor of purchases of material.'

As this account shows, designing and building a medieval castle was an enormous undertaking that required teams of highly skilled specialist workers and an army of labourers, all under the direction of a master mason. Also needed, as evident above, was a huge investment of time and money.

THE ROLE OF THE MASTER MASON

A key figure on the building sites of medieval castles, the master mason liaised directly with the patron – the king or lord who was to own the building. In some cases, the patron, too, played a very active role in influencing and determining aspects of castle design – down to minutiae. King Richard I of England, for instance, was a hands-on patron of this sort and was heavily involved in the design and building of his castle, Château Gaillard in northern France. However, it was more typical for the master mason to be the one responsible for making the decisions about design and building while both taking instructions from the patron and advising him on what was possible. As happens for almost all building projects today, as part of this process, the master mason would produce drawings, or sometimes build a 3D wooden model to give the patron a clear idea of what was feasible.

▼ *Beaumaris Castle on Anglesey was built on a virgin site, enabling engineer-architect Master James of St Georges to lay out the concentric castle as he pleased. (Alamy)*

▲ *This 15th-century tapestry illustrates the castle community – and the feudal system – and its specific roles for each person, whether peasant, artisan or noble. (Getty)*

In addition to his role in the planning stages, the master mason was in charge of the building site itself – from managing the teams of labourers needed to shift earth and move heavy stones around the site using horses and carts to checking that tiles had been laid correctly. As a result, he usually only oversaw one building project at a time although occasionally he might be in charge of a number of sites simultaneously. We know, for instance, that Master James of St Georges was managing several concurrent castle projects in North Wales from the 1270s onwards.

The master mason needed vision, contacts, leadership skills and patience. As indicated in Master James's letter, at various times he might need to find and oversee a huge array of craftsmen from the beginning to the end of the project. Earthworkers were adept at digging ditches and earthwork fortifications; dykers were expert in diverting and managing water, digging moats and overseeing water defences; and quarrymen were skilled in identifying and digging out the best stone. As the site developed, carpenters to make winches for lifting and placing logs and scaffolding elements, and laying floors and roofs, hoardings and wooden walkways would be employed, together with blacksmiths skilled in designing hinges and strapwork and making and mending tools on site. The masons who shaped the stone provided by the quarrymen into the building blocks of the castle walls, and carved elaborate keystones for vaulted roofs and beautiful tracery windows were the highest ranking in the workforce, while tile makers were able to deliver perfectly fired, long-lasting tiles for roofs and hearths and floors. Various other skilled workers, adept at making lime, mortar, paints and whitewashes, and coloured cloth would also be involved. The master mason also needed to be able to balance the books and control the flow of money, paying suppliers and labourers the correct amount at the correct time.

Symbolic status

In total, the building of Beaumaris cost £15,000. This was a staggering sum for the times, but one that would have been worth paying since Beaumaris and the other Welsh castles of King Edward I – including Rhuddlan, Conwy and Caernarfon – were military tools, used to enforce the English king's power

▼ *The motte and bailey castle at Dinan in Brittany, depicted on the Bayeux Tapestry, being captured by the soldiers of Duke William of Normandy (later William I of England). (Mary Evans)*

◄ *The White Tower – the iconic 36 x 32m (118 x 105ft) stone keep at the Tower of London – was probably begun in 1078 to replace an earlier timber fortification and was completed by 1100. It is England's earliest stone keep and was originally built in Kentish ragstone, with details in imported Caen limestone.*

over North Wales. A formidable building with imposing fortifications, accommodation, its own water and food supplies (as far as possible) and a heavily armed garrison, the castle was a show of force – a means of both settling a region by deterring and stamping out local resistance and of imposing political authority.

Castle building came to the British Isles with the Norman invasion led by the army of William the Conqueror in 1066. (There were a few English castles raised in Essex and Herefordshire before 1066, but they were the work of Norman associates of King Edward the Confessor.) The incomers did away with the Anglo-Saxon aristocracy of Edward the Confessor and Harold Godwinson, the king defeated at the Battle of Hastings, and introduced a new Norman ruling class tied to William I and his descendants by the feudal system.

These Norman lords subsequently built and held castles as vassals of a superior lord or the king in return for loyalty and military service. The edifices that duly sprang up across England and Wales were symbols of Norman power intended to cow the Anglo-Saxon population. In addition, over time castles also became embodiments of social status and feudal power on a more personal level.

Kings, too, were enthusiastic castle builders, from William I to Edward I in Wales – and beyond. William himself founded enduring royal castles at Dover, Windsor and the Tower of London as he embarked on settling the newly conquered country, and Edward aimed to stamp out lawlessness in Wales by establishing a string of forbidding castles.

Another reason for royal castle building was that this was an era in which travel was slow and communication a major challenge. This meant that the most efficient way for the king to maintain and exercise his authority was to tour the realm, for which he needed a geographically distributed group of royal castles in which to stay. In addition, the castles functioned as symbols of his authority long after he had passed by on the rest of his tour – so the more splendid they were, the better.

STONES AND MORTAR: THE EVOLUTION OF THE CASTLE

The first Norman castles were usually timber-and-earthwork constructions made to a 'motte-and-bailey' design. The motte was a mound, surrounded by a palisade or defensive barrier and usually with a wooden tower at the top in which the lord or the castle defenders were based. Around the motte was the bailey, an enclosure defined by a ditch and fence, which contained living quarters and key buildings such as a communal hall, chapel, kitchens and stables. The motte was often a natural hill – and sometimes motte-and-bailey castles were built on and around existing hill forts – but at other times the motte was a man-made mound, laboriously dug out and raised by soldiers or labourers.

Over time, timber-and-earthwork castle structures were replaced with more enduring stone fortifications. Where stone walls were raised around the motte, historians call the result a 'shell keep' – as at Restormel Castle in Cornwall, Totnes Castle in Devon or at the Round Tower in Windsor Castle. This shell keep usually enclosed wooden or stone buildings within a courtyard.

In other places, the lord's residence was in a great tower or 'tower keep', as at the Tower of London. This was raised within a few decades of the Norman Conquest, in the 11th century, and through the following century tower keeps – rectangular, circular or polygonal – were added to many

▲ *The formidable 38m (125ft) tower keep at Rochester Castle, built in 1127–36, once held a besieging army at bay for two months – even after the rest of the castle was overrun.*

castles. Some lower-lying structures, for example at Norwich and Castle Rising in Norfolk, were called 'hall keeps' rather than tower keeps.

The shell, hall or tower keep was – like the motte behind its palisade in the earliest castles – the inhabitants' main refuge, the place to which the lord and his retainers, or the castle defenders in his absence, could draw back to when the castle was under attack. For example, the defenders of Rochester Castle in Kent famously retreated to its vast keep when the rest of the castle was overrun in 1215 and there endured a lengthy siege during which they were reduced to eating horsemeat. This castle stronghold was also known as the 'dungeon' (taken from Latin *dominium* and French *donjon*, 'lord' or 'master'); the English word dungeon acquired its modern meaning, that of a dark and damp prison for the lord's enemies, only at a later time.

The bailey was enclosed by thick defensive walls fortified with defensive towers that, when they projected from the wall, provided a formidable position from which bowmen and crossbowmen could fire on those attempting to undermine or climb the castle walls. From the towers, defenders could also fire on attackers who had gained access to the top of the walls. Battlements ran along the top of the wall to defend the alure or wall walk – a walkway that connected the towers and doubled as a shooting platform – and these battlements or crenellations consisted of raised sections called merlons and gaps or lower sections called crenels. Soldiers took shelter from offensive fire behind the merlons and dodged into the

GATEHOUSE

The most vulnerable part of the castle was probably the entrance. Towers were built on either side to defend it and in time these gave rise to the heavily fortified gatehouse that became a significant feature of castle design. In some castles, such as those as at Caerphilly and Beaumaris, this was the most secure part of the castle and contained some of its finest residential areas. Hand in hand with the gatehouses' evolution was the development of an array of powerful defensive features, including the portcullis, reinforced gates, machicolations and so on.

▼ *The impressive twin-towered gatehouse at Caerlaverock Castle, Scotland. This moated 13th-century structure is triangular – the only castle of this shape in Britain.*

crenels to fire at the enemy. Many castles had a dry ditch or moat around the outside of the defensive curtain wall to further deter approach.

Other defensive measures included the concentric castle design, as can be seen at Beaumaris and Caerphilly in Wales. Edward I and others had seen first hand the effectiveness of this arrangement, which was as old as Ancient Egypt, while on crusade in countries such as the Kingdom of Jerusalem, where religious brotherhoods such as the Knights Hospitaller had perfected the design.

In the later medieval period the military importance of the castle declined, but at one time – for example, during the '19 long winters' of the struggle between King Stephen and Empress Matilda (1135–54) – waging war effectively amounted to a launching a series of castle sieges. The battle between King John and a group of rebel lords in 1215, for instance, culminated in the two-month siege of Rochester Castle. However, by the Wars of the Roses (1455–87), if not before, the battlefield was where conflicts were decided and castles no longer needed to be impregnable.

From around this period, lords correspondingly increasingly put comfort above security in designing or adapting their homes. They still wanted gatehouses and battlements on their properties, however, because these features remained symbols of power. In order to get permission to satisfy these desires, gentlemen such as Sir Edward Dalyngrigge, builder of Bodiam Castle in East Sussex, had to apply to the king for a 'licence to crenellate'. The result was places such as Penshurst Place in Kent and Stokesay Castle in Shropshire, which are considered fortified manor houses rather than castles proper; they have fortifications, but only sufficient to deter passing opportunists and not a besieging army. Sir Edward Dalyngrigge's castle, Bodiam, too, was designed with prestigious appearance more than defensive security in mind – its large windows and poorly defended rear approach meant it would not have withstood an assault for long.

FEUDAL POWER STRUCTURES

Under the feudal system imported to England by the Normans in 1066, the king apportioned pieces of land called fiefs to noblemen, who in return promised loyalty to the monarch and to carry out certain duties. These included: performing a number of days' military service for the king each year; attending the royal court and providing advice if requested on legal matters and other elements of policy; and making a financial contribution to the king's expenses – for example, if he were building a royal castle.

The nobleman was the king's vassal: he called the king his lord. Noblemen then assigned parcels of land to sub-tenants, who swore loyalty and committed to perform duties in their turn. The feudal system thus became a hierarchy – from the king to the leading dukes and counts; from those leading men to the lesser nobles; all the way down to the holder of a small fief and the vassals who held sections of his smallholding.

It sounds simple enough, but relationships could in reality become complex because a vassal could hold lands from more than one lord, and so have divided loyalties if two of his lords came into conflict. For vassals in this situation, one of

▾ *Symbol of lordly power and built for effect rather than defence, with morning mist rising from the waters of its moat, 14th-century Bodiam Castle really looks the part.*

the feudal superiors would be identified as the liege lord – the one to whom loyalty took precedence.

The liege lord had feudal rights over his tenants and they lived under his protection – he and his knights by their presence deterred lawlessness and were ready if necessary to fight to protect the lord's lands. On the flip side, tenants were required to offer service as labourers or provide a proportion of goods grown on the land or produced in workshops.

Castle building was an important part of the feudal system in England and Wales. By building and inhabiting a castle a lord settled the land he had been granted. He lived there with his family and servants and, in some cases, the knights and squires in his service. In the great hall he met his vassals, received homage, administered his estate and passed judgement on disputes. This was also the setting for communal meals for the castle population, and the place where the lord hosted magnificent feasts for his knights and squires, accompanied by music, poetry and tournaments that celebrated the cult of chivalry.

Feudal life

On a typical feudal estate, the lord controlled one or more manors around the castle. Part of the land within the manor he set aside for his own use: the demesne. His tenants at the manor were required to work on the demesne for a specified amount of time – perhaps two or three days per week. In return, they were granted land to work on their own account on other parts of the manor estate, although a proportion of the produce derived in this way was due to the lord and had to be brought to the castle, where it was stored for later use

▲ *In this illustration from the Grimani Breviary peasants work in fields around the castle. Castle life was a microcosm of feudalism, with strict hierarchies and social immobility. (Getty)*

A KNIGHT'S PLACE IN SOCIETY

The feudal system had its origins in the relationships between Charlemagne, king of the Franks (r.768–814), and the mounted warriors in his heavy cavalry, who served the king in times of war in return for grants of land. As the system developed, it became the custom for holders of fiefdoms (originally a lifetime grant) to pass them on to their sons. In this way, large noble families were able to establish substantial territories. Another development was the emergence of the fraternity of knights – warriors who were admitted in a ceremony to an exclusive chivalric brotherhood.

Within the brotherhood all knights were equal. Only a knight could make another person a knight through the ceremony of the accolade – using a sword or hand on the shoulder – and it also became possible to pass a knighthood on to one's descendants. In theory, anyone could become a knight by proving himself worthy of the honour, and some knights did rise from humble beginnings – Sir William Marshal, for example, had relatively lowly origins yet became one of the leading men in England and was hailed 'the greatest knight who ever lived'. Yet, in practice, knights were mostly members of a social elite – partly because of the fact that the title could be inherited at birth, bringing with it the right to valuable land, but also because actually being a knight and equipping oneself with armour, horse, lance and other equipment was hugely expensive and thus an option for only the wealthiest people.

In the feudal hierarchy, knights occupied the level between the great barons of the land and the squires, the latter being warriors who had not been admitted to the chivalric brotherhood or who were younger men preparing for knighthood. Many knights were builders and holders of castles, while others instead served great barons and noblemen who kept these establishments.

Knighthood was thus a complex combination of a mark of honour for military renown (your own or your predecessor's) and a social level. It involved abiding by a code of honour and a religiously sanctioned status – something that could be hard to do – since knights and their words were blessed by the Church as 'soldiers of Christ' and defenders of the Christian faith and they were expected to act accordingly.

THE PHILIPPIEN MODEL

In the early 13th century King Philip II of France embarked on a major military campaign to win back French territory lost to England when Eleanor of Aquitaine married the English king Henry II. Phillip regained a great deal of land and, in order to consolidate it, built several garrisoned castles, seeking to extend the power and control of the crown across the French regions.

He introduced a standardised castle model to cut costs and save time, and make it possible to build a large number of castles quickly and efficiently. It was essentially based on the fortress he had built in the late 12th century to protect Paris: the Louvre, a quadrangular castle with corner towers and an imposing donjon or tower in the courtyard. The original Louvre, completed in 1202, measured 72m x 78m (236ft x 255ft) and had a crenellated wall 2.6m (8ft 6in) thick, with machicolations. In later examples of Philippien castles, one of the corner towers acted as the Great Tower. The builders at Guédelon set out to follow this model.

◄ *Philip II's fortress at Paris, the Louvre, was the starting point for the Philippien model. This image of the Louvre in its prime is from the 15th-century manuscript* Les Trés Riches Heures du Duc de Berry. *(Getty)*

in the kitchens. There were typically two types of tenants: freemen and villeins, or serfs. The freemen could sell their land, manage it as they saw fit. and move away if they wished. In return, they were obliged to pay rent to the lord or provide a specified amount of produce. The villeins, on the other hand, did not have these liberties – they were tied to the land and needed permission to sell or make any alterations to the land or livestock.

THE GUÉDELON PROJECT

Most of what we know about castles and how they were built must by necessity come from ruined remains – supplemented by references from literature of the time. However, with the modern-day project of Guédelon Castle in northern Burgundy we now have a wonderful opportunity to gain an insight into the process and techniques of building a castle in the medieval period.

◄ *Saint-Fargeau Castle, 13km (8 miles) from Guédelon in Burgundy, France. Castle owner Michel Guyot oversaw its restoration, then had the idea for the Guédelon project when he was told that a 13th-century castle lay beneath the walls of Saint-Fargeau.*

Guédelon is a 13th-century-style castle being built, as much as possible, with the equipment, materials and methods that would have been used at the time. It is an exercise in hands-on, experimental archaeology: through the process of construction, the aim is to gain a new and practical understanding of castle building in the period. The idea for the project arose in 1995 and was the brainchild of one Michel Guyot, the owner of the magnificent Saint-Fargeau Castle in Burgundy – once owned by Anne-Marie d'Orléans, Duchess of Montpensier and cousin of French king Louis XIV (r.1643–1715). At that point, Guyot had spent more than 20 years overseeing the painstaking restoration of Saint-Fargeau Castle and as part of the project had commissioned a study of its medieval origins. This study, carried out by fortification expert Nicolas Faucherre and castle expert Christian Corvisier, concluded that beneath the brick walls of Saint-Fargeau was a medieval castle that had been built according to the criteria laid down by King Philip II of France (r.1179–1223). At the end of the report lay a single simple yet tantalising sentence, which would prove to be the spark that ignited the whole Guédelon idea: 'Reconstructing Saint-Fargeau Castle would be an amazing project.'

Together with co-founder Maryline Martin, Monsieur Guyot duly prepared to follow the standardised or 'Philippien' castle model established by Philip II and set about constructing a 13th-century-style castle.

Lord of Guédelon

As part of the process of creating Guédelon, Michel Guyot and Maryline Martin, working with master mason Florian Renucci and historical experts, came up with an imaginary but historically feasible backstory to justify, inspire and influence the castle's construction. To do this effectively, they also needed to invent a fictitious Lord of Guédelon, complete with plausible biography.

Born in 1199, this figure was a relatively low-ranking nobleman, a younger brother in the Courtenay family who had possession of some of the family's territories and had married into a junior branch of the illustrious Toucy family. The dowry that came with his bride brought him forests, mills and land from which he derived a decent income.

In 1228, he won honour fighting bravely in the royal army of Blanche de Castile against rebel barons. As a reward, his feudal superior, Jean de Toucy, granted the lord a licence to crenellate (permission to build a castle) and he thus embarked on building his castle at Guédelon. It was to be a relatively modest affair – large enough to accommodate 30 people – the lord, his wife and their four children, together with family members, their children, and about 12 servants, including guards, kitchen staff and other domestics.

Bringing history to life

Work on the Guédelon site began in May 1997, with a 25-year plan in which to complete the castle. Each year, as in the 13th century, the castle site closes down for the winter and reopens in March for a long summer's hard work, plus over 300,000 visitors who pay an entrance fee that funds the project. Year by year, the castle grows, with progress carefully monitored by a team of France's leading archaeologists.

This book combines the invaluable design and construction insights gleaned from the Guédelon project with our pre-existing knowledge of the great castles of the 11th to 14th centuries in England, Wales, Scotland and France, thereby vividly bringing to life the world of the medieval castle – how it was built, who lived in and around it, and what their life was like – in times of peace and of war.

▼ *Work began at Guédelon in 1997. By 2009 the foundations of the walls and their towers were in place, and the Great Hall was ready for its roof.*

1

BARBICAN AND DITCH

The castle's defences began outside the walls. In the earlier part of the castle-building era, when the ability to shield the castle from attack was key, the lord would require a ditch or moat to be dug around the curtain walls to serve as a first line of protection. A manned and fortified area – the barbican – was also often added. This was overlooked by the gatehouse and castle walls, elevated positions from which defenders could keep close watch on anyone who approached the barbican. In later castles, when defences were often more for show than for use, outer fortifications were still added to the castle for reasons of prestige and symbolic effect.

◄ Chateau Gaillard, a 12th-century fortress built by Richard the Lionheart, King of England. (Alamy)

OUTER FORTIFICATIONS

There were two main types of barbican in a medieval castle: the courtyard or passageway. The courtyard barbican was normally situated beyond the main castle ditch or moat and enclosed by its own wall or ditch, and was connected to the gatehouse by a bridge. The passageway barbican, by contrast, usually took the form of an extension to the gatehouse and was in effect a fortified corridor, typically surrounded by a crenellated parapet and allure (a fighting platform around the top of the walls).

The first barbicans were small, enclosed courtyards positioned right in front of the gatehouse. These provided added protection for the gate – a point of vulnerability when open – as well as being an area in which troops could mass in safety before venturing out. A good example can be seen at Dover Castle, where in *c.*1180 Maurice the Engineer built not one but two barbicans of this type, one at each entrance to the castle's inner ward, immediately in front of the gate. These were overlooked by defenders up in the gatehouse or on the curtain wall and provided additional protection to the castle.

The next stage of development was to move the barbican away from the gatehouse. At Dover Castle, some time around 1220, a new barbican was built in front of Constable's Tower on the outer side of the castle's ditch, as well as at Caerphilly Castle, Wales, where in *c.*1260/70 Gilbert de Clare commissioned a barbican that stood in the middle of the moat. This latter was accessed via a drawbridge that ran from the outer edge of the moat to the barbican and another from the barbican to the gatehouse.

Around this time, an engineer or master of works came up with the idea of introducing a right-angle turn in the approach through the barbican to the gatehouse – a development that was implemented at Sandal Castle in *c.*1265 by John de

▾ *Pickering Castle, Yorkshire, as it would have looked in the 13th century, when its wooden keep and walls were replaced by stone. It was originally a motte-and-bailey castle built in timber and earth by the Normans c.1070-1070. (Getty)*

► *The five-tower Constable's Gate at Dover Castle was rebuilt after the previous gate was breached in the French siege of the castle in 1216 (see page 35).Its associated barbican was beyond the ditch. (Getty)*

Warenne, 6th Earl of Surrey. Here, in order to enter the castle, you had to cross a moat via a drawbridge to access the side of the barbican, then make a 90-degree turn and cross a second drawbridge to reach the motte on which the castle keep stood. Similar barbicans incorporating 90-degree turns were built at Goodrich Castle in Herefordshire about ten years later in *c.*1275 and at the Tower of London at around the same time.

MASTER MASONS

The master mason in charge of planning and erecting a 12th/13th-century castle needed to be a man of many skills. Some were called engineers, and we know that in addition to building fortified edifices they were experts in making the terrifying siege engines and other machines of war used to attack these structures. The two went hand in hand; by devising and creating the mechanical assault weapons they were conversely able to construct effective defences to withstand and repel them. In addition, the master mason had to advise on geology and earthworks – in laying out the castle and preparing the site.

At other times called carpenters, these men may also have had to take down pre-existing timber fortifications while building in stone, as well as designing or at least controlling the production of wooden elements of the building, such as roof beams and floorboards, gates, doors, drawbridges, sockets, chases, scaffolding and hoarding.

However he was named, the medieval builder was, above all, a master mason – in charge of sourcing the right stone, quarrying it, bringing rocks to site, preparing them and overseeing the erection of the walls, towers, gateways and other defensive structures. He was in charge of teams of labourers – including quarrymen, stonemasons, carpenters, tile makers and blacksmiths – and in all his work he was answerable to the lord, the patron of the site.

Generally, the patron would declare what he wanted and the master mason would come up with a way of making it

▼ *The Tower of London in the 16th century. The barbican with 90-degree approach became known as the Lion Tower because of its association with the royal menagerie. (Getty)*

happen, which the lord could then either approve or not, in which latter case he would demand changes. Sometimes the patron took a detailed interest. For example, King Richard I of England – the king known as 'the Lionheart', who was celebrated for his military prowess and was a veteran of the Third Crusade – had many ideas he wanted to put into practice in the building of Château Gaillard in France in 1196–98, and played a key role in its construction. Indeed, Richard spent so much time at Château Gaillard while it was being built that some historians think he himself should be considered its architect or master mason. This was, however, unusual, since normally the patron could not always be present; whether a king or an important lord, he was likely to be called away to attend to other matters. We know, for instance, that Hugh of Tichemers, master of works in the building of a new keep at Knaresborough Castle for King Edward II of England in 1307–12, had to leave the site four times to get the king's approval for design elements.

PASSAGEWAY BARBICANS

Over time, the passageway barbican became popular and by the 14th century was the norm. This was probably because it was far more efficient than the courtyard barbican in terms of providing defence: anyone approaching the main gatehouse was confined into a narrow approach and could be attacked from the parapets along the top of the enclosing walls. Most passageways also incorporated a ditch and had a retractable drawbridge as part of their defences.

A forerunner, perhaps, was the barbican at the Constable's Tower, Dover Castle. This had a long walled approach running parallel to and overlooked by the castle's curtain walls. Another earlier passage barbican was also built at Conisbrough Castle, South Yorkshire, where a walled approach from a gatehouse on the edge of the moat led towards the main ward of the castle, turned at 45 degrees to adapt to the alignment of the curtain walls, then took a right-angled jink to approach the main gateway.

Other examples include Lewes Castle in East Sussex, where John de Warenne, 7th Earl of Surrey, commissioned a passageway barbican with a heavily fortified three-storey barbican gatehouse in *c.*1330; and Warwick Castle, where Thomas Beauchamp, 12th Earl of Warwick, built a similar walled barbican with an imposing three-storey outer gateway about a decade later. Here, archaeological remains suggest that the tower of the barbican stood in the middle of the moat and was connected to the outer bank and the main castle by drawbridges, as at Caerphilly Castle.

One of the best-preserved passageway barbicans of this period is at Alnwick Castle, Northumberland. Here, the outer gateway has square turrets and a recessed entrance that leads to a narrow passageway that is overlooked by an alure along the parapeted walls and by the main gatehouse. There was a ditch within the passageway.

TWIN BARBICANS

At Conwy Castle in Wales, built by Edward I of England in 1283–89, the castle layout and the shape of the barbicans were determined by the outline of the site on which it was built. The castle stands on a rocky promontory with one courtyard barbican at each end – east and west – both overlooked by the towers and walls of the main castle. The west barbican has its own gatehouse with twin turrets. Location was a hugely important consideration when selecting a site or adapting fortifications to existing conditions.

▼ The barbican at Goodrich Castle in Herefordshire required approaching soldiers to turn through 90 degrees when entering the castle. At Goodrich the timber-and-earth Norman structure was rebuilt in stone in the 12th century. (PD)

▼ At Lewes Castle in East Sussex the imposing three-storey barbican of c.1330 has round turrets, a rooftop fighting platform and cruciform arrow loops. It is connected to the 11th-century Norman gateway by a barbican passage. (PD)

▲ *The main outer east gatehouse at Caerphilly Castle in Wales was built in the 1280s by Gilbert de Clare. Holes to house drawbridge chains (see page 45) are visible above the opening. (Cadw)*

▼ *The ground plan of Conwy Castle shows the position of east and west courtyard barbicans, one at each end of the rocky promontory on which it stands. (Cadw)*

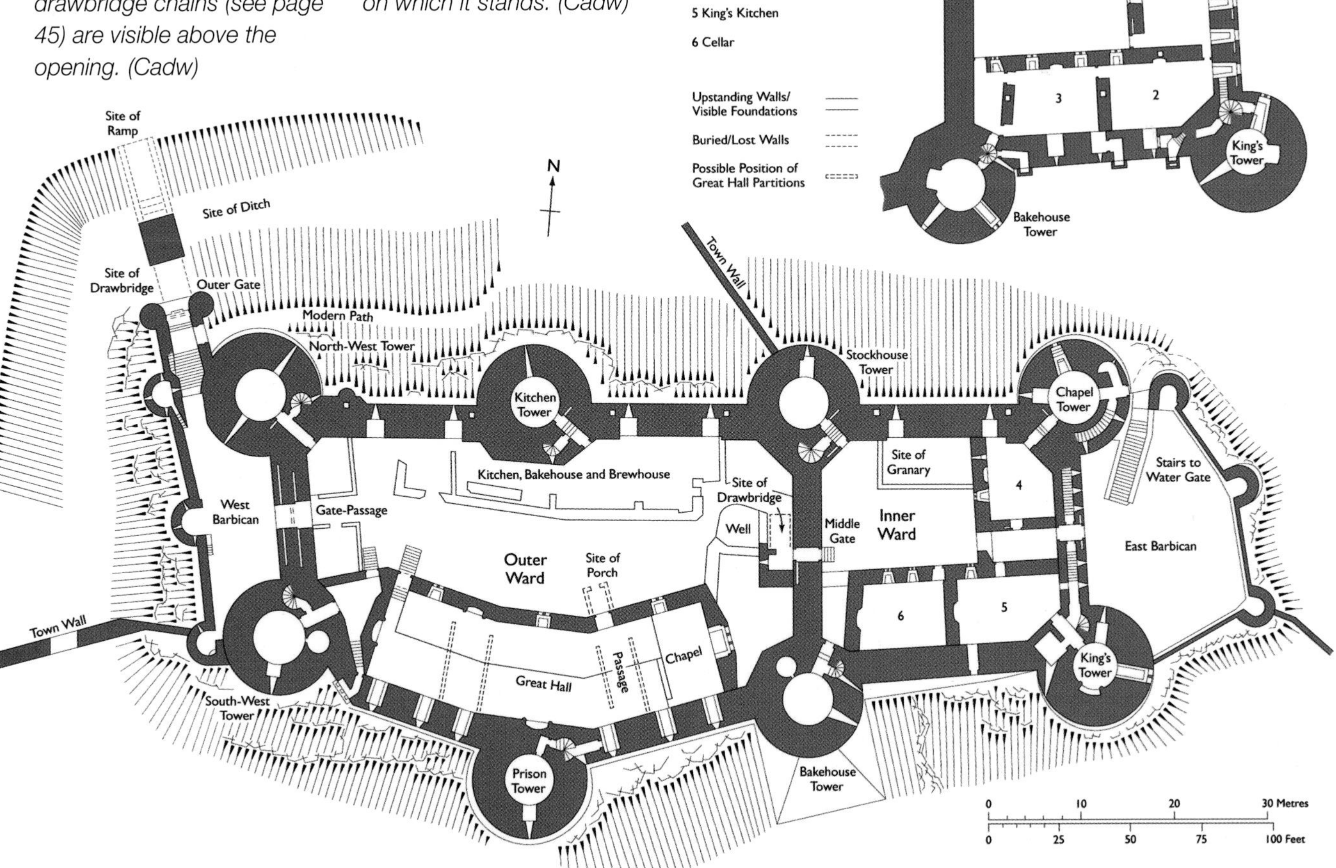

DUG DEFENCES: DITCHES AND MOATS

In many castles, the ditch was a pre-existing topographical feature, but in some it had to be laboriously dug out by teams of serfs or soldiers. Elsewhere, some lords used lakes or rivers as natural water defences, while others employed earthworks experts or water engineers to create and fill their moat. A castle's location was thus key – in determining whether or not an artificial ditch or moat would need to be created, but also for many other strategical reasons, too. For example, very often a lord would choose the site in an area that was best for defence – a hilltop or cliff, a place at the top of a slope, or a site with its own water defences, such as a lake or river. Of equal, or perhaps even greater, importance was the availability of supplies – both materials for building and water and food to support the castle's population.

Many formidable stone castles were built on the site of timber motte-and-bailey castles or even on top of much earlier British tribal or Roman defences. In these instances, the site was self-selecting, although adapting existing earthworks and building in stone atop a timber fortress was a significant challenge in itself. Lewes Castle, for example, was built on the site of a motte-and-bailey castle (unusually, one with two mottes or mounds); its curtain walls follow the line taken by the original wooden palisade, and the walls of the shell keeps on the twin mounds likewise take the line of the original defences. Castles at Berkeley in Gloucestershire and Farnham in Surrey were also built on and over existing timber motte-and-bailey castles.

In these cases, the master mason had to be adept in planning and overseeing the re-digging of earthworks – or else use an expert in the field. At some sites the master mason had to take down previous stone buildings in reworking a castle. An expert in earthworks often played an important role in selecting a new site, too, advising on the local countryside and geology and on the availability of stone and timber – and of water if a flooded ditch or moat was part of the plan. Some castle-building projects also involved specialist ditch experts – dykers.

At the beginning of the Guédelon project, the castle builders chose their site because of the availability of natural resources. Like their castle-building predecessors in the Middle Ages, they knew they would need a huge amount of timber and stone for the castle – calculated in Guédelon's case to be 10,000m^3 (350,000ft^3) of stone. The site they found – an abandoned quarry in many hectares of unspoiled

◀ *Early days at Guédelon. Work began clearing the quarry and preparing foundations in 1997–98. Managing water and preventing flooding was very important on many castle sites.*

▲ *The main courtyard well at Guédelon is 7m (23ft) deep. Masons use water for mixing building materials every day.*

► *The tripod above the courtyard well at Guédelon supports the rope pulley system used for raising water.*

▼ *The courtyard well at Guédelon incorporates a built-in spout for filling buckets with water drawn from below.*

oak woodland – was therefore perfect for their needs: from the quarry they could dig out sandstone, sand for making mortar, clay for crafting roof and floor tiles, and ochre for creating paints; from the forest they could harvest oak for roof timbers, floorboards and battens from which to hang tiles, and oak shakes for roofing houses. They also knew they would need copious amounts of water, so they brought in water diviners who found a source less than 6m (20ft) down; they duly set to digging wells.

In the Middle Ages, pitched battles were sometimes fought in order to gain control of quarries. Victory meant a king, lord or powerful bishop won both a source of building materials and of wealth – for a substantial fee he might grant other users rights to quarry stone there. Making use of local materials was commonplace: Conwy, Harlech and Montgomery castles in Wales, for instance, were built mostly from the rock in the immediate vicinity. This made sense, because transporting materials, where they were not easily accessible, was both difficult and expensive. Surviving documents show that at Caernarfon Castle in 1285–86, almost five times more was spent on transport than on materials – around £535 on transport, compared to just over £150 on materials. The mode of transport was usually horse-drawn carts and drays along uneven roads, which made progress slow, though where possible materials might have been transported by barge along rivers and streams.

NATURAL DEFENCES

Lords and master masons often wanted to make the most of natural features and would select a site based on its imposing position as well as for its other beneficial local conditions. In these instances, the site's footprint and other features usually determined the form of the castle, as can be seen in the French castles at Chinon and Gaillard, both of which were shaped by the rocky promontories on which they stand. In such places, builders might need to excavate a ditch or moat

▲ *The ruins of Dunstanburgh Castle command a breathtaking view from a headland near Alnwick in Northumberland. In the 14th century diggers flooded lakes along the landward side of the headland to provide very effective water defences.*

only around part of the site – although at Château Gaillard, Richard I dug additional ditches around the outside and between the baileys as an additional defensive measure.

Moreover, it wasn't just the elevated situation of a potential site that could be desirable. For example, Dunstanburgh Castle in northern England – built by Thomas, 2nd Earl of Lancaster in *c.*1313–22 in an imposing headland position on the Northumberland coast, the site of a former Iron Age fort – offered the additional benefit of nearby waterways. The earl, realising their potential, had his master mason and digging teams excavate and flood the line of lakes along the landward side of the headland, creating with comparitive ease effective water barriers, and establishing the castle position as a highly defensible island.

PREPARING THE SITE

The first major task in preparing a new site was to dig the ditches and ready the platform or mound on which the castle would stand. The principle purpose of digging ditches was to create defences, but it was also to provide earth with which to build up the platform. Another part of the process was to establish foundations for the curtain walls and castle. This was performed by teams of diggers who worked on the ditches, labourers who prepared the platform, and specialist masons who laid out the foundations.

Sometimes castles had to be put up in a hurry to secure control over land, but mostly building a castle took many years. At Guédelon, after work began in May 1998, the workers spent the first three building seasons just preparing the scarped base on which they would go on to build the castle walls. Teams of labourers carried out the hard physical work of digging and moving earth, using simple wheeled handcarts and drays pulled by carthorses. They did not dig a new defensive ditch, instead using the existing lie of the land; as an old quarry, the site was already substantially dug out.

An important part of this work was managing water onsite. Guédelon has a mainly dry, though sometimes muddy,

◄ *A drainage channel at Guédelon. The quarry site on which the castle is being built can get very muddy on a rainy day; if rainwater is not carefully channelled it will erode the masonry.*

defensive ditch; the water-management challenge here was to drain the site and keep work dry rather than create floods for a moat. The workers laid off-cut rocks from the adjacent quarry on the paths around the site to maintain their structure and dug ditches alongside them to channel rainwater away. Later in the process they built drainage systems at the start of preparing any space for building – for example, in the great tower they built a drainage channel 4m (13ft) long in the cellar. They also built up a sloping ramp of earth at the base of walls to protect the foundations from rainwater.

QUARRYMEN AND MINERS

On some sites, the master mason had to arrange for defensive ditches to be cut through rock, a task that required him to employ miners and quarrymen – experts in digging out and handling rock. These two roles were closely aligned – skilled professions both, in which knowledge was frequently passed down from father to son. Mining often took place on the surface and quarrymen sometimes carried out their work underground – although the typical quarrying technique was simply to clear the earth and dig out the bedrock.

▶ *The inner ward of Hubert de Burgh's Montgomery Castle, Powys, begun in 1223. An earlier motte-and-bailey castle, Hen Domen (1071–74), is nearby. (Cadw)*

BUILDING TECHNIQUES: HOW TO SPLIT SANDSTONE BLOCKS

Guédelon is being built in a sandstone quarry – once the quarrymen clear the sandy topsoil, they can access beds of sandstone of different sizes and hardness. The quarrymen work to the master mason's orders: he specifies the size and quality of sandstone he needs for a particular job or a specific part of the castle. It is hard physical work and a little expert knowledge goes a long way in saving time and energy. The quarrymen need to be able 'read' the rock. They look for natural fissures in the surface, which they then work to widen, carefully splitting the large slab of rock into two pieces.

1 Having inspected the rock and identified a fracture line, the quarryman positions a metal wedge and hammers it into the crack. The wedge needs to go in at just the right angle.

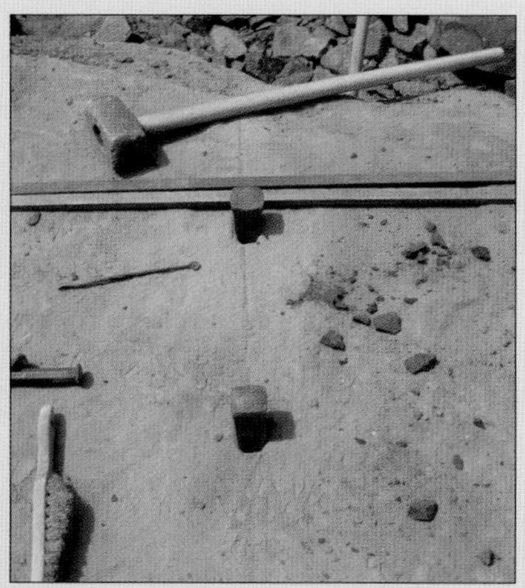

2 The quarryman keeps the line of the natural fracture in the piece of sandstone in mind as he places and drives in a second metal wedge around 12–18in (30–45cm) away from the first.

3 Once the wedges have been hammered fully in, the rock splits along the line of the natural fracture. You can see the marks alongs the edge of the rock where the wedges were driven in.

TOOLS AND EQUIPMENT: THE QUARRYMAN'S TOOLS

In the medieval period, quarrymen would pass on skills and techniques from master to apprentice, from father to son. The quarrymen at Guédelon had to learn more or less on the job, picking up the skills they needed as they went. At the start of the project in 1997–98, they found that using explosives produced fragments that were too small to use, and using expanding cement caused pollution. They mastered working with medieval-style tools like those below.

Wedges and chisels
The quarrymen use wedges to break apart large pieces of rock along a natural fissure. Chisels and punches are used to carve edge holes into the rock. The punches are pointed, while the chisels have a flattened end.

Sledgehammers
To split rocks the quarrymen work in pairs. One positions the concave surface of a long-handled quarrying hammer at an angle against the stone; his partner then strikes the other end with a sledgehammer.

Plug and feather
To ensure that the wedges have been tightly driven into the rock, the quarrymen first clear all the dust from the whole and drive the wedge between thin, iron wedges

Levers
Once larger pieces of sandstone have been split, they need to be levered from their natural position and lifted so they can be moved. The pieces of sandstone and other rocks are usually moved by horse and cart or by handcart.

▲ *At Corfe Castle in Dorset, King John employed miners to cut a forbidding defensive ditch. His predecessor Henry II built the stone keep before 1105, using local Purbeck limestone.*

▲ *The rock-cut ditch made around the southeast corner of Harlech Castle in Wales protected the fortress against attack. The castle was built in 1282–89 by Edward I. (Cadw)*

An example of the use of miners is Montgomery Castle in Wales, where, in *c.*1223, Hubert de Burgh used skilled labourers from the Forest of Dean – equipped with mallets and picks, wedges and levers – to dig ditches and foundations for the stone castle he was building for Henry III of England. Another is Corfe Castle in Dorset, where a few years earlier (1207 and 1214) miners were used to dig defensive ditches. These were very necessary, since Corfe was a substantial fortress in this period – so much so that it was where King John kept Eleanor, the 'Fair Maid of Brittany' – a potential rival to his rule – in captivity.

Quarrymen were essentially rock experts who knew how to grade, handle, split and work different types of stone. This required in-depth knowledge, since different types of rock require different treatment. In order to split soft limestone, for instance, quarrymen could create a crack in the rock by knocking it with a mallet, then insert wooden wedges and soak them with water. As the wood expanded, the stone split in two along the crack. However, this method would not work with harder rock, such as sandstone or granite. In these cases, they looked for natural fracture lines, hammered out one or two small inserts and then drove in metal wedges to split the rock. The quarrymen thus needed to be able identify rocks and see their natural qualities, and often used colour to judge: in a sandstone quarry, for example, the more blue colour there is in the rock, the harder it is and the more

DIFFERENT TYPES OF STONE

No stone was wasted on a medieval quarry or construction site – the best stone was reserved for dressed masonry for the most visible part of the castle, while poorer quality stone was used for rubble infill for the walls or the laying of paths. Quarrymen were experts in selecting stone – at Guédelon they can tell different qualities by colour.

Yellow
At Guédelon the softest sandstone is yellowish in colour. The master mason selects these stones for rubble infill.

Red
Reddish sandstone is of a medium-hardness. The banker masons dress this type to use as facing stones.

Blue
Blue-tinted sandstone is the hardest and most difficult stone to work. It is used for load-bearing elements, such as lintels.

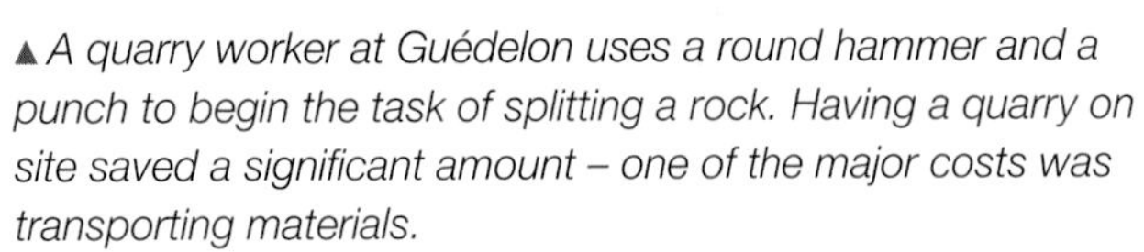

▲ *A quarry worker at Guédelon uses a round hammer and a punch to begin the task of splitting a rock. Having a quarry on site saved a significant amount – one of the major costs was transporting materials.*

▲ *Chinon Castle was rebuilt by Henry II of England in the 12th century. It has three sections, separated by dry moats. The castle was captured in 1205 by Philip II of France, who built the keep. A tunnel links the keep to the inner ward.*

difficult it is to work. In this environment they would look instead for dark-red sandstone.

At the quarry they usually worked to order, seeking rocks of a specific quality and size for the master mason. They would then produce dressed stone – sometimes worked to a square edge – for laying walls in horizontal courses, but they also provided the undressed rubble that was used to fill the interior of the castle walls. Moreover, in addition to working in the quarry, quarrymen were often also present on the castle site as masons or stonecutters.

TUNNELS

The master mason also used miners to dig tunnels in castles, as can be seen at the linked fortifications of Château de La Roche-Guyon in northern France, which controlled a crossing of the River Seine. Here, a tunnel was dug to join the 12th-century donjon on top of the cliff with the 13th-century fortified dwelling beside the river below. Elsewhere, tunnels provided access to wells, or an exit from the inner or outer ward to the outer reaches of the castle or to the area beyond the fortifications. At Château de Chinon in France, a tunnel links the cylindrical keep – the Tour du Coudray, built by Philip II of France – to a well in the inner ward. Meanwhile in England, at Windsor and Dover castles, tunnels were built in the 1220s to lead out from the inner or outer wards and were used by troops to surprise attackers. When designed for this purpose, tunnels were called 'sally ports'.

MOATS

While dry ditches were most common, lords incorporated water defences – moats – wherever local conditions made them possible. At Kenilworth Castle, Warwickshire, the benefits of these were demonstrated in the celebrated siege of 1266, when supporters of rebel Lord Simon de Montfort defied the attacking royal army led by Henry III and Prince Edward for almost six months, from 21 June to 14 December. This feat was achieved because the water kept the besiegers' trebuchets and other war engines out of range, and crossing the water, even at night, proved unsuccessful.

The water defences at Kenilworth Castle were originally created in the 1120s by King Henry I's treasurer, Geoffrey de Clinton, by damming nearby Finham and Inchford brooks, which flooded the land to the west and south of the castle. Meanwhile, a moat was dug around the north and east. Then, in the early 1200s, King John raised the dam and created a large, defensive lake about 1.5km (1 mile) long – the Mere.

Where water was to play a key role in castle defences, a specialist in managing water and ditches was often employed, as was the case at Robert of Mortain's motte-and-bailey Berkhamsted Castle in Hertfordshire, where, in 1066, a double moat that used water from a diverted stream and drained into the nearby River Bulbourne had been created.

Surviving documents show that Flemish ditchers and dykers – used to maintaining strategic dyke systems at home – were especially popular. For instance, one, named John le Fossour, was employed by Henry III to work on the water defences of the Tower of London in the 1240s. English water experts got a look-in too, however: Adam the Fleming (though actually an Englishman, from Suffolk, near the fens of East Anglia) was in charge of moat systems for Edward I's castles in Scotland at Dumfries in 1300 and at Linlithgow in 1302. We know from surviving documents that teams of 20–30 diggers, each with its own master, worked under Adam's direction at Linlithgow Castle.

Elsewhere, too, the trend for using water was taken up by lords when devising their castle defences. For example, Gilbert de Clare – a Norman lord known as 'Red Gilbert' for his hair, who had taken part in the 1266 siege at Kenilworth – flooded the area around Caerphilly Castle by damming local streams, and created three fortified 'islands': a central castle ward and an outpost each to east and west. At Leeds Castle in Kent, Edward I is thought to have created the extensive lake found there by damming the River Len after he took control of the site in 1278. A much later but no-less impressive example is Bodiam Castle, built by Sir Edward Dalyngrigge under a licence granted by Richard II in 1385, which has a defensive lake fed by local springs. By this stage, it should be noted, a castle's defensive features – which at Bodiam also included portcullis, battlements and drawbridge – were more for show than practical use. Bodiam, which also has big windows and a poorly defended rear entrance, would not actually have withstood attack.

▲ *Edward I is thought to have created the water defences at Leeds Castle in Kent, a favourite residence of his. Much of the castle was rebuilt in the 19th century.*

▼ *Caerphilly Castle in Glamorgan, Wales, begun in 1268, is celebrated for its artificial water defences, created by damming local streams, and for its concentric design. (Cadw)*

2

GATEHOUSE, TOWERS AND DRAWBRIDGE

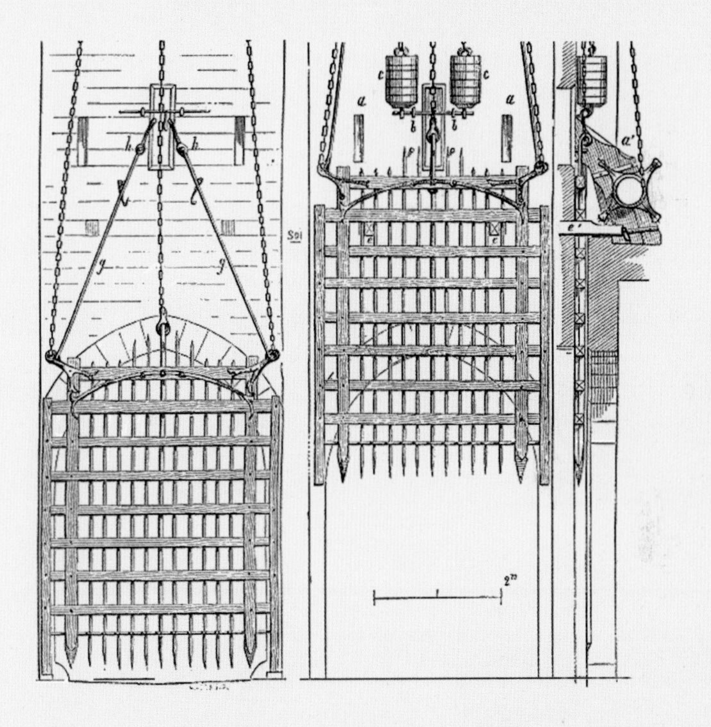

The castle's main entrance was a significant area of vulnerability. Earlier castles often contained the gateway within a single tower, but thereafter more secure twin-towered gatehouses were developed. Gateways were fully equipped for defence – with retractable drawbridge, iron-tipped portcullis and 'murder holes' in the vault of the entrance passage – while along the curtain wall, flanking and corner towers also provided cover.

GATEHOUSES

Master masons in the 1100s relied on a single tower gatehouse, but later that century the entryway was redesigned for more effective defence, with twin towers, complex, highly guarded approaches, and a forbidding array of defensive equipment, such as the drawbridge, portcullis, paired gates and machicolations. The process perhaps reached its peak in Britain c.1296 with the King's Gate at Caernarfon Castle, built by King Edward I to subdue the Welsh and most definitely a fortified site designed with effective defence in mind.

At Framlingham Castle in Suffolk, Roger Bigod, 2nd Earl of Norfolk, built a single-towered entrance to his new castle in 1190, with additional defence being provided to the gate itself by a portcullis. Elsewhere, however, around the same time, master masons began to appreciate the benefits of twin towers to defend the gateway; two entrances to the inner ward at Dover Castle had already been built with twin rectangular towers in the 1180s when in c.1190 William Marshal, Earl of Pembroke, erected a grand outer gatehouse with rounded twin towers at Chepstow Castle in Wales, on the cliffs above the River Wye. This reworking of the castle, which had been founded in 1067 by William FitzOsbern, 1st Earl of Hereford, was the direct result of the experiences gained by Marshal while fighting in France and in the Crusades. Dubbed 'the best knight who ever lived' by Stephen Langton, later the Archbishop of Canterbury, he brought to bear his knowledge of warfare when devising the modifications, and in addition to building the gatehouse, strengthened the defences elsewhere, too.

▲ *A labourer operates a treadmill winch to lift heavy materials to the top of a tower in this medieval miniature of a castle under construction. At ground level masons shape and transport stones. (Getty)*

▼ *The gatehouse at Chepstow Castle, built by William Marshal, c.1190, was the first in England and Wales with twin rounded gate towers. It was also equipped with formidable defensive machinery including two portcullises. (Cadw)*

The twin towers of William Marshal's gatehouse at Chepstow Castle stand forward of the arched gateway and had defensive arrow loops on two levels, meaning that guards could provide covering fire. The gateway passage is defended by a machicolation slot – an opening in the roof of the passage through which guards could drop missiles or use weapons against attackers. There were also two portcullises with a pair of gates between. This was a pioneering design: the first in England and Wales with rounded twin gate towers. At Guédelon, the gatehouse, when complete, will have twin rounded towers with a diameter of 8m (26ft) rising to a height of 15m (almost 50ft).

Other examples of twin towers soon followed: King John built a new gatehouse with two rounded D-shaped towers at the north-west of Dover Castle in 1204–16; and the master mason at Kenilworth Castle adopted a similar design there in c.1210–12, adding two D-shaped towers to the existing rectangular gatehouse (Mortimer's Tower). This new arrangement at the latter provided arrow slits facing forwards and sideways and lengthened the entrance passage so increased fortification could be installed – there are no fewer than three defensive gates and two portcullises.

MORTAR MAKERS AND MASON LAYERS

Two key groups of men worked for a medieval master mason – alongside the stonecutters – in getting the walls of the gatehouse and other parts of the castle built, and ensuring they remained standing once up. These were the mortar makers, who prepared the mortar; and the mason layers, who put the walls together using trowel, plumb line and mason's level. In some contemporary accounts, the mason layers were referred to as rough masons.

The mortar makers used lime, sand and water to create the binding material for the walls, typically working with a tool similar to hoes used by gardeners today to stir together the ingredients on large mortar boards on the ground. Local conditions could determine what was available, and the quality of the sand, and as a result proportions varied from place to place.

The mortar makers mixed three key types of mortar: a flexible sort that was needed for arches and vaults; a fine type for the facing walls; and a coarse variety for the rubble core of the walls. They kept the exact recipes they used secret and passed the know-how down from father to son, master to apprentice, though it is known that they adjusted the amount of lime, the grade of sand and the amount of water to make the various types. The coarse variety can take hundreds of years to set. Indeed, archaeologists have found that in the centre of some medieval walls the mortar is still not fully set even today, centuries after it was mixed. This flexible mortar allowed the stone walls to slowly settle into place. The mortar used at Guédelon is made with non-hydraulic lime, which once applied has a very long setting time.

MAKING MEDIEVAL MORTAR AT GUÉDELON

When the castle builders began at Guédelon they used sand from the River Loire and industrially produced hydraulic lime – less than authentic ingredients. However, the team were not happy with the results: the mortar was too white, compared with that found on local buildings, and it set far too quickly. An expert on the castle's scientific committee duly made contact with Christian Le Barrier, an archaeologist and researcher with a specialism in the making of mortar.

Le Barrier analysed samples of medieval mortar from the nearby chateaux Ratilly and Saint-Fargeau and compared the results to a batch he made himself on site using non-hydraulic lime putty and sand from the quarry at Guédelon. The results showed that the batch he made had the same composition as the historical mortar from Ratilly and Saint-Fargeau. From that time on, the mortar makers at Guédelon have used non-hydraulic lime, which is a close physical/chemical match to the medieval material they studied, mixed with local sand, with much more authentic results.

BUILDING TECHNIQUES: MAKING MEDIEVAL MORTAR

The team prepare the mortar, which bind the stones together. There are two types: one to bind the rubble in the inner part of the walls and one to hold stones in position in facing walls. The mix for the cores is made of one part gravelly earth, one part sand and one part non-hydraulic lime putty. Mortar for facing walls is made of two parts sand to one part lime.

1 Basketloads of quarry sand are laid out on the boards. The angular particles in the quarry sand will lock together when the lime binds them.

2 The lime is thinned with water and mixed into a smooth, creamy consistency.

3 The lime putty is than poured over the sand before they are mixed together using long-handled hoes.

BUILDING TECHNIQUES: HOW TO MAKE LIME

In 2015, the Guédelon team, with the help of archaeologists from the French National Institute for Preventive Archaeology, built an experimental lime kiln based on medieval designs.

The kiln is built against a bank of earth. On top of the firebox, masons constructed a dome out of small blocks of limestone. This dome was then covered with clay and a fire was lit in the firebox. This fire was kept burning for three days and three nights to produce quicklime. At the end of the firing, the masons carefully removed the blocks of quicklime and plunged them into tubs of water. This process, called 'slaking', produced the non-hydraulic lime putty used on site to make mortar.

1 Against an earth bank in the crafts village near the castle site, the Guédelon team construct a kiln to experiment with making lime. On top of the kiln, they build a dome from offcuts of limestone from the stonemasons' lodge.

2 The dome is then covered with an insulating layer of straw and clay and a fire is lit inside the kiln. For the first few hours the team 'smoke' the kiln, driving off water vapour in the limestone.

3 The woodfired kiln must be brought up to 900–1000°C (1650–1800°F). Teams work around the clock to maintain these temperatures for 72 hours (three days and three nights).

4 After the firing, the workmen remove the clay to uncover the quicklime. They wear protective masks against the fumes – in the medieval period simple kerchiefs would have been used.

5 The quicklime is plunged into buckets of water in the final stage of making the lime putty. The slaked lime will be left to mature for several months before being used to make mortar.

▲ *A reconstruction drawing of Dover Castle as it appeared in c.1300 gives a clear view of its concentric defences. Still standing today, although much changed, Dover was one of the most formidable of all medieval castles. (Getty)*

LINES OF ATTACK – AND DEFENCE

The positioning of the gatehouse was a key defensive concern. At Château Gaillard, Richard I and his masons did not position the gateway to the outer bailey along the main approach that an attacking army would have taken to the castle, but instead situated it on one of the side walls so that the attackers would have had to manoeuvre along the north-east wall of the outer bailey – under fire from bowmen on the curtain walls the whole way. At Dover Castle, Henry III's master mason moved the main gateway after the experience of the siege of 1216–17, when the twin-towered gateway, being directly in line with the main approach from outside, had proved vulnerable and been badly damaged and partially undermined. In the rearrangement, the entrance was moved to the west curtain wall, as at Château Gaillard, forcing those approaching to make their way along the curtain wall under the watchful eye of defending troops.

▶ *The defences of Prudhoe Castle proved their worth – Prudhoe was the only castle in Northumberland not to fall to the Scottish invasion under William 'the Lion' in the 1170s.*

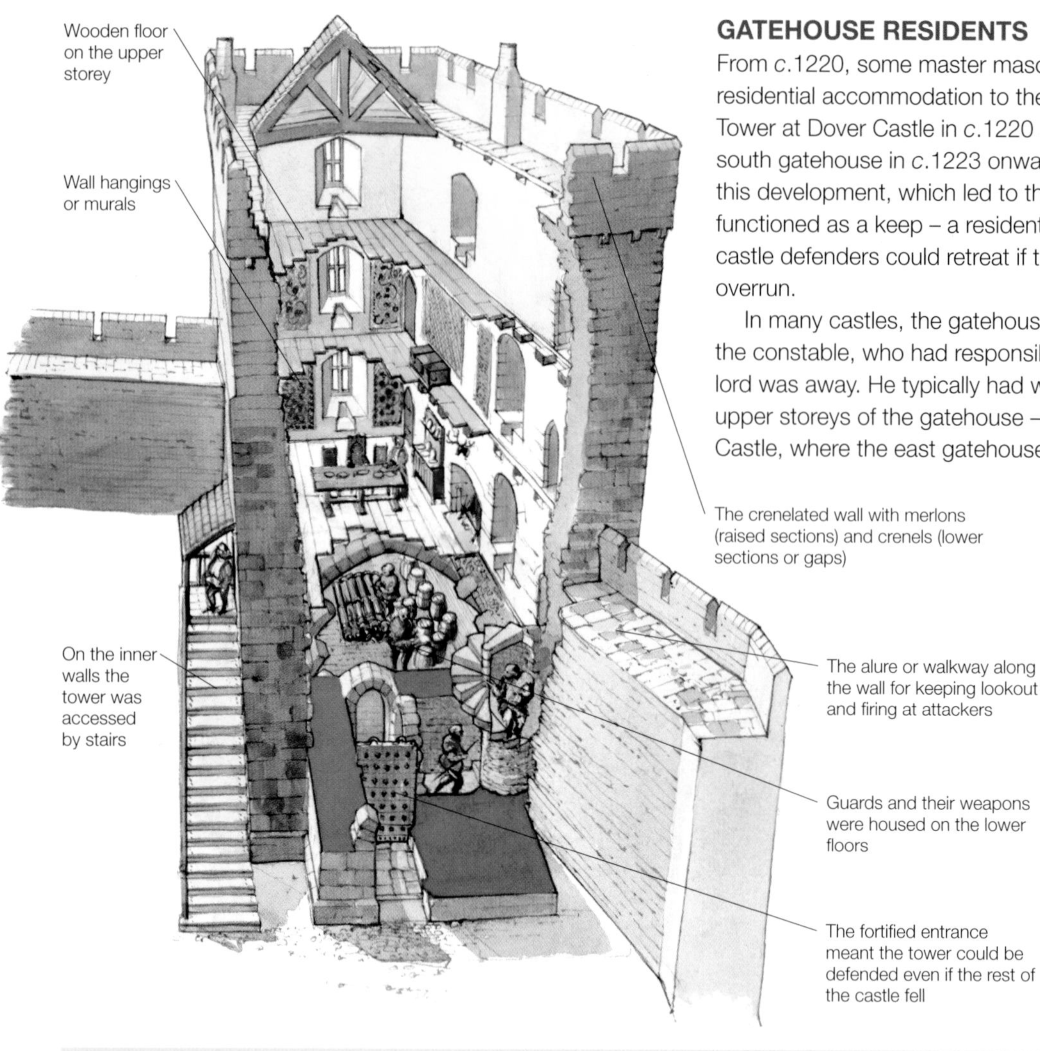

GATEHOUSE RESIDENTS

From *c.*1220, some master masons began to connect residential accommodation to the gatehouse. Constable's Tower at Dover Castle in *c.*1220 and Montgomery Castle's south gatehouse in *c.*1223 onwards were early examples of this development, which led to the great gatehouse that functioned as a keep – a residential stronghold to which castle defenders could retreat if the rest of the castle were overrun.

In many castles, the gatehouse contained the dwelling for the constable, who had responsibility for the castle when the lord was away. He typically had well-appointed rooms in the upper storeys of the gatehouse – as for example at Caerphilly Castle, where the east gatehouse, the castle's most strongly

◄ Fortifications could be combined with comfort in the gatehouse and other residential towers. This reconstruction of the residential tower at 14th-century Etal Castle, Northumberland, shows how defensive quarters in the lower part of the tower gave way to spacious dining and living quarters on the upper floors.

GREAT SIEGE OF DOVER

Dover Castle was besieged for ten months in 1216–17 by an invading force led by Prince Louis of France in support of the barons who were in revolt against King John. These barons had offered Louis the throne of England and he had even been proclaimed king in London, but Dover held firm under Hubert de Burgh, Justiciar of England, with a garrison force that included 140 knights. The siege began when Louis first attacked the main castle gateway in July 1216 with siege engines, then under cover of a 'cat' (a kind of wheeled hut that protected those under it from missiles and arrow bolts). This enabled Louis' men to access the barbican and undermine the oak stockade that defended it, allowing his army to pour into the barbican and capture it. He then set his diggers to undermine the gatehouse. They succeeded in bringing one of the twin towers crashing down, but found that the gap this created had been blocked by the defenders, who had built a barricade within. The attackers were thus driven back and never came that close to taking the castle again. A long siege ensued, and eventually Louis abandoned his attempts to take the English crown. (Getty)

▲ *An arrow loop in the outer curtain wall at Harlech Castle. A bowman inside had limited visibility but was well protected from enemy weapons. (Cadw)*

◀ *The rear, or inner, face of the east gatehouse at Harlech Castle. The rooms on the upper floors were comfortable – each had a fireplace and there were three windows per floor overlooking the inner ward. (Cadw)*

fortified structure, had rooms for this usage on the upper storeys, including a large second-floor chamber with a great fireplace. In some cases, fine rooms were also kept in the gatehouse towers to accommodate knights and noblemen captured in battle; they would often be confined in comfortable conditions and with the freedom to roam the castle, until their families or allies paid a ransom for their freedom. By contrast, beneath the gatehouse floor you might find the dungeon, where lesser prisoners were chained up, shivering and praying for mercy. The chapel was also often included in the gatehouse – for example, at Prudhoe Castle in Northumberland. One theory is that the lord and his master mason placed the chapel there in the hope that it would prevent evil or misfortune from entering the castle.

GUARDS AND DEFENCES

A porter had responsibility for managing incomings and outgoings on a daily basis, but guards flooded to the gatehouse if the castle came under attack or a warning was received of an impending assault. From a guardroom above

▶ *The remains of murder holes in the gatehouse passage at Harlech Castle. The arch springers indicate where the holes would have been. (Cadw)*

◄ *A besieging army attacks a medieval castle. Attackers load crossbows and fire longbows and, to the left, attempt to scale the walls using ladders. The defenders fight on the wall top, using swords and hurling objects and pouring liquids down onto the troops below. The miniature, from the* Chronicles of Jean Froissart, *depicts the Siege of Aubenton by the army of Count Jean of Hainaut in 1340. (Getty)*

the gateway, they fired bolts and arrows or dropped missiles or liquids on attackers. Sometimes there was also a water chute in the gatehouse wall, down which guards could pour water to put out the fires that attackers often tried to start.

Such defensive considerations, alongside the domestic ones, were very much part of the planning, as can be seen in the magnificent twin-towered gatehouse keep at Tonbridge Castle, Kent, built by Richard de Clare or his son Gilbert de Clare in *c.*1250–65. This combined D-shaped flanking towers containing three levels of arrow loops with first-floor private chambers and a hall on the second floor. It had a forbidding array of defences protecting access to the gatehouse passage: on either side of the passage there was a ground-floor guardroom and in each of these were two arrow loops to enable guards to fire at attackers. From every guardroom a stairway led up to a room on the first floor from which guards operated the portcullis and could use the inner set of machicolations or 'murder holes' to attack incomers below. The stairs continued to the upper levels and the parapet, from which guards could access the outer machicolations.

GATEHOUSE UNDER ATTACK

Attackers approaching from outside would thus encounter first a string of machicolations, then a portcullis, followed by an inward-opening gate and more machicolations before they had to negotiate the passage covered by the arrow loops. Doors to the two side rooms each had their own portcullis and between them was another line of machicolations. The passageway was designed to be defended from both directions – from the outside and from the courtyard. Coming out into the gatehouse from the courtyard a soldier would have encountered, again, first machicolations, second a portcullis, third another inward-opening gate and then further machicolations.

◄ *Handsome Herstmonceux Castle in Sussex, built in the middle of the 15th century, bears defensive features but dates from an era when gentlemen like its builder – Sir Roger Fiennes – wanted fortifications for their look and status, rather than from any concern about potential attack.*

GATEHOUSES OF EDWARD I

These measures meant that the gatehouse was defensible from either direction in case of the castle being overrun, and were clearly deemed desirable since Gilbert de Clare subsequently built another gatehouse along very similar lines in 1268–71 – the east gatehouse at Caerphilly Castle.

The gatehouses at Tonbridge and Caerphilly castles went on to be the models for those built by Edward I at his Welsh castles in the 1280s and 1290s, in particular at Harlech and Beaumaris. The gatehouse at Harlech Castle, guarded by twin D-shaped defensive towers in the Tonbridge style, had two upper floors divided into rooms, with fireplaces and three windows per floor looking over the inner ward. One theory is that the first floor was accommodation for the constable and the second for elite guests – possibly even the king.

The gatehouse itself was defended by three portcullises and two or more thick doors, the outer of which had two leaves and was secured with a horizontal drawbar that passed into the thickness of the wall. Then came two portcullises and a further door with drawbar; then another portcullis, probably with another set of heavy doors in front of it. The front two portcullises were lifted into the first-floor room at the front (which was a chapel) and the third into one of the two rooms at the rear. The first floor also contained the winches used for raising and lowering the portcullises and, on the inner side of the gatehouse, gave on to external stairs.

The King's Gate at Caernarfon Castle, built in 1296–1323, was even more heavily defended, introducing a right-angle turn into the sequence of defences: a drawbridge, with a pit in the passageway into which it descended when closed; two portcullises; machicolations; a set of gates; two further portcullises; then another set of gates giving into a hallway in which the passageway turned 90 degrees to the right towards another portcullis and a final set of gates leading into the lower ward. (The gatehouse at Caernarfon was never completed and so how it was intended to work can only be a matter of conjecture.) There were four guardrooms accessed from the passageway, two to the front and two to the rear.

These heavily defended Welsh castles of Edward I were very much working fortresses, which came under severe and frequent attack and so needed all of these mechanisms to repel invaders. Many of the modifications were developed in direct response to a failure of preceding defences. For instance, just prior to the building of the King's Gate by master mason Walter of Hereford, Caernarfon Castle had been captured by the Welsh under Madog ap Llewlyn in 1294, but was taken back by the king a year later. Moreover, Caernarfon was the capital of Edward I's administration in North Wales, so the defences erected there had symbolic as well as practical value.

Elegance and symmetry

Monumental gatehouses remained an important feature even after the defensibility of the castle became much less important in the 14th and 15th centuries. During this later period, handsome symmetrical frontages still featured martial-looking polygonal towers equipped with defensive features either side of a gateway – for example, at Maxstoke Castle, Warwickshire, built for Sir William de Clinton, 1st Earl of Huntington in 1345; and Herstmonceux Castle, Sussex, built for Sir Roger Fiennes, treasurer to King Henry VI, in c.1441. Both were noble residences built merely in the style of a castle, rather than being working fortresses.

▼ *Guédelon Castle as it will look when the building program is complete, in c.2025, with an imposing twin-towered gatehouse. The Great Tower at the right is shown fitted with wooden hoarding for defense against any attackers.*

DEFENSIVE TOWERS

Early stone castles relied on soldiers patrolling an alure atop the crenellated walls to provide protection, along with the forbidding defences built into the entrance gateway. As time went on, though, master masons increasingly placed towers along the walls of the castle and made sure that they were amply equipped with arrow loops, to increase the opportunity for defensive fire.

At Dover Castle, King Henry II built defensive towers on battered plinths in the inner curtain and a section of the outer curtain walls in *c.*1180. Here, the impressive Avranches Tower was raised in the eastern corner of the outer curtain wall. The tower was complemented by a series of rectangular wall towers, all with arrow loops. Moreover, the sections of wall in which these towers were built also had arrow loops incorporated – one of the first times this had been done. It gave a semi-octagonal profile to increase the field of fire for the defensive archers; the set of three loops on each level, for the use of one crossbowman, meant that he could fire in three directions by running from one loop to another. Galleries in the wall gave access to these firing platforms. However, despite this, since the Avranches and other defensive towers built at this time at Dover Castle were open on their inner side, towards the castle interior, they would have served no defensive purpose if the castle were taken.

BENEFITS OF ROUND TOWERS

Similar sections of wall with rectangular towers were built *c.*1190 in the inner bailey curtain wall at Framlingham Castle by Roger Bigod, 2nd Earl of Norfolk. A number of polygonal towers were also constructed around this time, for example the hexagonal Butavant Tower at Corfe Castle and the Bell Tower at the Tower of London in *c.*1190. Elsewhere, semicircular, D-shaped or round-wall towers were being built at Chinon in France, at Conisbrough in Yorkshire and at Chepstow, where William Marshal built round towers in the wall of the middle bailey from 1190 onwards. A few years later, in 1196–98, Richard I built Château Gaillard in France with a whole series of cylindrical towers along the curtain walls of the middle and outer baileys.

Master masons found that round towers were more stable than rectangular or polygonal ones – something that was especially desirable since an attacking army, if its soldiers could get close enough, might try to dig under the tower in the hope of making it collapse. This method was extremely effective, and was the very technique that worked for Prince Louis' besieging army at Dover Castle. Round towers were less vulnerable to this form of attack, and they also provided a wider line of fire for the defensive crossbowmen stationed within the tower to send crossbow bolts hurtling murderously out at attackers through the arrow loops cut in the walls. Another benefit was that missiles fired against the towers by siege engines were more likely to be deflected.

ROUND TOWERS

Master masons often began with simple geometry when laying out a tower and commonly created simple 3D models when in discussion with their patron, the lord, about the shape the castle should take. In addition, they sometimes built templates for certain features of building – for example,

◂ Chateau Gaillard. The great tower and the inner bailey are visible in the background, beyond the largely ruined middle bailey. Originally the wall in the foreground along the middle bailey featured a string of cylindrical towers.

► *Conisbrough Castle, South Yorkshire, was built in stone in the last half of the 12th century by Hamelin Plantagenet. This reconstruction drawing depicts the castle in the 13th century after Hamelin's son added the curtain wall with its semicircular D-shaped towers. (Getty)*

at Guédelon the carpenters made a wooden template for the shape of the steps in the chapel tower's spiral staircase. Simple geometrical drawings were also used to plot the shape of a tower.

The next stage was typically to mark out the shapes on the ground with wooden pegs and ropes. At Guédelon, the builders used a giant compass, created by erecting a mast in the centre of the laid-out tower and attaching a horizontal pole to it. As the central mast was turned, the pole and attached plumb line marked out a perfect circle on the ground. Once the dimensions were demarcated, the labourers could set to work digging out the foundations.

Often, master masons and stonemasons, carpenters and labourers had to adapt plans as they worked in response to local geology or to make the best of available materials. This was true at Guédelon, too, and the team frequently had to change their strategy and use common sense to overcome unforeseen problems. For example, at Guédelon an issue that arose as towers went up and floors were fitted was that it was easy to lose track of the centre of the tower, something that was not desirable since if this were to happen then the walls would gradually lose shape and structural integrity. However, by building corner towers in the largely rectangular plan of

▼ *The Avranches Tower in the eastern corner of the outer curtain wall at Dover Castle. This view shows one of the firing platforms built for crossbowmen, showing the choice of directions they had for firing. (PD)*

► *Marten's Tower, built for Roger Bigod, 5th earl of Norfolk in c.1287–93 in the lower bailey at Chepstow, looms over the approach by land to the castle. Substantial spurs protect the base of the wall from attack. It was later used as a prison.*

Guédelon, the master mason and his team found they could extend the lines of the walls that met at the corner to find the centre of the tower, at which point they could raise the Great Tower. They thus stretched ropes along the line of the east and north curtain walls and knew that the point at which they met was the centre of the tower.

D-SHAPED DEFENSIVE TOWERS

An alternative option for the defensive wall tower was a D-shaped profile, used by Philip Augustus at the Louvre in *c.*1190–92 and by King John on the wall of the West Bailey at Corfe Castle in 1201–04. At Corfe Castle, these towers did not have a solid back: they were for archers, who could fire from four arrow loops – two giving a line of fire along the curtain wall and two outwards. John also had towers of this profile raised on the west and north walls of Dover Castle, but here they had solid backs that protruded within the curtain wall. D-shaped towers were easier to build within the line of the curtain wall than a fully round tower, while retaining many of the military defensive advantages of the latter – such as improved lines of fire, reduced vulnerability to mining, and the capacity to deflect missiles.

ARROW LOOPS

In castles built in France in the 13th century to the standard set by Philip II, arrow loops typically had a different design to those built by the Plantagenet kings. The design used by Philippien castles – and at Guédelon – prioritised the solidity of the walls above ease of use and range for vision for the bowmen. The slits at these places are about 60–120cm (24–48in) tall and just 5–10cm (2–4in) wide and are set in a V-shaped embrasure – an opening that is splayed out on the inside of the wall. Bowmen using these could fire only in one direction, but this was offset by the fact that slits of this type were easy and quick – and therefore cheaper – to build. The Plantagenet arrow loops, meanwhile, were easier to access because they were set in the thickness of the wall, and had a support on which the bowman could rest his foot to steady himself for firing. Some had a horizontal opening halfway up the vertical slit – so they looked something like a crucifix – which increased the angle at which the bowmen could fire. Both types of loop were strategically positioned in corner towers and along sections of curtain wall to maximise the range of fire for the castle defenders.

The loops were designed for use by crossbowmen. This was because the crossbow was easier to use in the confined spaces within the castle than the longbow and delivered a powerful shot that could drive clean through the armour of an attacking knight. Skilled crossbowmen were extremely accurate. In the castle, they kept their crossbow 'arrows' – hard metal bolts or 'quarrels' – in a barrel close at hand for grabbing, fitting to the crossbow and firing.

TYPES OF ARROW LOOP

The arrangement of the arrow loops was clearly an important consideration for their effectiveness as a means of defence. The sturdy, twin-towered gatehouse at Tonbridge Castle (see page 38) had its arrow loops arranged in three tiers and staggered – that is, not arranged one above the other but in a kind of diamond pattern on the front of the towers. This made it possible for the bowmen to cover an arc of ground with defensive fire. A ditch, to be crossed with a drawbridge, also lay in from of the tower, making an attack more difficult. In the impressive barbican at Lewes Castle (see page 20), built *c.*1330 for John de Warenne, 7th Earl of Surrey, the barbican tower and flanking turrets either side of the gate arch all had Plantagenet-style cross-shaped arrow loops at first-floor level to provide effective cover fire.

▾ *The gatehouse at Tonbridge Castle built 1250–65 by Richard de Clare, Earl of Gloucester, or his son Gilbert, has three tiers of arrow loops in its rounded flanking towers. (Alamy)*

▸ *It was so difficult to fire an arrow in through the slit to injure anyone inside that when it happened it must have been as much by chance as by skill.*

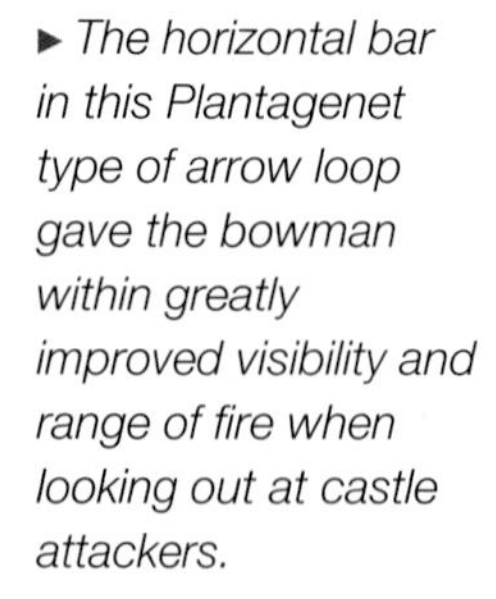

▸ *The horizontal bar in this Plantagenet type of arrow loop gave the bowman within greatly improved visibility and range of fire when looking out at castle attackers.*

BUILDING TECHNIQUES: DESIGNING AND FITTING AN ARROW LOOP

The narrow, vertical openings in a castle's wall are variously called loopholes, arrow loops or arrow slits. At Guédelon the arrow loops have narrow embrasures like those built in the castles of the French king, Philip II, which reduce the field of vision, therefore the arrow loops are offset on each level of the tower to increase the archers' range.

1 A mason has laid out the embrasure – the widest inner part of the arrow loop opening in the wall of the chamber.

2 He fixes the sill (the bottom of the opening) in position. He is careful to ensure that it is absolutely flat.

3 He begins to build up the side walls of the arrow-loop opening. He uses the long wooden guide to check alignment.

4 The 'staightedge' – a long wooden ruler – is one of the most important tools for working and checking.

5 A mason places the stones around the jamb. He uses mortar mixed according to 13th-century methods.

6 The masons have fixed corbels on the jambs to support the front lintel, and the back lintel has been fixed.

7 A team of four masons lowers a lintel very gently on to temporary wooden supports.

8 A sandstone lintel spans an arrow loop in Guédelon's Great Tower. It rests on sculpted corbels.

9 Relieving arches are built above the lintels to distribute the load throughout the wall.

DEFENSIVE EQUIPMENT

The defensive machinery of the gatehouse was integral to its design and construction. Machicolations and arrow loops giving from guard rooms on to gatehouse passages clearly needed to be incorporated into the structure – as did spaces in the stonework to hold the portcullis machinery and the drawbridge. All these elements had to be planned for from the very start.

Since castles were typically defended by a moat or ditch, a bridge was needed to access the gatehouse – and the retractable drawbridge was developed to maintain security. The simplest type was the lifting bridge, which pivoted on the gate's threshold. The outer end of this was linked by chains to a windlass in a guardroom above the gatehouse passage that was operated by soldiers, who wound the chain around an axle to lift the drawbridge. In its vertical position the bridge provided an additional barrier in front of the gatehouse.

Openings in the wall above the gateway are usually all that survive of this type of drawbridge mechanism. They can be seen, for example, at the inner gatehouse of the White Castle, Monmouthshire, where Hubert de Burgh, Justiciar under King John, carried out rebuilding in 1229–32.

The trouble with this type of drawbridge is that it took the guards some time to wind the chain and raise the bridge and the process could be too slow in a crisis. Another type of bridge was thus developed – the 'turning bridge'. In this

◄ *A reconstruction of the gatehouse at Goodrich Castle, Herefordshire (c.1275), shows the winch devices in the upper chamber used to raise the twin portcullises, as well as guards on duty in the gateway passage below. There were two portcullises: one at the gateway entrance and a second behind, partway along the passage. (Getty)*

▲ *The 15th-century gatehouse at Chateau de Vitré in Brittany shows chains for raising the double drawbridge and slots in the masonry into which the lifting arms were raised. (Getty)*

▲ *The holes in which the drawbridge chains were stored when the bridge was raised are visible above the raised portcullis of the outer gatehouse at Caerphilly Castle. (Alamy)*

▼ *Upstairs in the gatehouse at Caerphilly Castle a replica portcullis shows how these barriers were constructed and how sturdy they were. (Cadw)*

▼ *The gatehouse passage looking towards the inner ward at Harlech Castle. Note the groove in which the portcullis ran up and down, and arrow loops for firing at attackers. (Cadw)*

design, the bridge pivoted around its midpoint: the inner section was weighted and there was a pit on the castle side of the ditch/moat or in the gate passage. Because it was weighted, this drawbridge would swing closed unless it was held open – so if the bridge had to be raised quickly, the guards simply released the locking element that was holding it open and it would immediately and automatically shut.

The use of the weight was markedly similar to the mechanism used in the trebuchet siege machine; as we have noted, castle builders in this period were often skilled military engineers, too. As the weighted inner section of the bridge descended into the pit, the counterbalancing outer side raised up and, as with the retractable drawbridge, in its vertical position it provided an additional barrier to entrance. Quick and easy to operate, this type of bridge was fitted in many castles, such as the donjon at Château de Coucy in *c.*1225–50, as well as in another part of the White Castle, the outer gatehouse, which was probably raised in *c.*1256 by the future King Edward I. Versions of it were also installed at about the same time in the Black Gate in Newcastle Castle and in the 1270s by Edward I at two of his Welsh castle – Flint and Rhuddlan.

In some places, it appears that a combination of the two systems was used – for example at the main gateway at Caerphilly Castle. Here, we find both a pit in the gateway passage for the inner end of the drawbridge to drop into and square holes above the gateway for the chains of a lifting bridge. The evidence at the gate-next-the-sea at Beaumaris Castle also suggests this double system was in place.

▲ *A version of a lifting drawbridge at the 10th-century Soncino Castle in Italy. The chains are attached to wooden arms that are wound up to retract into a vertical position in cavities cut into the masonry to raise the bridge.*

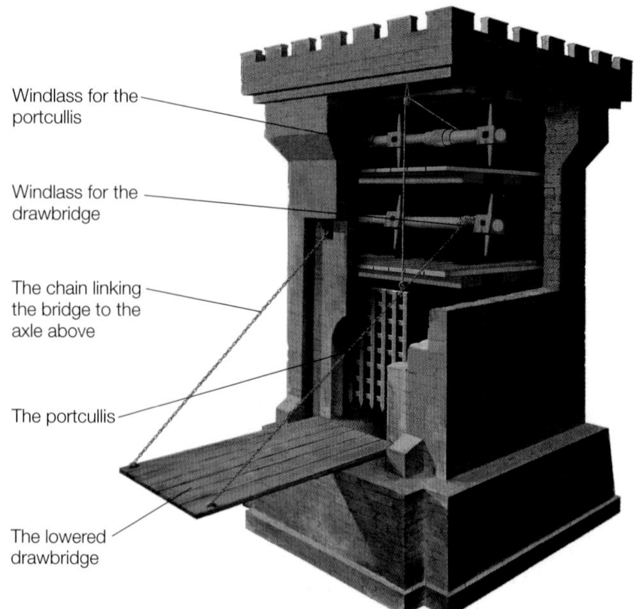

▲ *Cutaway reconstruction of a lifting bridge. When in a vertical position it was a sturdy barrier with a portcullis dropped down behind. The inner end of lifting bridges was usually weighted underneath to make lifting them easier.*

◄ *Corbelled machicolations against the wall above the Gate-next-the-Sea at Beaumaris Castle allowed defenders to fire weapons and drop missiles from above, should the castle come under attack. (Cadw)*

From around 1300 onwards, a third type of drawbridge used a counterbalanced beam that pivoted above the entrance: a weighted section on the inner side and an outer section attached to the bridge by a chain. As the inner section was lowered, the outer section pulled the drawbridge up. When vertical, the beams fitted into specially designed slots. The arrangement was used in the entrance to the keep at Raglan Castle, and in the entrance to the north-east tower at Bothwell Castle, Scotland, as well as in many French castles.

MURDER HOLES

Openings in the vault of the gateway passage made it possible for defenders to attack intruders from above and there were often several rows of these in the entrance passage. At the main east gate at Caerphilly Castle, for example, an intruder would pass through an opening, then encounter a portcullis and, behind that, the gate. In the vault overhead were two lines of murder holes, one above the opening and one between the portcullis and the gate. There was also a slanted opening or chute above the gateway entrance, down which water was poured in case of fire. Guards accessed the outer line of murder holes and the water chute from an opening behind the window above the entranceway and the second line from a guardroom over the gateway passage. The holes could also be used for handing up supplies to guards if necessary.

PORTCULLIS

The gateway was also defended by the portcullis – a grill-like framework gate made of wood with a spiked lower end. The portcullis was set in grooves in the walls on either side of the entrance and raised by chains using a windlass set in a guardroom immediately overhead. The wooden framework of the portcullis was often covered in beaten iron, as in a surviving 14th-century example at the outer gatehouse at Carlisle Castle, England. This would have made it longer lasting and was a precaution against fire. There were various systems for raising and lowering the portcullis, but generally ratchets were used to hold it in position once it had been raised and a counterweight system meant it could be released to fall either swiftly or more gently.

If attackers caught the castle guards by surprise, the portcullis would be sent thundering down into the entrance. More foolhardy troops might be injured by its spikes, while others would have to back off or rush forwards into the gateway to avoid it – either way they would be split up. Those trapped in the gateway would face attack from either side by crossbows fired through arrow loops or from above via the murder holes, while those shut outside would be assailed by bowmen firing from the top of the gatehouse, the alure along the castle wall or arrow holes in the flanking walls and towers. In response, all the attackers could do was try to set the portcullis on fire to gain entrance.

During more peaceful times, the portcullis was usually raised out of sight when not in use – with only its metal-covered spikes protruding. However, some designs allowed for the portcullis to remain in view when raised. Surviving evidence suggests that the portcullis was assembled and fitted while the gatehouse was being built and that carpenters and masons worked side by side to get this key piece of defensive equipment into position. If the portcullis was badly enough damaged during a skirmish to need replacing, it would have been dismantled in situ. A new one would then have needed to be assembled piece by piece to fit in the existing stone framework of the gateway.

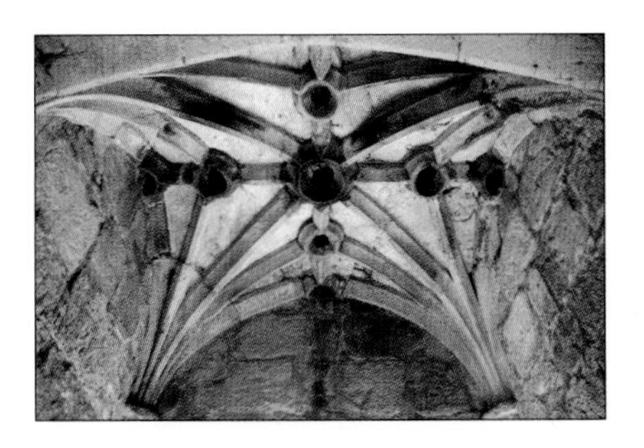

◂ *Murder holes for dropping missiles or pouring liquids on attackers in Bodiam Castle, probably never used in earnest.*

◂ *Portcullises were sometimes kept visible in a raised position when not needed, as here at the restored 12th-century Château de Beynac, France.*

◂ *This forbidding portcullis is at the vast Malbork Castle in Poland, built by the religious order of the Teutonic Knights in the late 13th century.*

▾ *The 14th-century gatehouse at Bodiam Castle may have been designed more for its appearance than actual defensive effectiveness, but it gives a good idea of an attacker's view of machicolations (above) and spiked wooden portcullis.*

3

CURTAIN WALLS AND BATTLEMENTS

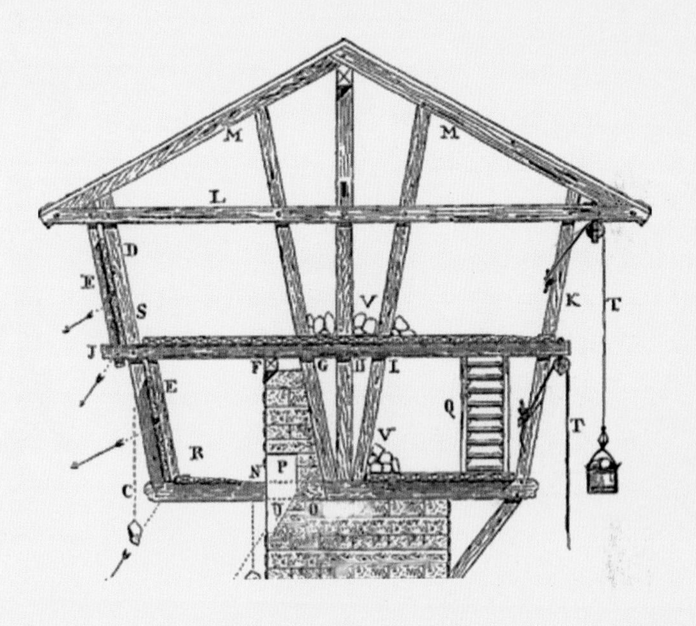

The castle courtyard or bailey was protected in the earliest castles by a wooden palisade, and later by a thick stone curtain wall topped by a crenellated parapet. Arrow loops, through which bowmen fired at attackers, were inserted in the curtain wall and the defensive towers placed strategically along its length. Master masons also built sections of wooden hoarding and, later, stone machicolation, from which guards and bowmen could fire directly from above.

◄ *Harlech Castle, in Wales, built on a near-vertical cliff face, was impregnable from every angle. (Alamy)*

BUILDING A CURTAIN WALL

The curtain wall was a key part of the enceinte – the name given to the round of fortifications that enclosed the castle bailey. This could include outer fortifications, such as water defences or ditches, and there could also be more than one round of walls. In the concentric castle design, master masons laid out inner and outer baileys together with two rounds of curtain walls.

The outline of the shape enclosed by the curtain walls was often determined by the site. Many castles were built on imposing defensible sites such as hilltops, cliffs or rocky promontories and local geography and geology determined the shape of the enceinte. The crusader castle of Krak des Chevaliers in Syria, built by the Knights Hospitaller from 1142 onwards on a rocky spur accessible only from the south, is an impressive example. Another is Stirling Castle in Scotland, begun in the 12th century on a crag guarding a crossing of the River Forth.

LAYING OUT THE WALLS

At other sites, of course, the lord and his master mason could shape the castle as they chose. In laying out the castle at Guédelon, the master mason was working to an architectural plan established by Philip II of France that called for a quadrangular courtyard with four corner towers connected by high curtain walls, with one tower – the Great Tower – being

▾ *The Philippien-style layout of Guédelon is based on a quadrangular layout. The four corner towers, one of which – the Great Tower, in the northeastern corner – is larger at 28.5m (93ft 6in) tall, are connected by high curtain walls with walkways. The chapel tower is in the northwestern corner, and beside it the postern gate provides the chance for a rear exit.*

▾ *Krak des Chevaliers sits atop a 650m (2,130ft) high spur near Tartus in Syria. Its natural position plus strong concentric fortifications built by the Knights Hospitaller gave it a formidable reputation.*

▸ *After the Guédelon castle site was cleared of vegetation and the land prepared in spring 1997, the quadrangular layout was marked out on the ground and the walls were begun over the following seasons. Two large winches were already in use for lifting heavy materials.*

taller and of larger diameter than the other three. The quadrangular layout combined curtain wall lengths of 52.5m (172ft), 39m (128ft), 49.5m (162ft) and 47.1m (155ft).

Typically, the layout was first marked on the ground using pegs and ropes, then the foundation pits were dug by labourers under the supervision of the master mason and, where he was available, the ditcher or dyker who had overseen the excavation of the castle ditch or water defences. The depth of castle foundations could vary tremendously. For instance, at Warkworth Castle in Northumberland, possibly built in stone by Robert fitz Richard between 1150 and 1200, we know that the foundations for the curtain wall were dug roughly only 50cm (20in) deep. By contrast, the rectangular stone keep at the Tower of London – begun in 1077, and which came to be known as the White Tower after it was whitewashed in the 13th century – had much deeper foundations. We can surmise this because a sheriff in the reign of Henry II wrote of it, 'The walls and keep rise from the deepest foundations and are secured with a mortar mixed with beasts' blood.'

At Guédelon there are no foundations, the castle was built directly on the bedrock of the quarry. As a requirement of planning permission the master mason brought in machinery to compact the soil – an example of the occasional deviations from the 13th-century methods that are required by 21st-century authorities.

Occasionally the carpenters were involved in this formative stage and would sink oak piles deep into the foundations to stabilise the structure. Archaeologists have found remains of oak piles of this type in the foundations of Saint-Verain castle in Burgundy, France. We also know that the walls were sometimes built up all round the building's planned outline to a height of about 1m (3ft) before the team concentrated on one area. Typically, castle walls were about 2.5m (8ft) thick.

At Guédelon, the curtain walls, which are 3m (almost 10ft) high, are 2.4m (7ft 10in) thick at the base and 2m (6ft 7in) thick at the top. This thickness differential is typical of medieval castles, and was used as a way of giving them added protection against mining and further attacks at ground level. The bases of the walls were typically built with a tapering shape – a plinth – and the tower walls were usually even thicker – for example, the Guédelon Great Tower is 3.8m (12ft 6in) thick at the base.

To construct the walls, mason layers built up the outer and inner faces of the walls at the same time and filled the inner part with a rubble core. They also periodically placed a bonder or header – a stone that is placed at right angles to the wall's face and lies across the rubble infill, and serves to bind the facing stones to the infill. Medieval builders must

▸ *The north curtain wall at Harlech Castle in Gwynedd, Wales. The horizontal line indicates where the wall originally finished before it was made taller between 1282 and 1283 (Cadw).*

have discovered the need for these bonders by trial and error – without them, the rubble infill, which is bound with wet mortar, moves, making the facing wall lose its verticality. As the walls rose taller, the wall builders also had to make putlog holes in the masonry. These were present to allow for the insertion of the timbers of the wooden scaffolding that the carpenters built to enable the masons to work on the higher sections of wall.

MASONS AT WORK

Teams of mason layers worked with trowel, plumb line and mason's level to raise the walls, using the trowel to apply the mortar that bound the rubble infill and the facing stones together, the plumb line to check that blocks and the wall itself followed a vertical line, and the mason's level to check that the tops of the blocks were flat, perfectly horizontal.

There were generally two types of facing. Ashlar blocks were finely cut, regularly sized and expertly finished with square faces and edges. Rubble or rough walling, by contrast, consisted of undressed stones of irregular size and shape, together with offcuts from the quarrymen. Sometimes master masons directed their workers to use ashlar blocks on the outer walls for a prestigious appearance and rough walling on inner-facing walls. For the same reason, ashlar may have been reserved for towers.

▲ *Some of the authentic medieval masons' tools at Guédelon: a masons' level, a lump hammer, a punch and a chisel. The level is used to ensure that a horizontal stone or course of masonry is perfectly even.*

▼ *Using a round hammer and chisel, a Guédelon mason works a piece of limestone. While the castle is mainly built of sandstone, limestone from a neighbouring quarry is used for vaults and windows.*

At Harlech Castle in Wales, the builders mainly relied on local grey-green sandstone, using dressed blocks for the towers and rougher material, perhaps excavated from the ditch, for the curtain walls. On some sites, you can see ashlar masonry and rough walls side by side – for example, at Conisbrough Castle, where a section of curtain wall with a rough finish abuts the ashlar masonry of the keep. The curtain wall was the later addition, and was probably built by William de Warenne shortly after 1202; the fine cylindrical keep was already standing, having been built by William's father and Henry II's half-brother, Hamelin Plantagenet, between 1180 and 1190.

When building coursed rubble walling, the masons inserted a continuous horizontal row of dressed stone every 3m (9ft 10in) to ensure that masonry remains level: this is called a levelling course. These courses both strengthen the wall and allow the masons to check that the wall is level. A mason's level is placed on the dressed stones to help guide the subsequent rough walling.

Herringbone and petit-appareil

In addition to ashlar and rough walling, there were other types of finish used in curtain walls and the masonry of keeps and towers. Herringbone masonry, for instance, used smaller stones at an angle of about 45 degrees, leaning left in one course and right in the next with a levelling course of flat stones in between. Examples are found at Pevensey Castle (East Sussex), Exeter Castle (Devon) and the inner bailey wall of Tamworth Castle (Staffordshire). Some historians argue that this technique, which derived from Roman *opus spicatum* ('spiked work'), was used when buildings needed to be erected quickly.

Petit-appareil consisted of regular rows of smaller, square blocks and was a technique that was popular in France, where it was used in the walls of the donjon at Langeais (Centre-Val de Loire), built as early as c.1000, and at

▶ *The latrine shaft protrudes from the wall on the north wall at Guédelon. Note the putlog holes and the levelling course in the masonry between two sections of rough walling.*

▲ *Zig-zag herringbone masonry was a stonebuilding technique derived from the Romans, who called it* opus spicatum *('spiky work'). This example is at Pevensey Castle, originally built by the Romans.*

▼ *Conisbrough Castle keep and curtain wall. The wall has a rough finish while the keep is faced with fine ashlar blocks. Here the keep (1180–90) preceded the wall (c.1202).*

◄*A miniature from a French manuscript of c.1450, the* Bouquechardiere Chonicle, *purports to depict the building of the biblical Tower of Babel. The builders use pulleys, putlog scaffolding and handheld wickerwork baskets, exactly like those developed at Guédelon. (Getty)*

▼*An image from the 15th-century manuscript* Les Tres Riches Heures du Duc de Berry *represents Spring. In the background is Dourdan Castle, one of the examples studied by masons at Guédelon. (Getty)*

Avranches (Manche), another 11th-century donjon. In Britain, the keep of Chepstow Castle, built c.1085, also used this type of stonework.

Stitching

If the castle layout required two lengths of rubble wall to meet at an angle, a structurally vulnerable spot was created. Master masons solved the problem by building a tower at that point or using a sequence of dressed stones at the angle to 'stitch' the walls together. At Conisbrough Castle in *c.*1190, the master mason used single-faced cornerstones arranged right then left in sequence for the stitching.

Hard labour

Raising the castle walls was labour intensive, requiring large numbers of masons and labourers to work together. If enough money was available for maximum manpower then wall building could be done at speed, as happened at Harlech Castle in Wales. The haste in this instance was because the structure was urgently needed by Edward I both to function as a working fortress and to be a show of strength intended to subdue North Wales. The initial 4.6m (15ft) of the inner walls at Harlech Castle were raised in 1282–83 by a team of 35 stonemasons and accompanying carpenters; archaeologists can see from a line in the stonework where they stopped. By this stage, the castle could be defended against attack. Work then continued until 1289 to complete

the superb concentric castle, with the walls being thickened in some places and built to their full height. Seemingly no expense was spared: documents show that in 1286, when labour was most intensive, the building work at Harlech Castle required no less than £240 every month to pay for the 227 stonemasons, 115 quarrymen, 30 blacksmiths, 22 carpenters and 546 labourers. In total, the building work during the period 1282–89 cost £8,190.

At Conwy work began within days of King Edward I's decision in March 1283 that he would construct a castle and walled town on the site of the Cistercian monastery of Aberconwy Abbey. Under master mason Master James of St Georges and Sir John Bonvillars, labourers began on digging out the ditches, then raised the curtain walls and towers for the castle in the first season, 1283–84. The next phase over two years 1284–86 involved raising the buildings within the castle walls and laying out the town walls for the adjoining settlement. The huge army of labourers needed for this was imported from England – each year they were required to gather at Chester and then make their way by foot to the castle site. Overall the cost of the castle and the town walls was £15,000. This huge sum was necessary despite the fact that Master James saved costs by building mainly in local grey sandstone and limestone – stone that did not prove good enough for detailed carving on windows, so he imported better sandstone from as far away as the Wirral.

At Guédelon, it took four years to complete the lower part of the walls of the curtain and towers at the scarp (the inner

BUILDING TECHNIQUES: EDGE BEDDING

Quarrymen and masons pay close attention to the direction in which the sedimentary layers run through the rock. Masons lay stones according to their 'bedding planes' (the surface that separates each layer of stratified rock from its preceeding layer). These beds are similar to leaves in a book: a book supports more weight when laid flat than when stood on end.

When building a wall, the masons lay the stones so their sedimentary layers run horizontally along the wall face. This is because stone is strongest when it is laid in its natural position – with the layers travelling as they would have done in the ground rather than vertically, which would weaken the wall. Sometimes, however, they are placed vertically – at right angles to the wall face – in a process called edge bedding.

Masons only place stones in this way when laying coping (the top section of wall) or sills (the base of a doorway or window) because these rocks are exposed on their top sides and there is a chance the beds will separate..

▲ *The edge-bedded stones will eventually form the webbing of a cross-rib vault on the chapel tower.*

▲ *The masons carefully position edge-bedded stones on a curved formwork.The stones are fixed in position with mortar.*

▲ *A section of the curtain wall shows naturally bedded stones on the facing wall and edge-bedded in the rubble core.*

▲ *A thick layer of sacrifical mortar is spread over the top of unfinished walls at the end of a building season, to protect the work from winter weather.*

◄ *A 15th-century painting shows labourers operating a hand winch in the construction of a castle. On the wall to the right masons are standing on scaffolding secured using putlogs.*

bank of the ditch). The mason layers by this stage were getting weary, so the stonecutters tried to raise their spirits by engraving upbeat messages in the final stones they supplied – including 'keep going, lads' and 'this is the last one!'

During this phase of the construction they also found that they needed to adapt their methods to fit requirements – in other words, to 'get real'. For instance, initially the masons were preparing the dressed sandstone blocks so meticulously that they produced at most one stone a day. It dawned on the team, though, that at this rate the building of Guédelon Castle was not practicable: it would simply take too long.

SAFETY FIRST

Authenticity is of utmost importance to the builders of Guédelon, both in terms of materials and techniques. However, some modern safety features do apply to the treadmill winches, which are used every day for heavy lifting. These come in the form of drum brakes fitted to the treadmill winches, which the overseer can order to be applied. Moreover, while Guédelon craftsmen and women make rope for general use on the site, in the case of the treadmill, modern industrial rope and modern pulleys and axles are fitted instead. While in use, this potentially dangerous piece of machinery is supervised by the overseer, who stands at the foot of the wheel and directs proceedings, issuing orders to both the workers operating the wheel and brakes and those receiving the materials that are being lifted.

Fortunately, a research trip to Dourdan Castle in Essonne made them realise that the stones on the scarp needn't be perfectly finished – the ones there had a rougher, tooled finish and it was still possible to see some of the wedge holes made while quarrying the stones – this meant they were able to speed up their work rate considerably.

Sacrificial mortar

Even when erected in haste, building a castle inevitably took several, if not many, years. This was in part because master masons and their crews did not work through the frost and bad weather of the winter, which meant that walls could not be finished in a single season. Before closing down the site, therefore, mason layers sometimes opted to protect their work against the frost by applying a layer of manure and straw, which could be cleared off the following year – as happened at Builth Castle in Wales, built for Edward I in 1277. Builth was built in stone on an existing motte-and-bailey castle with two baileys within a boundary wall. Edward's work was overseen from 1278 by Master James of St Georges, who arrived in Wales that year and took over building work at Aberystwyth, Flint and Rhuddlan as well as Builth. Work continued at Builth until 1282, but was left incomplete because of lack of funds and because Edward was concentrating his resources on operations in Gwynedd. The recorded cost at Builth, interestingly, is relatively low – just £1,666, due to the fact there were existing earthworks from the earlier motte-and-bailey castle.

Another technique was to apply what was called 'sacrificial mortar' – a thicker layer of mortar on top of the unfinished

BUILDING TECHNIQUES: SCAFFOLDING AND PUTLOGS

The holes to support scaffolding struts, when building high walls, were normally arranged in a grid pattern. The gaps between the different levels of putlog holes in a wall was typically around 1m (3ft) to 1.2m (4ft). The putlog holes were designed into the wall at the correct intervals, with masonry built around them.

1 Masons preparing a putlog hole. They build around a block of wood; which can then be removed, leaving a hole in the masonry that the carpenters use to insert a putlog during installation of the scaffolding.

2 Putlog scaffolding on the Chapel Tower. The putlogs support the working platform around the top of the tower as well as the pulley system that is used for lifting and lowering materials as construction progresses.

3 Carpenters fit a putlog in the masonry. They then lay planks on the horizontal putlogs, forming a platform on which the masons can work. The platforms can be raised or lowered using the different layers of putlogs in the walls.

4 Putlog scaffolding on the Chapel Tower. Note the large number of putlog holes, now not in use, lower down the face of the tower and along the western curtain wall. Part of the scaffolding includes a safety barrier around the top.

BUILDING TECHNIQUES: OPERATING THE DOUBLE TREADMILL

The double-treadwheel winch has been in use at Guédelon since 2010. Inside the two large wheels – known as the squirrel cage – two workers walk at a steady pace to turn the wheels. As the wheels turn, they wrap rope around the machine's central axle and the load is lifted. The winch is used on average ten times a day.

▲ *A trial run of the double treadmill winch is carried out, early in the 2010 building season, to ensure that it had been fitted safely in its new position.*

▲ *Everyone using the treadmill winch has to work very carefully and keep in mind what the other members of the team are doing as the huge weights are being moved.*

▲ *While the squirrel cage is moving and the rope is wrapping around the wheel, the foreman on ground level and the brake operator make sure that they are communicating with one another.*

▲ *The double treadwheel winch hoists a heavy load to the top of the tower. Workers prepare to unload it. Some materials have already been lifted on to the scaffolding.*

▲ *The winch has a slewing action; the jib can be pivoted through 360 degrees to deliver its load to the most convenient spot.*

▲ *A diagonal sequence of putlog holes on the south drum tower of the east gatehouse at Harlech Castle, probably used to construct a sloping ramp of woven branches. (Cadw)*

▲ *Workers use a single treadwheel winch on the ground to raise parts of the timber ceiling to the top of the Great Hall in the North Range.*

wall. At the beginning of the next season, the masons scraped this off before resuming work, although they were not always completely thorough in its removal – a fact that has meant historians can identify season breaks in building by the presence of thicker lines of mortar in castle walls.

RAISING MATERIALS

As walls rose, the challenge to be met was how to hoist the heavy stones and other materials to masons and others working on the top of the wall. The answer was pulleys, hand winches and treadmills operated by labourers. At Guédelon, the carpenters built and installed a range of onsite lifting machinery. After they had fitted scaffolding on the wall, simple pulleys were installed for raising small loads, such as a bucket of rubble infill for the curtain walls, and there was also a hand winch that could be easily moved and was used by two men working side by side to raise medium-to-small loads. Treadmill cranes were used for heavy loads.

As in the Middle Ages, the Guédelon masons include putlog holes – used for supporting the wooden scaffolding – in the masonry as they build the walls. At other sites, archaeologists examine these putlog holes to work out how the scaffolding was installed at a particular location. In some castles, the holes run in horizontal lines along the wall, and probably supported level platforms of scaffolding. In others – at Conwy, Beaumaris and Harlech castles, for example – they run in diagonal lines or go up in spirals around towers. On these holes, archaeologists believe, were placed ramps made of woven-together branches that provided a surface from which labourers could haul up materials. The arrangement of putlog holes at Harlech is one of a number of features in the Welsh castle that are typical of the work done in Savoy at this time, others include the use of corbelled towers, the style of the windows, and semicircular door arches. From the start of work there in 1282 the master mason at Harlech (as at Builth) was Master James of St Georges, so historians have suggested he probably directed the import of Savoyard techniques into the Welsh castle. However, some of the typically Savoyard elements seen in Wales originated after Master James had left his homeland. These are probably the work of craftsmen who followed him and brought with them techniques familiar in Savoy.

The onsite machinery at castles may also have included a single- or double-wheel treadmill crane and/or the ‘sheerlegs’ – a pulley system mounted on tall poles that are joined at the top and splayed at the bottom, which was used for raising delicate loads – for example, a bell to the top of a bell tower. The treadmill was the ancestor of the modern crane and consisted of one or two large vertical wheels attached to a central axis, which are turned by one or two men walking within the wheels. The movement operates a pulley, which in the two-wheeled version was capable of raising loads of up to 500kg (1,100lb).

In addition to their capacity for lifting, the treadmills had the advantage that they could be operated either on the ground or mounted in scaffolding high on the wall. This meant that carpenters would dismantle and rebuild the treadmills at different points of the site, as required. In the medieval period, historians report, some treadmills were not dismantled at all, but were instead kept permanently available – for instance at Mont St Michel (off the coast of Normandy) or Beauvais Cathedral (Hauts-de-France).

CONSTRUCTING A CURTAIN WALL

Building the curtain wall at Guédelon was a huge job requiring work over many building seasons. The total length of wall in the quadrangular layout is 188m (617ft); the walls are 6m (almost 20ft) high and 2–2.4m (6ft 7in–7ft 10in) thick. The base of the towers are in dressed stone and the walls are of coarsed rubble. The rubble cores consist of lower-quality stone and off-cuts from the quarry, bound together with mortar.

▲ *Early in the 2013 season, work began on the western section of the curtain wall. The masons started by scraping back the old mortar. In the background a header – a long stone that will bind the wall's rubble core to its outer section – is being positioned.*

▲ *Wicker baskets filled with lime mortar. Made by the basket weavers at Guédelon, these are light and flexible; much more practical for carrying up ladders and scaffolding than heavy wooden buckets.*

1 A mason carefully positions a large stone in the top part of the wall. He uses mason's lines strung along the upper level to maintain the shape of the wall as he builds it up. He judges by eye how the stones will best fit together.

2 The mason packs the joints between stones with lime mortar. The mortar has a very long setting time, which allows a small amount of movement in the wall, which helps stability. A pointing trowel is used to apply mortar in small spaces.

3 A plumb line is used to check that the stone is positioned vertically. Afterwards a mason's level will be used to check that the wall is perfectly horizontal.

WALL DEFENCES AND FEATURES

The curtain wall enabled communication between different parts of the castle defences. It usually connected a series of towers and sometimes had hidden mural passages within towers or sections of wall to make it possible to get around safely even when the castle was under attack. The alure or walkway along the top of the curtain wall was a lookout spot as well as a fighting platform.

Providing an eagle's-eye view of the surrounding countryside as well as a lofty vantage point from which to assail attackers, the wall walks that ran around the inside of the curtain walls were a vital part of a castle's defences. Marked out by the iconic crenellations so distinctive to castles, the parapets that rimmed the wall walks provided the guards with both shelter – behind the merlons (raised sections) – and suitable firing locations – in the crenels (lower sections or gaps).

◂ *The remains of a mural passage can be seen in the east gatehouse of Harlech Castle. It made it possible for guards and reinforcements to move around out of sight of any attackers. (Cadw)*

MURAL PASSAGES

The curtain walls usually included mural towers, equipped with arrow loops, from where crossbowmen had a better angle of fire along the wall. Some towers also had a mural passage – a passageway running within the thickness of the tower's outer wall that linked the wall walk on either side and enabled safe, rapid movement by the garrison. As an added protective measure, many of these passages were equipped with heavy doors that could be closed, locked and barred to try to halt the enemy if they had penetrated that part of the castle. Examples of mural passages can be seen at Beaumaris Castle, both on the first floor of the inner curtain walls and in the outer curtain wall beside the dock that stands to the right of the main entrance, the gate-next-the-sea. Mural passages also thread the formidable walls and towers of Caernarfon Castle's south front.

HOARDINGS

A wooden construction called a hoarding was often mounted on the outside of the curtain wall and on some towers. Sometimes these structures were permanent, in France there are still a few castles that have preserved or reconstructed

▾ *The outer curtain wall of the concentric Beaumaris Castle has a mural passage in the section near the dock situated to the right of the Gate-Next-the-Sea. (Cadw)*

▲ *Putlog scaffolding along the western section of the Guédelon curtain wall supports workers constructing the crenellated alure in the 2016 building season.*

▲ *The same section of the western wall from outside the castle in the 2017 building season. The crenellated wall walk is now complete. Scaffolding is still in place.*

their medieval hoarding, sometimes they were rapidly put together when the castle was under attack. Bowmen could use them as an elevated firing platform, while other castle defenders could drop weapons and burning substances, such as hot sand or quicklime, through the openings in its floor. Other missiles sent into orbit from the hoarding included firepots – clay pots containing flammable liquids such as tar that were set alight and then hurled at people and siege machines – or simply heavy rocks and stones that could kill and maim the enemy below.

The main evidence of the use of hoardings in British castles comes from surviving sockets found at the top of walls by the parapets in castles such as Pembroke Castle, where putlog holes survive at the top of the early 12th-century keep, and Rochester Castle, where recesses still exist beneath the battlements on the formidable tower keep.

Through these sockets or in these recesses the carpenters would have inserted the supporting beams of the hoardings, which had recesses at their outer ends, before laying a flooring of planks on top. Next, using a small pulley crane mounted on the parapet, vertical posts would have been lowered into the mortices at the beams' outer ends, and timber planks would then have been fitted in between the vertical posts to form the outer wall of the hoarding. The 'floor' was situated at the level of the crenels, so bowmen simply jumped on to the crenels and stepped out on to the hoarding, the floor of which extended out on both sides of the parapet. We know from manuscript illustrations that some hoardings had a protective roof, which was occasionally covered in animal skins in an attempt to protect it against flaming arrows fired from below – but even with this precaution the hoardings were vulnerable to catching fire.

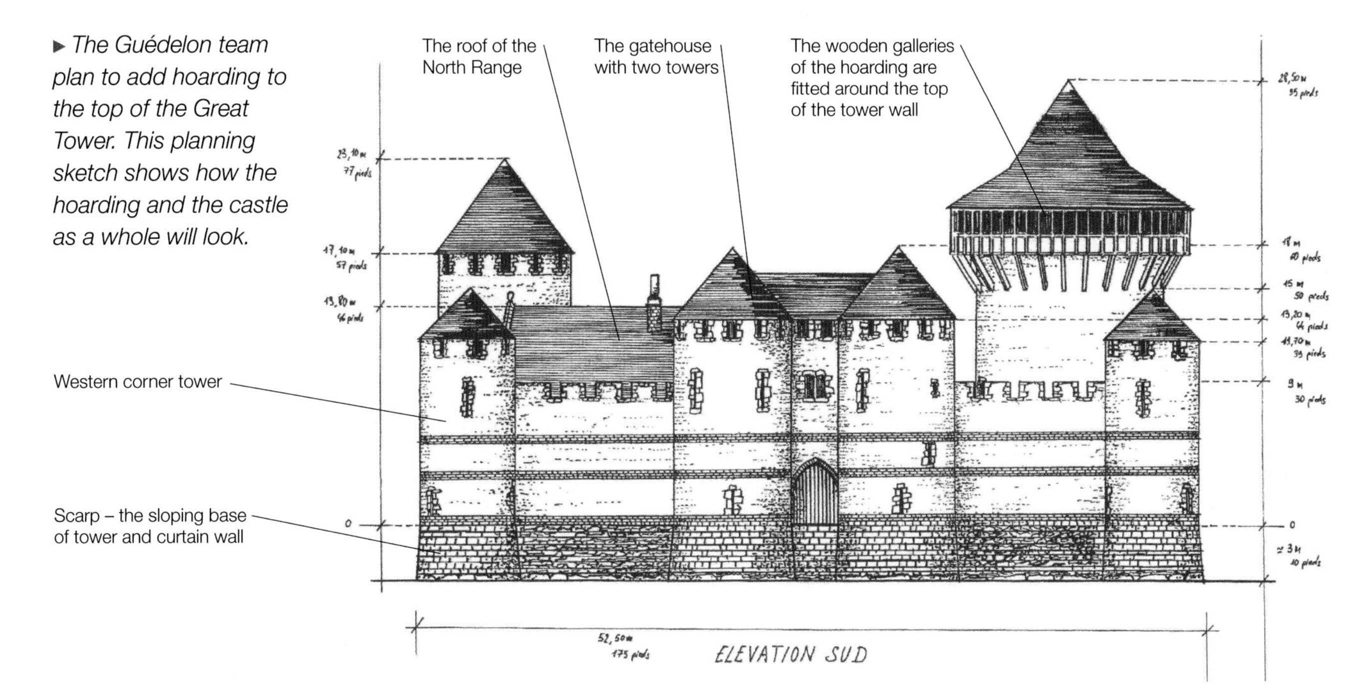

► *The Guédelon team plan to add hoarding to the top of the Great Tower. This planning sketch shows how the hoarding and the castle as a whole will look.*

▲ *A rare surviving medieval hoarding, dated c.1220, on the donjon at the Château de Laval.*

▼ *Slot machicolations – a stone version of wooden hoardings – on the northeast tower in the inner enceinte at Krak des Chevaliers.*

▲ *Internal view of the hoarding on the donjon at the Château de Laval. Various modern features such as railings have been added. The roof covers the top of the hoarding, which was definitely built as a permanent, not removable feature.*

Sometimes hoardings were added to the walls and towers at other times, too, such as when the castle was readying itself to face a siege: presumably the construction materials were kept ready in a store within the castle so that, when needed, experienced carpenters could put the hoardings up at speed – even as a besieging army approached. In other cases, wooden hoardings were simply always kept in place. At Guédelon, when the castle is finished, the plan is to have permanent wooden hoarding around the top of the 28.5m (94ft) Great Tower.

A notable surviving example of a medieval hoarding is on the donjon at the Château de Laval (Pays de la Loire), which was built *c.*1220. Elsewhere, only hoarding sockets survive, such as those found in sections of the curtain enclosing the outer ward at Château Gaillard, although in some places, for example the donjon at Château de Coucy (Picardy), stone corbels rather than sockets were used to support the floor beams. Their presence is particularly significant since it represents the first step towards the corbelled machicolations that eventually took the place of wooden hoardings.

MACHICOLATIONS

Corbelled machicolations were a stone version of the wooden hoarding and comprised stone corbels – in place of the timber beams that previously supported the hoarding – and a stone parapet with machicolations – downward openings used for attacking from above. These were, for obvious reasons, less vulnerable to destruction by missiles and fire than the wooden hoardings, and are found, for example, over the gateways at Conwy Castle and above the Gate-Next-the-Sea at Beaumaris.

Another version was slot machicolations, which consisted of a stone parapet supported by a buttress sticking out from the wall. These were built in the northeast tower in the inner enceinte at Krak des Chevaliers in the 12th century and at Château Gaillard in 1196–98.

GUTTERING

Dealing with the rain, as well as pooling water left by rainstorms, was a major challenge for builders since it could undermine foundations, make carefully laid stones move, weaken masonry, wash away joints and turn the lime within the walls into liquid, causing crystals to form on facing walls. Installing drainage systems was therefore not an afterthought but a matter that needed to be dealt with early on in the building of any feature of a castle, including at Guédelon.

The first line of defence against water was to make the lowest parts of the walls sloped in order to protect the foundations. In addition, while building the curtain walls around the courtyard and bailey at Guédelon, guttering spouts were laid in the base of the walls. The masons also installed guttering in the southern curtain wall to drain water from the courtyard and send it out into the ditch, and constructed a settling basin, a sandstone gutter and a guttering spout leading out into the ditch. Molten-lead sealing joints – created using a clay mould – held the stones securely in position.

BUILDING TECHNIQUES: GUTTERING

Beside the corner tower on the southern curtain wall, the masons built a drainage system to collect rainwater, which was collecting in the courtyard, and send it gushing into the surrounding ditch outside the wall. The settling basin traps sand in the runoff, while the water runs down the sandstone gutter and splashes through the spout into the ditch.

1 As part of the drainage for the southern curtain wall a mason pours molten lead from a pan into a clay mould to create joints for a section of guttering.

2 The lead joints are used to seal the joints in the section of stone guttering installed in the southern curtain wall to drain water from the courtyard.

3 The complete drainage system in the southern curtain wall – with settling basin, gutter and (at the far end) the guttering spout through which the water pours out.

4 A stone guttering spout has been installed high up on the northern curtain wall. It directs wastewater into the surrounding defensive ditch, where it drains away.

CONCENTRIC FORTIFICATIONS

A formidable sight and very difficult for an attacking army to penetrate, concentric castles are considered the ultimate in castle design. They consist of a fortified enclosure or inner ward with a higher wall that overlooks and dominates an outer ward, which is in turn surrounded by a lower curtain wall. This arrangement provided two barriers for an attacking army to overcome and also gave castle defenders an inner sanctuary should the castle came under sustained attack.

The concept of concentric fortifications goes back to the ancient world and is found, long before the era of castle-building, in many tribal hill forts. However, it really came into its own with the layout of the two-ward concentric castles of the late 12th and the 13th century.

Maurice the Engineer at Dover Castle and Richard I at Château Gaillard experimented with the design, and provided outer walls to enclose an outer ward that was defended and overlooked by a dominant inner ward, though neither design was a fully concentric castle. For the defences to be fully concentric, the outer wall needed to surround the inner wall entirely so that there was a continuous region between the two walls.

The first dateable castle of this kind was Belvoir Castle in the crusader Kingdom of Jerusalem, built by Gilbert of Assailly, Grand Master of the Knights Hospitaller, from 1168 onwards. Now ruined, the castle was constructed on a high, wind-battered basalt plateau about 20km (12 miles) south of the Sea of Galilee – it is now in northern Israel. It overlooks the River Jordan some 500m (1,600ft) below and perches in a place likened by Muslim writers to an eagle's nest or home of the moon because of its elevated, inaccessible location.

The Hospitallers in the crusader kingdoms were pioneers of the concentric castle and went on to rebuild the renowned Krak des Chevaliers in Syria as a concentric castle in the early 13th century, adding an outer curtain wall. (The name Krak des Chevaliers dates only from the 19th century; originally a Kurdish garrison, it was previously known as 'fort of the Kurds' and then, after the Hospitallers took possession, as 'Crac de l'Ospital'.)

Siege defences

One theory to explain why the Hospitallers and others adopted the concentric design is that they were affected by the brutal siege warfare they experienced in the crusader states. In a structure built to this design, the outer wall provided at least partial protection from siege machines while from the higher inner curtain wall crossbowmen could maintain a devastating defensive fire against attacking forces. Moreover, these vast establishments were designed to withstand the most punishing sieges: at Belvoir, 450 soldiers and 50 knights were resident, together with supporting workers and family; while at Krak des Chevaliers the garrison was 2,000 strong at its peak.

And the design worked. Belvoir withstood a siege by the army of Muslim general Saladin for a full 18 months before the defenders finally surrendered. Then, during the same campaign, Saladin was forced to turn away from Krak des Chevaliers, too, deciding it was too well fortified to be besieged successfully.

◄ *Concentric defences at Krak des Chevaliers, comprising a lower outer wall and higher inner wall (on the right). Defenders on the inner wall commanded the land between the two fortifications, and attackers were very vulnerable to assault from above.*

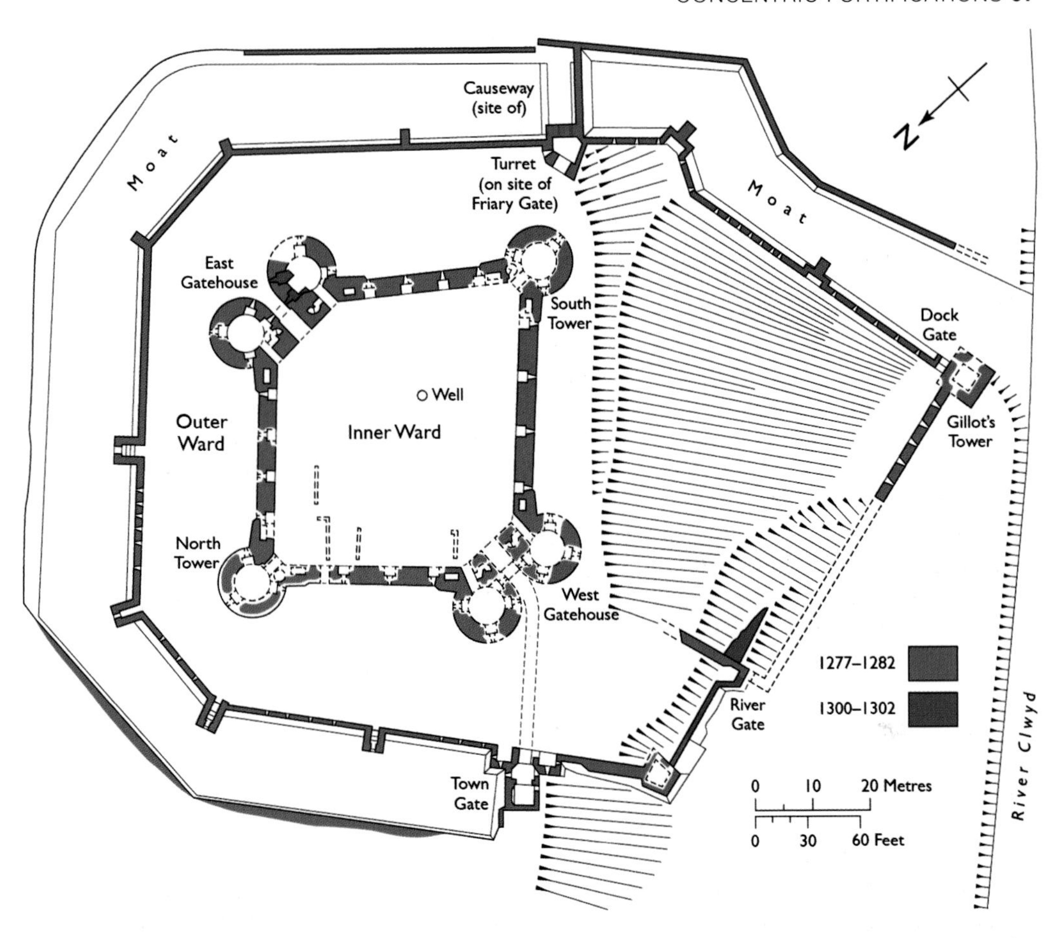

▸ *The ground plan of Rhuddlan Castle shows the concentric design with two sets of walls and two wards or baileys. The inner wards had two gatehouses and two towers. There are turrets along the lower outer wall.*

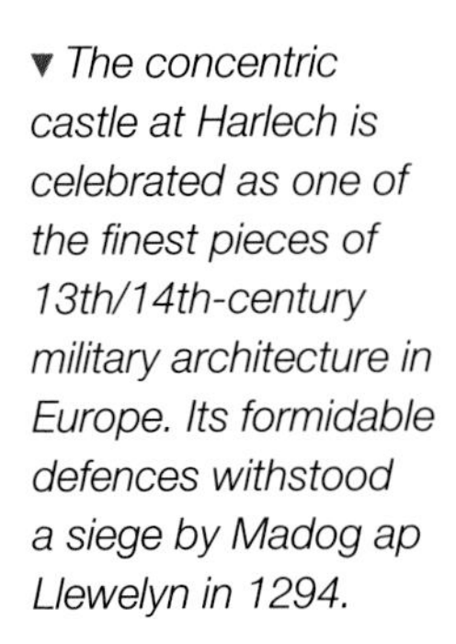

▾ *The concentric castle at Harlech is celebrated as one of the finest pieces of 13th/14th-century military architecture in Europe. Its formidable defences withstood a siege by Madog ap Llewelyn in 1294.*

EDWARD I IN WALES

Building a concentric castle was a major undertaking that was probably beyond the means of the nobility and limited to major military orders, such as the Hospitallers or Templars, as well as prominent members of the nobility and to kings. Edward I, for instance, built a series of widely admired concentric castles in Wales: Rhuddlan, Harlech and Beaumaris.

Pre-dating these royal edifices, however, was the concentric castle of Caerphilly, which was built in 1267–71 by Gilbert de Clare, Earl of Gloucester and Hertford. This featured an inner ward containing four corner towers and two gatehouses – influenced, it is thought, by the quadrilateral castles of Philip II in France that serve as the model for Guédelon. The outer ward has a similar configuration.

At Rhuddlan, a quadrilateral diamond-shaped inner ward has two gatehouses, at east and west, as well as a tower at each of the other two points of the diamond – north and south. The higher inner wall overlooks the outer curtain wall, beyond which is a dry moat on three sides of the castle, while the fourth side faces the River Clwyd. The outer curtain wall has regular turrets, and some of these contain stairs giving access to sally ports through which defenders could venture out into the moat to launch a counterattack.

At Harlech the walls of the inner ward have four corner towers and a substantial gatehouse with D-shaped defensive towers either side of the entrance. Directly opposite the inner gatehouse, two bridge towers guarded a stone bridge across the ditch cut to the east. Originally, the castle rock ran down to the sea, meaning that the castle could have been resupplied by water; today, however, the sea has receded. Roughly in line with the northwest tower of the inner ward a sea gate stood in the outer wall, giving on to a 127-step stairway running down to the foot of the cliffs.

THE PERFECT CONCENTRIC CASTLE

Beaumaris Castle on Anglesey is considered to be the perfect example of a concentric castle of the period. The curtain wall of its inner ward, 11m (36ft) high and 4.7m (15ft 6in) thick, has six defensive towers in addition to two gatehouses with twin D-shaped towers. The eight-sided outer ward curtain has 12 towers and two gatehouses and overlooks a moat; its south gate (the gate-next-the-sea) faces the sea and was

protected by a barbican. The castle could be supplied by sea via the tidal dock that was protected by a wall and a firing platform, which historians believe may have been the base for a trebuchet. After fighting their way across the moat, attackers would have faced arrows and quarrels fired by defenders on both the inner and outer walls – the bowmen on the inner walls could fire over the heads of the guards on the lower outer walls.

The castle was begun under the celebrated Master James of St Georges in 1295, following a Welsh revolt led by Madog ap Llywelyn in which Roger de Pulesdon, sheriff of Anglesey, was killed. Work continued until 1300, but then stopped because Edward I's attention and resources had been diverted to his wars in Scotland. Building was relaunched in 1306, when Edward was concerned that Scottish troops might launch an invasion via North Wales, and continued until 1330, first under Master James and then, following his death in 1309, under Nicholas de Derneford. In total the building of the castle cost £15,000.

◂ *Harlech Castle is one of the masterpieces of military design built in Wales by Master James of St Georges, and includes elements imported from his native Savoy. (Cadw)*

▾ *The ground plan of Harlech Castle shows the inner ward with four corner towers, a large gatehouse and a narrow outer ward. Note the water gate allowing supply by sea – in line with the northwest tower. (Cadw)*

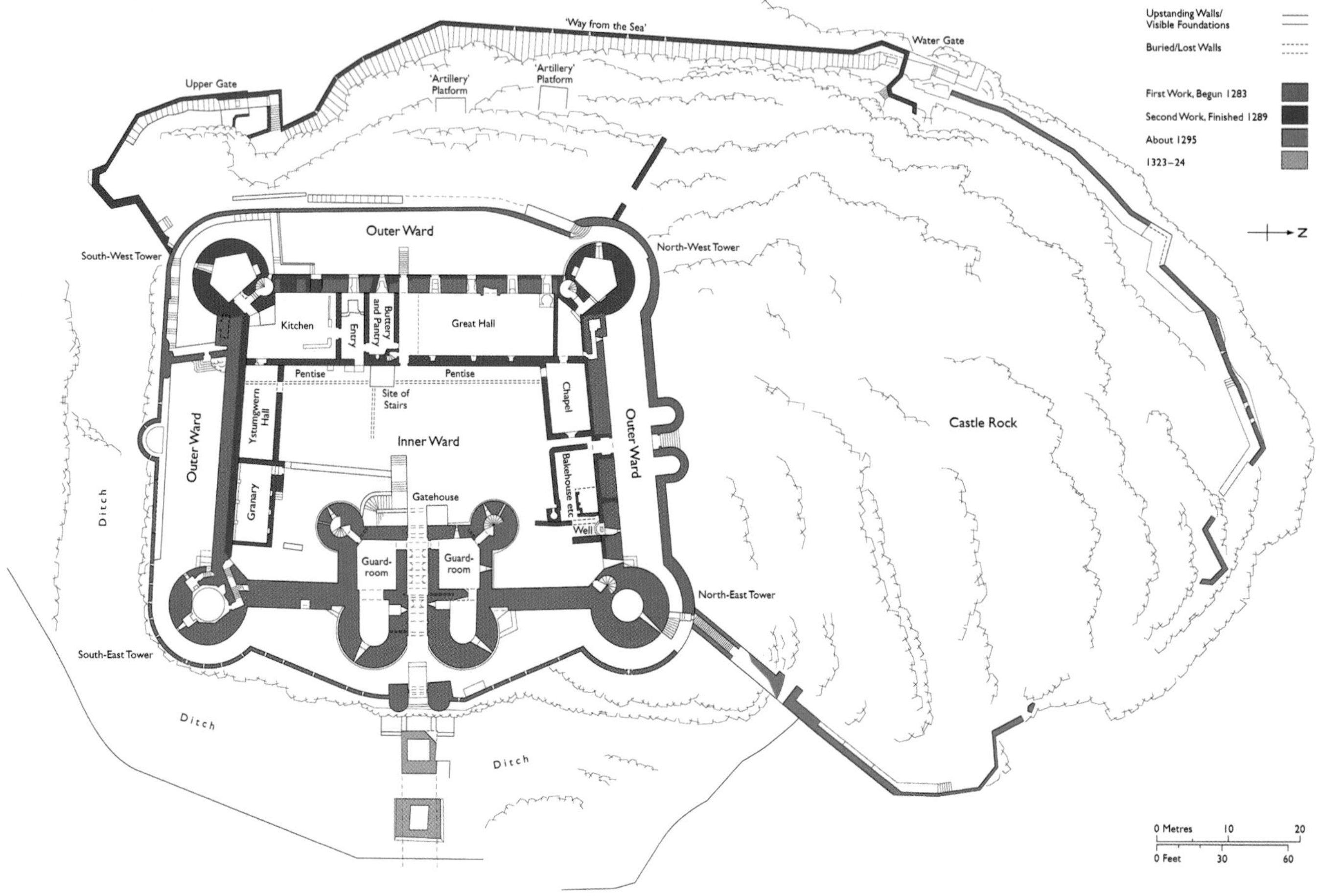

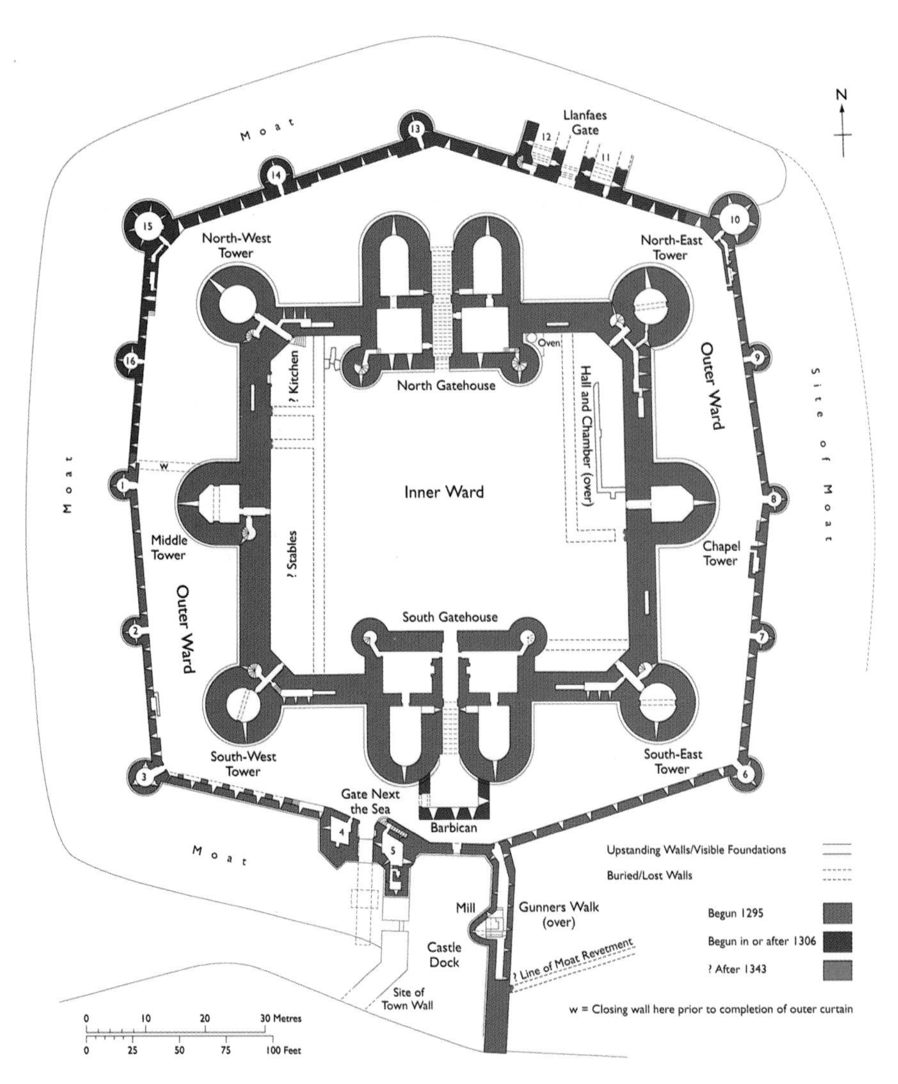

▲ *Inner and outer walls at Beaumaris Castle, with the outer ward in between. There were originally 164 arrow loops in the inner walls. (Cadw)*

◄ *The ground plan of Beaumaris Castle shows the heavily fortified inner curtain, with six towers and two gatehouses, all contained within the outer walls. (Cadw)*

► *Beaumaris is seen as the perfect example of a concentric castle. A fortified tidal dock, crucial for supplies, is at the top of the picture. (Cadw)*

4

THE BAILEY

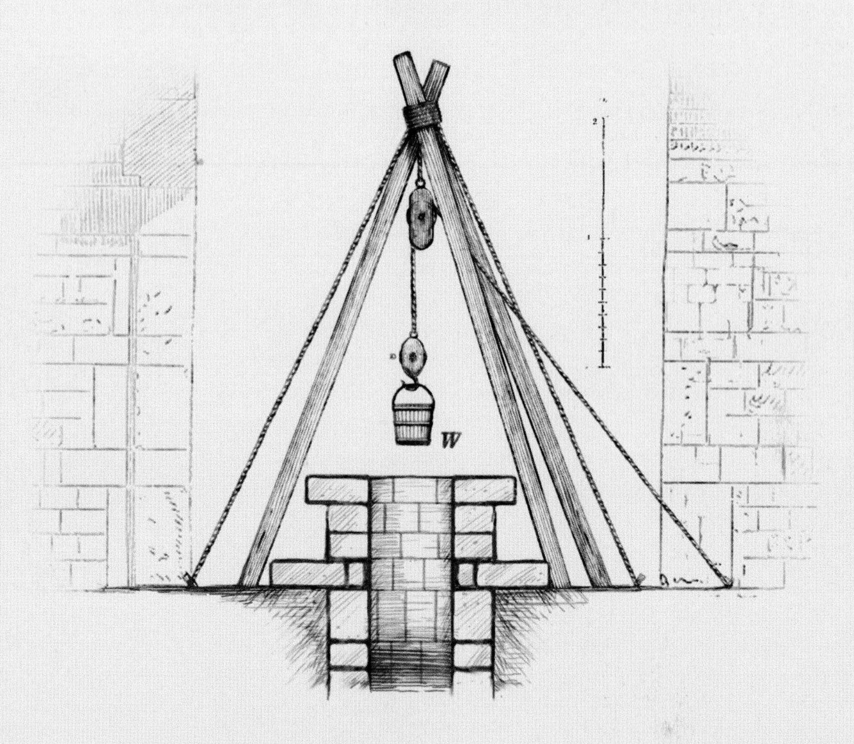

The bailey or courtyard was the area enclosed by the defensive curtain walls. The heart of the castle, its shape depended on the structure's ground plan: on some sites this was determined by geographical position, but on others the lord and master mason chose their design. At Guédelon, the quadrangular courtyard layout with four corner towers follows the architectural style established by Philip II. Some castles had two baileys or a series of separate courtyards, with the lord's accommodation situated in the most remote and secure of the enclosures.

◄ *The bailey of Caernarfon Castle, built by Edward I to consoidate his power in Wales. (Cadw)*

CENTRE OF CASTLE LIFE

Within the walls of the bailey, much of the castle's daily life took place. You might find barracks, stables, kitchens, granary, animal pen, the blacksmiths' forge and stonemasons' lodge, the base of operations for the lime makers and mortar makers, the tilers' kiln and the centres for many other essential activities. Residential quarters and a great hall overlooked the bailey, some of which contained a chapel, though this was usually – as at Guédelon – situated in one of the towers.

A visitor to the castle entering the courtyard would encounter a bustle of activity. If he were a knight or lord, he would probably dismount after riding through the gatehouse and hand his horse to a stable hand. Standing on foot, he would see the main features of the castle laid out before him.

Visitors would know what to look for – how to 'read' most castles of this period – even though the particular arrangements of individual castles differed. In many, the main hall would be opposite the courtyard, raised above it and accessed via an imposing sweep of steps. In corner towers or in towers erected along the curtain walls, or sometimes in rooms stretching along the side of the bailey, the visitor would see the residential quarters, perhaps identifiable by their large windows giving into the courtyard; in some castles there would be rooms, together with guardrooms and prisons, in

▲ *The granary in the inner ward at Harlech Castle, which once also contained a kitchen, bakehouse, two halls, a prison and a chapel. (Cadw).*

▼ *The inner ward of Conwy Castle, from the Chapel Tower, showing the lower-level cellar and kitchen areas with royal apartments above. (Cadw)*

Food was grown within the bailey as well as in farmlands outside the castle walls

The castle stood on a spur commanding the valley of the River Fowey

The shell keep, containing hall, kitchen and guest chambers

A defensive wall and an outer ditch also protects the bailey

The keep was defended by a deep ditch

▲ *Restormel Castle in Cornwall was converted from a Norman motte-and-bailey castle to a shell keep in the 12th–13th century. This reconstruction drawing shows the castle in the 13th century, showing the extensive bailey overlooked by the shell keep, all set within a wall and deep ditch. (Mary Evans)*

the main gatehouse through which he has just passed. He might be able to see a chapel window in a wall of one of the towers. At Chepstow Castle in Wales, a chapel window in Marten's Tower would have been clearly identifiable from the castle entrance. At Guédelon, too, a new arrival would be able to identify the chapel's gothic tracery window in the Chapel Tower. Distinguishing towers by their use was a common feature – as in the Prison Tower at Harlech Castle, and the Kitchen Tower at Kenilworth Castle.

FOOD PREPARATION

In some castles, food was cooked more or less in the open air in makeshift lean-to kitchens along the walls off the bailey. In others, however, the kitchen was in the lower part of the great hall or one of the other buildings lining the bailey. At Guédelon, the kitchen stands next to the storeroom and gives directly on to the courtyard, on the ground floor of the north range. Facilities for making butter and cheese, and for grinding flour ready for bread making could also be present in the bailey. The butcher might set to work nearby, as could the candle maker, who used wax or tallow (rendered-down animal fat) to make his wares. Even the animals – cows, pigs, geese, goats, sheep – could be brought within the safety of the curtain walls in times of war. Food waste needed to be carried out and slung somewhere – as far away from the kitchen and residential quarters as possible. In castles of more than one bailey, the waste could be carried to a good distance; for example at Barnard Castle in northern England, built in stone by Bernard de Balliol in the 12th century, the kitchen waste was carried to the lower court.

KNIGHTS AND SQUIRES

In many castles, the bailey would include the stables where horses kept by knights in the lord's or king's service were housed and cared for by the stable master. The blacksmiths'

▼ *Access to the kitchen at Guédelon is from the northeast corner of the courtyard. Vegetables from the garden and foods prepared in the kitchen are laid on the table.*

lodge would be in the same location; one of their tasks would be to ensure that the horses were well shod. In many castles, lists (an enclosed area) were kept for the lords to exercise their horses and practise jousting. They could be in the outer ward of a concentric castle or one of the more distant baileys of a castle with more than a single courtyard.

During jousts, armoured knights would ride their horses at speed while attempting to strike a dummy (the quintain) with their lances, or try to use the lances to pierce a hanging loop. Tournaments at larger castles – in which knights jousted against one another in the lists – could be held within the castle boundaries.

Other structures associated with chivalric engagement were also sometimes found in the bailey. For example a tiltyard, an area near the stables for knights and squires to practice fighting and jousting techniques. In the 14th century, when founding a chivalric order, King Edward III of England began work on a circular building in the upper bailey at Windsor Castle to be its headquarters. It appears that this building was never finished but the chivalric order, the Most Noble Order of the Garter, was formed in June 1348, and consisted of 26 knights: Edward; his son, the Black Prince; and 12 companions each.

At different times in the medieval period and in different castles, the role of knights and squires varied. In some castles, knights were permanently resident in the service of the lord; in others they lived temporarily on site in order to perform their feudal duty for the lord by guarding the castle for a limited period. Squires could be either less-wealthy warriors not admitted to the chivalric brotherhood, or young men in training to become knights one day.

The latter were often sons of the nobility who had been singled out to become knights, and would be sent to the castle of another lord at the age of seven to be trained in chivalry. Here, they would wait on the castle womenfolk, and have lessons in languages including Latin and in music and poetry. They would also undergo physical training and play outdoor games.

Once they reached the age of 14 they would learn how to use and repair weapons, look after armour and groom horses, as well as how to take part in riding practice, hunting and jousting. They served the lord in the great hall and were required to go to war with the men when battles arose. In these situations, they would serve knights by helping them mount and taking care of their horse and weapons, and might be required to look after enemies taken prisoner. When they reached their majority, if they had proved themselves worthy, they would be acclaimed as knights themselves

THE CARPENTERS' WORKSHOP

Carpenters were very important during the construction of castles. They had to work in close cooperation with the masons in order to install scaffolding and make the formworks required for the construction of arches and vaults. They were also responsible for working on flooring and roof timbers as well as larger structures such as hoarding, or drawbridges.

Carpenters were respected, well-remunerated, craftsmen capable of mastering the complex geometry required to build strong wooden frameworks. Carpenters selected trees to be felled to order according to their construction requirements.

▼ In this 14th-century illustration, knights joust in the lists, while courtiers watch from a grandstand, musicians play fanfares (left) and King Richard II of England presides. (Getty)

▲ Here a blacksmith forges an iron nail, just one of the thousands needed for the wooden structures that the carpenters create on site.

▲ *The carpenters also look for curved trees. This curved trunk is being hewn into a wall plate for a round tower. Following the grain of the wood produces a stronger finished product.*

▲ *A carpenter uses a hand axe to shave a tapered oak peg. Pegs are used by the carpenters to hold together tenon and mortice joints.*

Trees were chosen for their height and girth for specific uses on the building site. Woodcutters would then fell the trees using axes and wedges. The timber would have been worked soon after being felled while the wood was still green. It would have been impossible to work seasoned oak with the hand tools available to medieval woodworkers.

At Guédelon, the woodcutters and carpenters work together in a workshop just 100m (35ft) to the southeast of the castle, on the edge of the forest. The carpenters set to work on making beams, joists and rafters, using axes and side axes to hew the trunks. They removed the outer sap wood, retaining the heart wood. As a result, if making a curved section such as a curved angle brace, the carpenters would select a curved tree. By following the natural grain of the wood, the finished piece would be stronger. A supply of wood was also required for scaffold poles and putlogs (horizontal supports for scaffolding).

At Guédelon, oak is used for all the permanent wooden stuctures in the castle: roof timbers, doors and hoardings, and to make shakes (split wooden tiles) for certain roofs. The woodcutters split the wood using a mallet and froe. Oak pegs are used to fix the shakes to the roof which shelters the

▼ *The carpenters' workshop at Guédelon stands on the edge of the forest opposite the castle. On the left is the large tracing floor and on the right the workshop.*

BUILDING TECHNIQUES: HEWING A BEAM

The beams for the castle are hand-hewn. The carpenters convert round logs into flat-sided squared-up beams using axes and side-axes. Trees which match the rough dimensions of the finished piece are sought out in the forest: long straight trees for rafters and joists; curved trees for angle braces or the curved wall plates of the towers. The trees are not transported far. They either come from the woodlands around Guédelon or from near-by Bellary Forest.

▲ *A woodcutter swings his felling axe in Guédelon forest. He angles the axe blow to create a V-shaped notch on the side that he plans for the tree to fall.*

▲ *Woodcutters and carpenters use a ruler (left) and plumb bob (right) to establish the level and plumb lines on each end of the log.*

▲ *Chalk lines are snapped over the log to connect both ends of the timber. Note the 'iron dog' (right) securing the log to sleepers.*

▲ *A woodcutter begins the initial stage of roughing out the first face. He chops out notches with an axe to the depth of the chalk line.*

▲ *Once the sections between the notches have been removed with an axe, the woodcutters and carpenters use a side axe to create a smoother finish on each face.*

▲ Carpenters' tools: a mallet and a metal implement called a froe are used to split short lengths of oak to make the wooden tiles, or shakes, for roofing.

▲ A side axe (left) and a chopping axe (right). A side axe has a single bevel like a chisel. It is used as a finishing tool.

▲ A side axe, or broad axe, has an off-set handle to protect the woodcutter from scraping his fingers as he works.

▲ A carpenter uses a frame saw to cut a log to length. Saws were in existence in the Middle Ages but were used less than axes.

▲ The head carpenter uses a double-bitted mortise axe. This double-ended chisel is a powerful, precise tool used for cutting joints.

▲ An auger is used to bore a hole in a piece of wood. An auger ressembles a huge corkscrew. It has a long bit and a wide handle.

postern gate entrance in the courtyard and the roofs of the workshops. A roof made of oak shakes is as waterproof as one covered with terracotta tiles.

It was important for the Guédelon carpenters to find trees which corresponded to the tall thin trees used in 13th-century roof timbers. Not enough oaks of the right height and girth were to found in the immediate vicinity, but a supply was found near Guédelon in the 100-year-old Bellary Forest, in Nièvre, and transported a few miles to be hewn on site. No less than 30 cubic metres (1,060 cubic ft) of prepared oak was used to make the roof timbers above the Great Hall. In total, 250 cubic metres (8,830 cubic ft) of standing wood were felled and 90 cubic metres (3,180 cubic ft) of wood, or 13-metre lengths from 150 trees, were squared up.

THE STONEMASONS' LODGE

In the medieval period, one of the carpenters' first tasks when a castle was being built was to built the stonemasons' lodge. Here, the banker masons – those who shaped the stones provided by the quarrymen for use in construction – worked patiently on their current task, whether it was finishing a piece of masonry or shaping a design for a keystone in a vault, with pitching tool, chisels, punch and hammer.

The stonemasons stored their tools in the lodge and could shelter under cover from bad weather so that they could continue working. They also gathered there to eat and socialise. In this sanctuary, secrets and techniques could be shared and passed on between masons and from master to apprentice. It was understood as part of the masonic way of life in this period that the masons would look out for one another and aid those who needed a helping hand because they were starting out, injured or fell ill.

At a modestly sized castle such as Guédelon, many of the buildings that would have been in the yard or bailey of a large medieval castle are situated instead in the immediate vicinity of the castle walls. The stonemasons' lodge is one such example, and lies just beyond the ditch, about 100m (325ft) southwest of where the gatehouse will stand. This is a lightweight, open-sided wooden building, easy to erect and easy to move if needed.

▲ *The masons use double-headed stone axes as finishing tools when working in limestone.*

▲ *A mason's round hammer, a pointed punch and two flat chisels. The chisels are used to create sharp edges.*

▲ *A mason uses the straight edge of a set square to set out the shape of a voussoir on a block of limestone*

▼ *In the masons' lodge to the north of the castle a mason dresses limestone on a wooden table called a banker; the stonemasons who dress stone are known as banker masons.*

▼ *The masons use compass and ruler to set out full-scale designs on the tracing floor.*

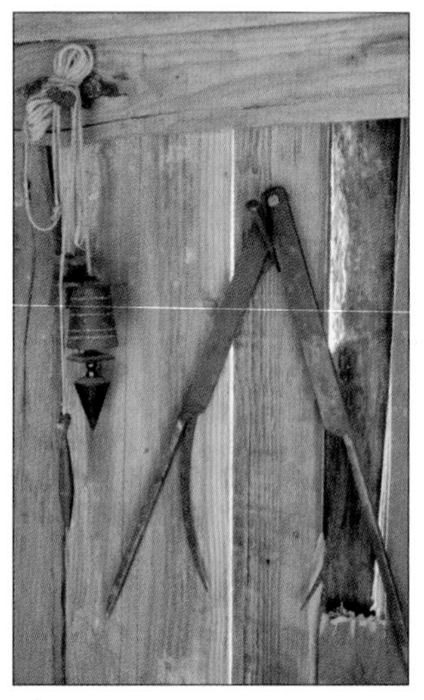

▼ *The stonemasons make wooden moulds from these designs to use as templates.*

In addition to the workspace inside the building, there is a tracing floor on which the stonemasons sketch, draw up full-size designs and make wooden templates or moulds for particular features. Using these templates, masons can draw on to a stone the shape it needs to be cut to and then follow the lines while carving. These moulds can be used several times to produce corbels (projecting supports used for arches and cornices) and voussoirs (wedge-shaped stones used to make an arch) on different sites. The masons work on flat, work tables called 'bankers' that can be dragged into the open air or under cover in bad weather.

Wages were negotiated in the lodge in discussions between the lodge master and the master mason or the lord himself. When a new stonemason arrived at a site, he would normally be paid 'at task' – that is, piecemeal – while the master mason assessed how fast and skilfully he could work. If he passed this test, he could be given a weekly rate. Sometimes masons negotiated to be paid not in cash but in

BUILDING TECHNIQUES: STONE DRESSING

In a medieval castle the chapel was often one of the most elaborately decorated rooms. At Guédelon the chapel contains three lancet windows and a finely carved tracery window, beneath a quadpartite cross rib vault. Banker mason Jean Paul was given the task of "dressing" (the art of shaping and surfacing) the keystone for the vault. It is decorated with finely carved foliage, a design based on a 13th-century original at the Cluny Museum in Paris.

1 Jean-Paul uses a stone axe to ensure that the surface is completely level before he begins the process of roughing out the keystone.

2 Jean-Paul then uses a pointed iron punch and a hammer to form the four branches of the ribs.

3 Jean-Paul has dressed the profile of the voussoirs (the stone wedges which form the ribs of the vaulted ceiling) into the keystone.

4 The keystone is positioned on thick braided robes to cushion the edges of the stone while it is being dressed.

5 Having carefully sketched out the design on the flat disk, Jean-Paul begins the task of sculpting the foliage.

6 The blacksmiths forged a range of small-headed chisels for the intricate carving of the decorated boss.

7 Jean-Paul uses a hand drill to gently bore into the stone in order to produce the keystone's undercut foliage.

8 The master mason produced clay models of the 13th-century design to guide Jean-Paul during the final phase.

9 The finished keystone is ready to be transported to the castle. It required five working weeks to complete.

MASONS' MARKS

In the Middle Ages, each stonemason had a signature – a letter or symbol such as a star or cross that he marked on the top face of every stone he finished. These were often covered over when the stone was placed in position, but before that they were used by master masons and senior stonemasons both to follow their apprentices' progress and to check on the quality of different masons' work. Sometimes they were used for calculating how much a mason should be paid. Archaeologists and historians are able to use the marks to track the movement of different masons – for example, the same marks are found at Krak des Chevaliers and in the cathedral of Tartus on Syria's Mediterranean coast. In Wales, masons' marks have been studied at the 13th-century Montgomery Castle and in the gatehouse of Raglan Castle, which dates to the 1460s.

A second type of mark was the positioning mark, or 'setting mark', used to show how a stone should be positioned and in which alignment. Quite a long time could elapse between a stone being finished in the masons' lodge and it being inserted in position in the castle wall, and it might need to be moved around the site and stored for a while, so these marks were necessary to ensure the stone ended up in its intended location.

◂*A selection of 13th-century masons' marks found in English castles. A mark needed to be quick and easy to cut and simple enough to reproduce over and over.*

goods – accommodation, food and firewood, say. Masons were freemen and could travel where they wished, though on occasion they could be forced to stay in one place and work on a particular project – for example, when a castle had to be put up in haste for military reasons. An example of this occurred when the Lord of Coucy (in Picardy, northeastern France) compelled a group of masons to work on his castle in the 13th century: they were paid a piece rate but were not permitted to leave the site.

The fact that masons could generally move across local and national boundaries freely, and earn well, played an important part in the spread of architectural ideas and types of fortification. Many masons travelled between England and France and worked on castles in both countries – and even further afield to the independent crusader kingdoms in what are now Israel and Syria and Lebanon, where they crafted fortifications for the military brotherhoods, such as the Knights Hospitaller, and Knights Templar on castles such as Belvoir and Krak des Chevaliers.

COIN MAKING

The bailey was not only the physical centre of the castle, it was also at the heart of the castle's economy. Much of the administration of the lord's estate typically took place in the great hall, which gave on to the bailey. At Guédelon this is reflected by installing a castle mint, situated along the eastern curtain wall in the courtyard. Here, the coin maker demonstrates to visitors all the different stages of medieval minting, from producing alloys to striking the coins, and in doing so provides Guédelon with its own currency.

In the Middle Ages a coin's value was determined by its weight and precious metal content – the precious metal being silver. In France, the coins in circulation were deniers. One sou was equivalent to 12 deniers; 240 deniers made a livre. The denier was the equivalent of the English penny, the sou matched the shilling, and the livre was the French version of the pound.

We can gain a fascinating insight into the castle economy, revealing who was the best off and who was at the bottom of the economic pile, by studying bailiff accounts for Gisors and Peyrepertuse castles in the 13th century. Here, records show that labourers on the castle site would receive 10 deniers a day, while a mason could get up to 18 deniers a day and a carpenter around 24 deniers. The Gisors accounts also reveal that a banker mason could receive 15 pounds a year. On the military side, while a foot sergeant was worth up to 12 deniers a day, a tower guard might get three times as much (3 sous daily) and the castle captain 5 sous a day.

At Windsor Castle in the mid-13th century, accounts list building craftsmen and eight chaplains each earning 50 shillings a year – less than 2 pence a day; sergeants were paid considerably more – 9 pence a day. Surviving documents from Chepstow Castle show that Master Ralf Gogun, the master mason in charge of the building works carried out for Roger Bigod, 5th Earl of Norfolk in 1270–1306, was paid 2 shillings a week. At Rhuddlan Castle in *c.*1250, skilled craftsmen such as master masons and builders of siege engines were getting as much as 12 pence a day; sergeants got 7½ pence a day and watchmen a more modest 2 pence a day.

MEDIEVAL SKILLS: COIN MAKING

Medieval mints were often fortified buildings themselves, for obvious reasons. At Guédelon Nicolas uses 13th-century methods in its own mint, which sits within the protection of the castle walls. His work is a good example of the ethos of archaeology in practice that informs the Guédelon project, gaining insights into how our medieval forebears worked.

1 In the first stage, Nicolas pours the molten copper and silver alloy into a mould. It is then set aside to cool.

2 The cooled metal lingot is hammered out with a club hammer to the thickness of the coins.

3 He regularly reheats the lingots to prevent them becoming too brittle before the next stage.

4 Using heavy-duty cutters, the lingots are cut into square blanks called planchets.

5 The monnayer weighs each planchet to make sure it is the right weight. He uses the large clippers to adjust them.

6 The iron dies are engraved with inverted images and text to be struck on the coin.

7 Having adjusted and hammered flat the blank, Nicolas places it between the pair of engraved dies and strikes them with a hammer thus imprinting the designs on both sides of the coin.

8 Guédelon now has its own currency! The coins are available in the mint for visitors to the site to pick up and examine and they can also watch Nicolas making them. Unlike these, medieval coins were often made of silver.

CHEPSTOW CASTLE AND BAILEY DESIGNS

On a limestone ridge commanding a key crossing of the River Wye, Chepstow Castle was built over three baileys between its foundation in 1067 and work being carried out by Roger Bigod, 5th Earl of Norfolk, in *c.*1270. In a wide range of castles of differing size and date, bailey designs, dictated by local topography as well as patron's preference, generally focused on the security of an inner sanctum and on controlling access to the king or lord, who occupied the most reserved area.

The idea of the enclosed bailey goes back to the motte-and-bailey castle design, in which the bailey was the area found at the foot of the motte or mound and was enclosed by a wooden palisade. At a later date, some castles were rebuilt in stone to mostly the same layout as an earlier wooden motte-and-bailey structure. In these instances, a keep was constructed where the fortifications had stood on the motte, and the new bailey was enclosed with a stone curtain wall in place of the wooden palisade.

Right from the start, some castles had more than one bailey. At Windsor Castle, for example, William the Conqueror built the first keep on a man-made motte between two baileys situated to east and west. Alnwick Castle in Northumberland was also built as a motte-and-bailey castle with two baileys, in 1096. At a later date, the motte was subsequently partly demolished and a shell keep built in its place, standing between the two baileys. Then, in the 13th century, a third enclosure was created when apartments were added to the inner part of the shell keep to create a courtyard.

Nottingham Castle was built in stone in the reign of Henry II on the basis of an earlier Norman wooden castle set up in 1067. This had three baileys: the inner one occupied the highest point of the castle rock; the middle bailey, to the north, contained the main royal apartments; and the outer bailey, which was much larger, lay on lower ground to the east. In France, the 13th-century Ortenbourg Castle (in Alsace, France) was built in 1260–65 to a similar three-bailey layout that was determined by local topography: its inner bailey is on the highest ground; a middle bailey lies to the south; and a larger outer bailey runs around to the south and east.

King Richard I's Château Gaillard (1196–98) was another castle with three baileys: an outer bailey that was separate from the other two and was essentially a barbican – although it contained the main castle gatehouse; a middle bailey accessed by a bridge; and an inner bailey, again accessed by a bridge, which contained a heavily fortified donjon.

▾ *Ground plan of Chepstow Castle shows its three bailey layout from the upper bailey on the left next to the upper barbican, through the Great Tower and middle bailey and down to the lower bailey, which contains the residential buildings added by Roger Bigod. (Cadw)*

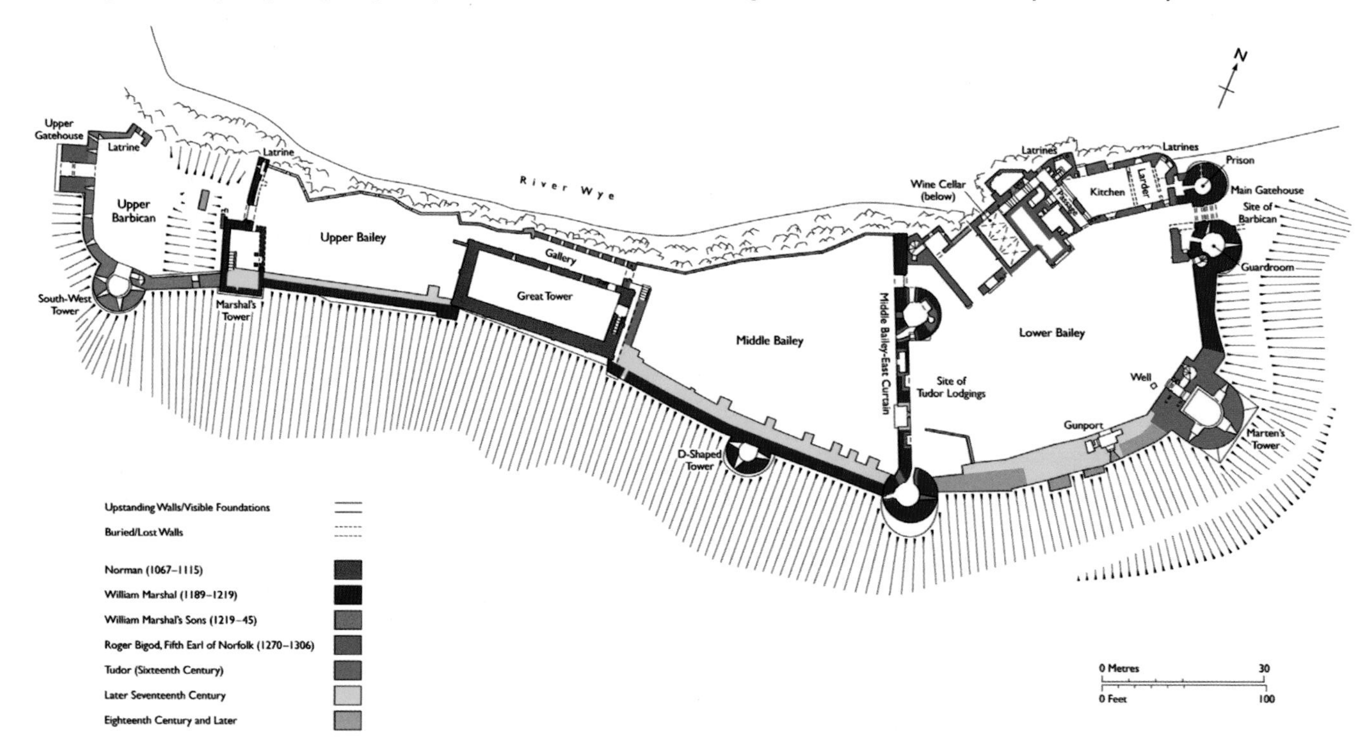

▲ *The impressive remains of Chepstow Castle cast their shadow on the curve of the River Wye alongside. The castle takes its shape from the ridge on which it stands. (Cadw)*

THE BAILEY AT CHEPSTOW CASTLE

William FitzOsbern began building work at Chepstow Castle in 1067 and the oblong two-storey Great Tower was completed, at the narrowest part of the ridge, by 1090. He also enclosed the upper and middle baileys to the west and east of the tower, occupying the full width of the ridge. William Marshal, 1st Earl of Pembroke, built the gatehouse, added defensive round towers to the middle bailey and reworked the defences of the upper bailey, with gateway and rounded mural towers. In this period, Henry III stayed in the castle for a few days, in July 1217.

William Marshall's sons subsequently rebuilt and fortified the Great Tower and largely rebuilt the middle bailey curtain wall, while also strengthening the upper bailey, adding a splendid rectangular tower at its western gateway. In addition, they laid out its lower bailey to the east.

▼ *The Upper Ward at Windsor Castle extends to the right of the Round Tower, which stands on the central motte. The Lower Ward runs down to to the left. The enclosure at the far right is the East Terrace Garden. (Alamy)*

SECURITY OF THE INNER BAILEY

In concentric castles, where a heavily fortified inner ward or bailey was surrounded by an outer bailey for added defence, the domestic buildings were generally concentrated in the inner ward. At Harlech Castle, for instance, the inner ward contained all the facilities needed for communal life: granary, bakehouse, kitchen, chapel, prison and two halls. There were four towers – the Weathercock Tower, Garden Tower, Prison Tower and Chapel Tower. The immense, highly fortified three-storey gatehouse contained accommodation for the castle constable; in 1290–93 this was Master James of St Georges, who had been in charge of construction.

At Beaumaris, meanwhile, the domestic buildings and accommodation were concentrated in ranges along the east

▲ *A reconstruction shows the luxurious courtyard house built in the 1130s by Roger le Poer in the bailey at Old Sarum Castle, near Salisbury in Wiltshire. The deep fortifications of the hill fort are visible, and the formidable gatehouse of the castle stands beyond the courtyard house. (Getty)*

and west sides of the inner ward, a fact that is evidenced by the remains of fireplaces that survive in these buildings.

Conwy Castle, built 1283–92, was interesting in its linear plan, which was dictated by the long thin ridge on which it stood. Here, the castle had two completely separate baileys divided by a cross-wall, which meant that if one bailey was overrun by attackers, the defenders could still defend the castle from the other bailey. The outer bailey contained a great hall and the accommodation for the garrison, while the royal apartments were sequestered in the inner bailey. The two baileys each had their own barbican, at either end of the narrow site.

Likewise, Caernarfon Castle could not be built as a concentric fortification due to the site on which it stood, and it also featured an inner and outer bailey laid out side by side. Both the formidably equipped King's Gate and the Queen's Gate opened into the outer bailey, while the Great Hall and the Eagle Tower (containing a postern) stood in the inner bailey. The whole, built as a symbol of English power in Wales and fitted out to house a permanent garrison, was protected by stupendous 6m (20ft) thick curtain walls. These walls featured no fewer than 12 towers, of which four contained accommodation on several levels.

STRUCTURES WITHIN THE BAILEY

At Old Sarum, north of Salisbury in Wiltshire, the Normans built a motte and bailey castle in 1070 within the defences of a Saxon hillfort. Then in the 1130s Roger le Poer, chancellor to Henry I and bishop of Sarum, built a palace within the castle bailey. The commanding hilltop, around 3km (2 miles) north of modern Salisbury, had been settled since the Neolithic era by hunters and later farmers. Then an oval-shaped Iron Age hillfort was built there c400BC, roughly 400 x 360m (1,300 x 1180ft) and enclosed by two banks with a ditch in between. It was a major site, close to several barrows (burial mounds) and also to the important stone circles at Stonehenge and Avebury. In the Saxon era it was a hilltop town, with its own mint.

Within a few years of the Conquest the Normans built a motte-and-bailey castle inside the Iron Age fortifications. And after medieval cleric Herman was appointed the bishop there, he and his successor Osmund built a cathedral in the site's outer enclosure. A service to consecrate the cathedral was held on 5 April 1092, but according to traditional accounts the building was badly damaged in a great storm just five days later. In the 1110s Bishop Roger rebuilt and expanded the cathedral in the outer enclosure of the hilltop. Then in the 1220s, a new cathedral was built in the valley close by and the present city of Salisbury grew up around it.

The castle at Old Sarum was an important place: in 1070 William I assembled his army there to pay them off after their campaign in northern England. Some authorities hold that William was presented with the Domesday Book there in 1086. And in August that year he convened a meeting at Old Sarum of major English knights, sheriffs, nobles and churchmen to swear allegiance to him.

▲ *The outer ward of Harlech Castle still shows the footprint of the buttery (bottom), the entrance hall (middle) and the kitchen range (top). The entrance hall may have been where the food was checked by the household officers. (Cadw)*

COURTYARD HOUSES

The palace Bishop Roger built in the castle bailey in the 1130s was substantial, measuring 170m x 65m (560 x 210ft) and enclosed a central courtyard. It contained a room 60m (200ft) in length that likely served as a great hall, with a tower attached to it. Roger had constructed a similar castle, with a hall, first-floor chapel and an attached tower, in the inner bailey at Sherborne in Dorset, southwest England. (The ruins of these structures, now known as Sherborne Old Castle, lie within the grounds of a 16th-century Tudor house that is more generally known as Sherborne Castle.)

Castle historians call the residential developments built by Bishop Roger at Old Sarum and Sherborne – and a similar development at Wolvesey Castle at Winchester – 'courtyard houses'. Wolvesey Castle, now known as the Old Bishop's Palace, was built in 1130–36 by Henry of Blois, brother of King Stephen, and Bishop of Winchester. Wolvesey was a substantial fortification and withstood a three-week siege by the army of Empress Matilda in 1141 – during which the castle defenders launched fireballs at houses in the city close to the castle. Inevitably most of the city was burnt down, in what became known as the 'Rout of Winchester'. Henry II later breached the walls and probably removed the gate defences to make Wolvesey unusable as a castle, but the splendid bishops' accommodation was left standing.

These courtyard houses influenced many royal chambers, such as that built by Henry II in the Upper Ward at Windsor Castle, and were part of the gradual change in the role of the castle, from defensive symbol of power to palatial home, which showcased the owner's wealth and luxurious tastes.

▼ *The lower bailey at Chepstow Castle, laid out by William Marshall's sons and showing the domestic buildings added by Roger Bigod from 1270 onwards. (Cadw)*

THE COURTYARD AT GUÉDELON

When Guédelon is completed, visitors will enter across a fixed bridge through the twin-tower gatehouse. Once inside, they will find a roughly rectangular courtyard laid out before them. Opposite the gatehouse is the north range, which contains the great hall and antechamber – the lord's chamber. Beneath these grand chambers are service rooms: the storeroom and kitchens.

To the visitors' left, as they stand within the gateway, a section of curtain walls leads to the western corner tower, which will be topped by a pigeon loft. From there, the western curtain wall connects to the chapel tower in the northwest corner. A wooden walkway runs high along the curtain wall. In front of it in the courtyard, mortar makers and lime makers are hard at work. In the chapel tower there is a water reservoir in the basement, and a shooting gallery or guardroom liberally equipped with arrow loops in its walls on the ground floor. The chapel occupies the first floor and on the second is a crenellated lookout post with a conical roof.

The Great Tower stands in the northeast corner of the courtyard, to the east of the Great Range. The eastern curtain

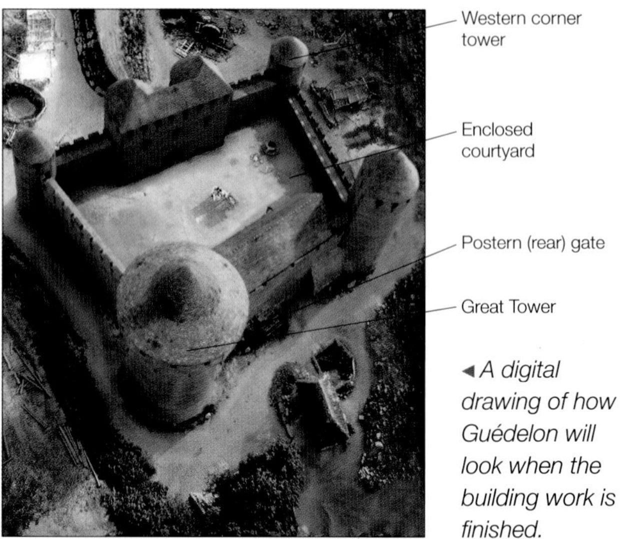

◀ *A digital drawing of how Guédelon will look when the building work is finished.*

▼ *The courtyard at Guédelon is visible through the unfinished front walls. The fixed wooden bridge crosses the dry ditch where the twin-towered gatehouse will stand.*

wall connects to the eastern corner tower. In front of it, the mint is set up, and the worker presses coins.

A wooden walkway runs high along the curtain wall. This was added in 2014. The carpenters dismantled the scaffolding in the courtyard and resused some of the wood in the structure. Wooden structures like this played an important role in medieval castles. Other examples of building using wood in the courtyard include the covered passage between the Great Tower and Great Hall and the postern's lean-to.

ROPE MAKERS

At Guédelon, the rope makers supply hemp and flax ropes for the site. Their hut is situated about 200m (yards) due south of the main entrance, where the gatehouse is being built, but in a medieval castle this would likely have been located within the bailey – for security, in case the castle was attacked. The ropes made on site at Guédelon are used for tying things together on the construction site (though for safety reasons the ropes used in the scaffolding are modern, industrial-strength ones), and also for attaching shutters, making belts and hanging shelves.

The ropes generally consist of either eight or 16 strands. These are fairly thin; to make thicker ones, the craftsmen increase the number of strands. To create the ropes, yarns are fixed to four hooks on a hand-cranked jack and to a single-hooked wooden traveller at the other end of the 'rope

▲ Stonemasons work on the gothic tracery window in the chapel. The window overlooks the courtyard from the chapel tower. This beautiful window is a tremendous achievement – the masons had to dress 36 stones for it.

► The floor of the walkway along the western curtain wall rests on putlogs inserted into the stone, while stone corbels support the roof.

MEDIEVAL SKILLS: ROPE MAKING

Many of the ropes used at Guédelon are made in the ropemakers' centre in the crafts village around the castle. Modern safety standards require stronger ropes for use on the treadmill winch and when building scaffolding.

1 The rope makers work steadily at the 'rope walk', winding the ropes on the machine installed outside their lodge. One of them has hooked the strands around the hooks on the jack.

2 At the other end of the rope walk another worker cranks the jack's handle. As the yarns twist into strands, they pull the traveller along.

3 A selection of finished lengths of rope, made entirely using 13th-century materials and methods. To make a thicker rope, the workers increase the number of strands. (Getty)

walk'. Rope makers turn the jack's handle and the yarns twist into strands; while this happens, they pull the traveller towards the jack.

DRAINAGE AND DRINKING WATER

Water management was a key skill, important both in terms of preventing flooding and in ensuring a supply of safe drinking water for the lord, his retainers, the garrison and other inhabitants of the castle, even when under siege. We have seen that water supply from a spring, natural wells or fast-flowing river was an important consideration when choosing a site for building a castle. Many castles, of course, were surrounded by water in a moat – but given the amount of liquid refuse (including used kitchen water as well as human waste) that could be directed into the moat this was never a source of drinking water.

During castle construction works, the master mason and labourers would take care to ensure good drainage systems would direct water away from the courtyard and the foundations of the walls. In addition, installing guttering to

▲ *The water cistern in the Great Tower's cellar. There is no stopping the rain, but the master mason's task is to devise ways to keep the site well drained.*

◄ *The 7m (23ft) deep courtyard well, on a snowy day. Water from the well is used every day in building work. Work stops on the site in the winter because the lime-based mortar cannot be used in freezing temperatures.*

direct rainwater away into the ditch or the moat was an important stage in laying out the structure of curtain walls around the bailey.

The same principles were applied at Guédelon where, early in the work on the curtain walls, towers and courtyard, the master mason and his labourers installed water cisterns to drain water away from the courtyard. They also dug a courtyard well to a depth of 7m (23ft). This supplies the water used in the daily building work. In planning the layout, the master mason and his advisers decided to construct water cisterns in the basements of the towers – in the scarped walls at the foot of the chapel tower and another in the base of the Great Tower. In addition, rainwater is collected and stored in barrels. As much as possible, nothing is wasted on site. The masons use the rainwater in the barrels to clean tools and the mortar makers use it for mixing their mortar.

► *Visitors look on as four carpenters prepare to carry a heavy tie-beam up the stone staircase on the southern wall of the North Range, the building which houses the Great Hall.*

GUÉDELON'S FIXED BRIDGE

Guédelon Castle's courtyard is accessed by a fixed bridge rather than a drawbridge. In France in the 13th century, when the imaginary lord of Guédelon would have been building his castle, drawbridges were used only in royal castles or significant towns. At Guédelon, the wooden bridge was built in 2000–1, after the completion of the castle's scarped base, and was designed by the Guédelon carpenters. It was the first large-scale wooden structure in the castle. Consisting of two sections of roadway that meet at a wooden pier, the structure, complete with guard rails, is supported at the castle end by an abutment built by the masons. The bridge needed to be strong enough to support heavy loads of stone hauled by carthorses on to the main castle building site. The horses had to be specially trained to make the crossing between the guard rails and over the narrow bridge.

To provide the necessary materials, the woodcutters used wood axes and two-man saws to cut down 57 specially selected oak trees. The carpenters then honed their skills, using side axes to work the wood, before laying out the sections, according to the design, on the drawing floor in the carpenters' lodge. They then assembled the bridge in their workshop before taking it apart and reassembling it in its proper place. Meanwhile, the blacksmiths made the 700 iron nails that were needed to put the roadway in place.

▼ *A fixed bridge was the first major wooden structure built at Guédelon. A wooden pier supports the two lengths of roadway that meet in the middle.*

▼ *More than 300,000 visitors a year walk across the bridge to access the courtyard at Guédelon. It is also in constant use by carts carrying loads of building materials.*

5

THE KEEP

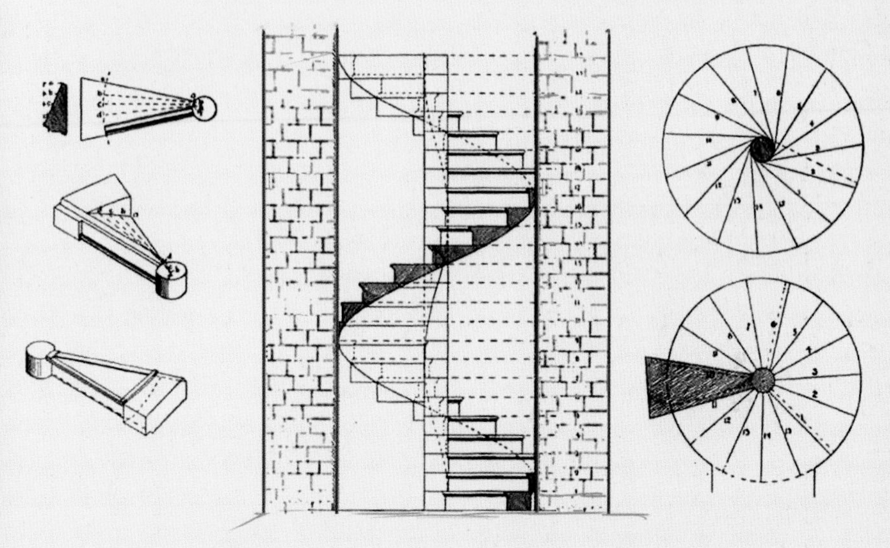

In many castles, the great tower or keep contained the lord's residential quarters and was the most secure part of the fortified enclosure – the place to which defenders could retreat if other parts of the castle were overrun. In castles derived from motte-and-bailey fortifications, the stone keep stood on the mound or motte, often on the site of an earlier wooden tower, or else enclosing the motte in the form of a stone 'shell keep'. In the castles built in line with the architectural principles established by Philip II of France – such as Guédelon – the great tower was the largest and most formidable of the four corner towers, equipped with a ground-floor defensive shooting gallery and elite accommodation on the upper floors.

THE SHELL KEEP

An early form of the castle keep was the shell keep – an enclosed area of varying shape and size set within the perimeter wall that contained the lord's accommodation and other important domestic buildings, such as barracks, kitchen and chapel. Protected by the newly erected stone wall that replaced the wooden palisade of the traditional motte-and-bailey castles, this space would have provided a relatively safe haven in which the day-to-day life of the medieval household could go on.

When creating the shell keep as part of the work to rebuild the castle in stone, the master mason typically sunk foundations 1.8–2m (6–6½ft) into the earth to support the keep's curtain wall, which was often as much as 3–3.6m (10–12ft) thick and built to a height of 4.5–9m (15–30ft).

The shape of the shell keep these walls enclosed varied, according to the lord's taste but also to the site conditions, as can be seen in the outlines left behind today. For instance, at Wiston Castle in Pembrokeshire, a shell keep was built in the early 12th century around the flat top of the 9m (30ft) motte of the motte-and-bailey castle that had been put up by Flemish Lord Wizo on land granted him by King Henry I. Here, the shell keep was outwardly polygonal in form, with 18 sections, but circular on the inner side of the wall. There was an arched gateway on the south side, and cavities are still visible in the walls into which bars would have slotted to secure the gate. This polygonal keep enclosed a sizeable oval bailey some 18m (60ft) in diameter, where the buildings of the castle – including the hall and chapel, barracks, stores and guests' accommodation, probably mostly made of timber – would have stood.

▲ *The motte-and-bailey castle, Wiston, in Pembrokeshire, built in the first half of the 12th century. (Cadw)*

▼ *Windsor Castle's majestic Round Tower, originally built as a shell keep by Henry II, is now mostly 19th century. (Alamy)*

Elsewhere, the same thing was happening as wooden structures were replaced with more robust and permanent stone ones. At Arundel Castle in West Sussex, for instance, William d'Albini II, husband of King Henry I's second wife and widow, Adeliza of Louvain, built a stone shell keep atop the 20m (66ft) motte of the original motte-and-bailey castle established by Roger of Montgomery in 1068. This shell keep had walls 9m (30ft) tall and was 20 x 18m (66 x 59ft) in size. Accommodation was ranged around the inner walls of the keep, with windows looking inwards towards the courtyard.

Other notable examples of shell keeps include the Round Tower at Windsor Castle, built by Henry II in *c.*1170 to replace a wooden Norman keep of 1070–86, but since much altered; and Totnes Castle, the shell keep of which was probably built by William de Braose, 3rd Lord of Bramber, on the site of a motte-and-bailey castle raised by Juhel of Totnes, a baron in William the Conqueror's retinue who was granted the territory by his lord in 1068.

▲ *The remains of the inner rooms added by Edmund of Cornwall are still standing within the well-preserved walls of the shell keep at Restormel Castle.*

Restormel Castle

In Cornwall, on high ground commanding a crossing of the River Fowey, Restormel Castle was built originally as a motte-and-bailey fortress in *c.*1100, then converted to a shell keep in the late 12th or early 13th century by Robert de Cardinham. Its well-preserved walls are 7.6m (25ft) tall and 2.4m (almost 8ft) thick in places – making an enclosure 38m (125ft) in diameter – and were sunk deep into the motte. The shell keep is set within a vast ditch which measures 15m (50ft) across and about 4m (13ft) deep. After being twice taken during the Second Barons' War of the 1260s, Restormel was passed to Henry III's brother, Richard of Cornwall, and then to his son, Edmund, who added inner chambers within the perimeter wall. These included a hall, solar (upper-storey private quarters for the lord) and kitchen as well as a guest chambers.

MANY-SIDED SHELL KEEPS

The Windsor tower and Totnes shell keep – like Restormel – were both roughly circular, while many other shell keeps were polygonal, such as Wiston. Other examples of polygonal keeps include the one at Tamworth Castle and Carisbrooke Castle on the Isle of Wight, where the 11-sided shell keep, 18m (60ft) across, was built by Richard de Redvers in the early 12th century on a motte-and-bailey put up by William FitzOsbern. At Lincoln Castle in the East Midlands, the polygonal keep was built in the 12th century on one of the castle's two mottes; it has 15 faces, divided by buttresses.

▼ *Cardiff Castle. A 9m (30ft) stone shell keep was built c.1150 on the motte that previously supported a wooden structure, possibly built by William the Conqueror himself.*

TOWER KEEPS

Lying at the heart of the castle and usually the most magnificent of the structures, a castle's tower keep or great tower served as a symbol of the power of lordship to both other members of the elite classes and to the local population. Important in a practical sense, too, it typically contained several storeys of residential accommodation and served as a formidable defensive fortification that could withstand sustained attack by enemy forces.

One of the most impressive tower keeps of the 12–13th century was built at Rochester Castle in southern England in 1127–36 by William of Corbeil, Archbishop of Canterbury. Measuring some 38m (125ft) in height, the keep withstood a brutal siege for two months in 1215, when King John and the royal army surrounded and attacked rebel barons who had holed up there.

ROCHESTER CASTLE

The first castle at Rochester, probably a motte-and-bailey fortification erected around the time of the Norman Conquest in 1066, had been rebuilt for the king in stone in 1087–89 by Gundulf, Bishop of Rochester – the probable builder of Colchester Castle and the White Tower at the Tower of London. In 1127, Henry I granted the castle to William of Corbeil and his successors as Archbishop of Canterbury, on the condition that the site was fortified.

William thus began work on the tower. He and his masons built to a square outline, 21m (70ft) on each side, with a pilaster buttress at each corner. The crew worked for a decade or more to raise the walls to a height of about 38m (125ft) – making it the tallest tower of the Norman era in

THE SIEGE OF ROCHESTER, 1215

The imposing tower keep at Rochester Castle was the scene of a two-month siege in the autumn of 1215, when King John and the royal army besieged rebel barons who had taken refuge there. After penetrating the outer walls and capturing the castle bailey, the king's men attacked the tower with five great siege engines, battering it day and night, and set miners to dig under the walls of the keep in the southeast corner. The king famously sent for 'forty of the fattest pigs of the sort least good for eating to bring fire beneath the tower'. Having killed the pigs, his men set them alight and caused a blaze that devastated the wooden supports they had put up in the mined area, bringing the corner of the tower crashing down. In response, the castle defenders retreated within the keep behind the cross wall that divided it internally. The siege dragged on for two months, and conditions grew so bad within that the defenders were reduced to eating their horses. Eventually, they surrendered on 30 November 1215.

▼ The impact of the square keep at Rochester Castle comes from its height. The turrets tower 3.7m (12ft) above the rest of the battlements. The curtain wall was built by Bishop Gundulf, but the imposing keep was the work of William of Corbeil. (Alamy)

▼ The huge keep at Rochester included a series of apartments over two of its four storeys.

England. Four corner turrets were raised 3.7m (12ft) above the battlements, and small windows in the lower part were cut larger in the higher areas of the walls. These were made of Kentish ragstone with fine Caen stone-facing especially imported from Normandy.

The walls were 3.7m (12ft) thick at the base and about 3.5m (10ft) thick at the top – deep enough for rooms to be built into them. Internally, the building was divided by a cross wall running east–west, which had an important structural role in supporting the huge tower as well as splitting it into a set of two-room apartments split over four storeys; it also provided a final line of defence in dire need – and proved useful to the castle defenders in 1215.

The ground-floor apartments were probably used for storage, while the first floor held a great chamber and a hall. On this floor was accommodation for the constable, who was responsible for maintaining and defending the castle in the absence of the lord – a room built into the northwest corner wall, and now known as 'Gundulf's Chamber', was probably the constable's chamber.

The second-floor chamber was 8.2m (27ft) tall, with a gallery around the upper half built into the walls; there was also a chapel measuring 8.5 x 4.6m (28 x 15ft), possibly for the archbishop's personal use. The cross wall contains openings with semicircular arches and cylindrical columns. Within the cross wall was a well shaft connecting to the well in the basement, which was 18m (59ft) deep, and from which water could be drawn even on the third floor. Also on the third floor was a secondary chapel, further accommodation and a way out onto the roof.

DEFENDING THE KEEP

The entrance to the tower keep at Rochester was accessed via a staircase leading into the first floor of a forebuilding on the north face. The staircase began on the keep's west side and turned around its northwest corner through a small defensive tower about 3.7m (12ft) square that is now almost completely dismantled. This two-storey tower's role was to defend the entrance and ensure that incomers were covered by defensive fire; its upper floor gave into the so-called Gundulf's chamber.

A 2.7m (8.9ft) gap in the approach was crossed by a drawbridge over a ditch that was 4.6m (15ft) deep. The way in continued through a fine arched doorway 1.8m (6ft) wide beneath a round arch decorated with chevrons; the door could be secured using a drawbar and was further protected by a portcullis. The doorway gave into an imposing entrance

◂ *Chepstow Castle's huge door, dated to 1159–89, is Europe's oldest. It originally barred entry to the 12th-century castle gatehouse, built by William Marshall.*

▾ *The door in the Great Tower at Guédelon was made by the carpenters from hand-hewn rather than sawn planks, finished with a side axe and decorated with strapwork.*

BUILDING TECHNIQUES: CRAFTING AND FITTING THE STRAPWORK DOOR

At Guédelon, the onsite carpenters and blacksmiths cooperated in making a heavy door for the Great Tower that featured both strapwork and ornate carvings. The decorative design – featuring 20 unique animal and human heads as well as foliage – was carefully researched and based on church doors from Lignac, Jaleyrac, Ydes and Serandon in central France. The carpenters employed 13th-century techniques, using hand-hewn planks cut with a saw, and finishing the faces with a side axe. In doing this they ensured that they worked with the grain of the wood rather than cutting across it – a time-honoured technique that makes the door more weather resistant and less likely to rot.

1 More tree than door at the start of the process, the surfaces of the thick planks are finished with a side-axe.

2 Over to the blacksmiths, who make the wrought-iron hinges and bend the strapwork into its sinuous design.

3 The blacksmiths fit the hinges to the door in the carpenters' lodge, and check the strapwork on the surface.

4 The heavy hinges are visible on the door as it is loaded onto a cart to be moved to the Great Tower.

5 The door is hung in place in the tower, and the blacksmiths nail their strapwork into place.

6 Hammer and nails, made in the forge, secure the strap work, which would protect the door against an attack.

7 The strap work includes a serpentine head. The metalwork shows wealth and prestige as well as provides protection.

▸ *A tool blade is forged on the anvil in the blacksmiths' lodge. The blacksmiths holds it with tongs while he hammers it. The blacksmiths have a constant turnover of repair and sharpening tasks for the masons and carpenters.*

▾ *It is hot, dirty work in the blacksmiths' lodge. Here one of the team works orange/red-hot metal using a lump hammer. As well as mending old tools, and making new ones, the team find new ways to recycle worn-out pieces. Nothing is wasted.*

hall 4.3m (14ft) wide and 7.9m (26ft) long, which had five windows. From here visitors passed into the main keep.

There was increasing emphasis in this period on strengthening the defences guarding the entrance to the keep or great tower. For example, doors and gateways could be protected by the presence of drawbridges, portcullises, murder holes and gates. A thick door in and of itself was an important aspect of the keep's defences, and this was often secured in the wall with a drawbar and reinforced with wrought-iron strapwork. This addition not only made the door stronger and more resistant to physical attack, but was also for show: it was a thing of beauty and a status symbol – a sign of wealth and power.

Ironworkers

Like a master or banker mason, the blacksmith was a free man, respected and sometimes even revered for his craftsmanship. The blacksmiths' forge would have been in the bailey of a castle at war, or at the heart of the building site that surrounded a castle under construction; in peacetime, the

HANDS-ON HISTORY

The keep door was the third one made at Guédelon and proved quite a contrast to the first, which had been inserted in the ground floor of the chapel tower. This was much less hardy, being made from sawn planks and without any strapwork, and it was also fitted with a lock on the outside, which would have made it far less effective as a defensive barrier.

This process is a good example of how valuable the experimental archaeology practised at Guédelon is for our understanding of 13th-century castle building. To produce a credible medieval structure, they feel, it is necessary to sometimes 'unlearn', to take something apart and start again before finding the right technique or finish. Designing, making and using castle elements from one building season to the next – and seeing them age in regular, daily use over several years – gives historians and craftspeople hugely valuable insights.

▲ *Masons and carpenters place their tools In these pigeon holes at the forge, at the end of a working day when they need sharpening or repairing. Each of the workers has a spare set to use in the meantime.*

blacksmith may well have been based in the local village – but could take refuge in the castle as necessary.

At Guédelon the blacksmiths' forge stands about 200m (yards) south of the eastern corner tower. There they work with the anvil, hearth and bellows, using tongs to hold the red-hot pieces of iron and a hammer to beat them.

Just as in the Middle Ages, the blacksmiths at Guédelon are essential to keeping the castle building site running. Fore example, each banker-mason has a kit consisting of pitching tools, chisels, punches and a lump hammer. When working the abrasive sandstone from the quarry, a stonemason can wear out an entire set of tools in the course of a single day. The blacksmiths' principal task, therefore, is toolsmithing: the making and repair of tools.

To ensure that work can continue, there are spare kits for the banker masons to use while the blacksmiths are at their repair work. The forge contains a set of wooden pigeonholes, one for each mason, in which they can leave tools that need sharpening, tempering or repairing.

BLACKSMITHS' COLOUR CHART

The blacksmiths keep a close eye on the colour of the metal they are working, since this indicates its temperature and tells them when it is the right time to work the metal in different ways. When it is scarlet, at about 270ºC (520ºF), the blacksmiths can begin working the metal. When it is turning cherry red, at about 750ºC (1,380ºF), it is ready to be tempered, a process that involves hardening it by immersing it in oil or water to rapidly cool it down. Much hotter again, at about 1,200–1,300ºC (2,190–2,370ºF), the metal turns pale yellow to white-hot. At this point, it is ready to be welded into shape.

In the Middle Ages – just as at Guédelon – producing iron was time consuming and labour intensive. Iron objects were therefore never thrown away, but instead refashioned so the metal could be used again. At Guédelon, the blacksmiths report that they remake damaged lump hammers as nails or scribe awls, a pointed metal tool used for marking metal or wood to show where it should be cut.

The Guédelon blacksmiths are also charged with making all the forged elements needed in building the castle and with fitting hinges and grilles, which are embedded in the masonry using molten lead. This latter substance was also provided by

▼ *A blacksmith pours molten lead into a mould. Lead is heated until it is liquid on a transportable hearth, and then carefully poured where needed before it has time to cool.*

▲ The Norman arch on the second floor of the square keep of Hedingham Castle is the largest in Europe. The hall also has fine windows and an imposing fireplace. (Hedingham)

◄ Hedingham Castle boasts what is probably England's best-preserved Norman keep. Two of the four 7.6m (25ft) corner turrets remain. Note the fine ashlar facing. (Hedingham)

the blacksmiths, who have a transportable hearth which can be taken to where the lead is needed. Molten lead – which is strong but malleable and does not rust – is also needed for the setting of stained-glass windows.

OTHER NOTABLE TOWER KEEPS

A square keep on an imposing scale similar to Rochester was built at Hedingham Castle in Essex at almost the same time – in the 1130s and 1140s – and to a similar plan. Aubrey de Vere II, master chamberlain of England under Henry I, was the likely lord in charge of this building. The keep at Hedingham is not quite square, measuring 16m (53ft) by 18m (58ft). Four storeys tall, it is about 21m (70ft) tall and the turrets rise a further 7.6m (25ft) above the parapet.

Masons built the walls 3.5m (11ft) thick at the base and 3m (10ft) thick at the top using flint rubble and lime mortar

◂ *The keep at Colchester Castle was probably designed by Gundulf, Bishop of Rochester, who also built part of Rochester Castle. The builders used brick and clay from the Roman colony of Camulodunum. The keep is the largest of any great tower.*

and facing blocks in very high-quality ashlar stone from Barnack quarry in Northamptonshire. On the second and third floors it contains a magnificent great hall, with a large fireplace, windows decorated with chevrons and an 8.5m (28ft) Norman arch – the largest in Europe.

Other important tower keeps of the period include the originally three-storey White Tower at the Tower of London, built between the late 1070s and 1100, and the keep at Colchester Castle, begun *c.*1074–76, both of which are strikingly similar in outline, with an apsidal projection at the southeast corner. Architectural historians have traced the influence on both English keeps to the French tower keep of Ivry-la-Bataille in Normandy, built in *c.*1000 for Aubrée, Countess of Ivry by a gifted master builder named Lanfred.

The Colchester keep has the largest ground dimensions of any great tower, measuring 46 x 33.5m (151 x 110ft), and was laid out around a pre-existing structure, the podium of a temple that once stood in the Roman colonia of Camulodunum (the forerunner of Colchester).

Sometimes, lower-lying keeps, such as the one at Colchester, are identified by historians as being 'hall keeps' rather than tower keeps. Fine examples of hall keeps are found at Norwich Castle and at Castle Rising Castle in Norfolk. The keep at Norwich Castle was built for William II and Henry I in 1095–1115. It measures about 29 x 27m (95 x 90ft) and stands about 21m (70ft) tall and is highly decorated – finished in ashlar blocks and with four levels of blank arcading. The entrance was on first-floor level via a forebuilding on the eastern side, Bigod's Tower, which is no longer standing, and was approached by a stone staircase. The interior has been gutted but historians believe it contained a hall two storeys in height, as well as a chapel, a kitchen, and no fewer than 16 latrines.

Castle Rising was built slightly later, from c.1138, by William d'Aubigny, 1st Earl of Arundel, as a hall keep set over two storeys. It measured 24 x 21m (79 x 69ft) and had walls of brown carrstone rubble (a local rock) with ashlar facing to a height of 15m (49ft). The residential accommodation – including a great hall and gallery, chapel and kitchen – was located on the upper floor. The keep was entered via a splendid, highly decorated forebuilding.

The tower keep at Dover Castle

In 1181–87, King Henry II's master mason, Maurice the Engineer, built the regal tower keep at Dover Castle. An imposing structure, this was just short of 30m (100ft) square and 25.3m (83ft) tall, with walls as much as 6.5m (21ft) thick at the base. There were three floors, connected by spiral staircases in the corner turrets, with the king's lavishly decorated chamber located on the second floor.

As in the keep Maurice built in Newcastle in 1168–78, a well shaft provides water on the second floor and from there is connected to lead piping that carries the supply to other parts of the building. The Newcastle and Dover keeps also share another design feature: a second-floor entrance accessed via an extended staircase within a heavily fortified forebuilding defended by a gatehouse.

This forebuilding at Dover made a magnificent setting for formal arrivals and departures. Historian John Gillingham argues that Henry built the keep at Dover as an embodiment of royal authority and a place of fitting splendour in which to entertain visiting royals and nobles coming to England via northern France, and so arriving at Dover, in order to pay homage at the shrine of St Thomas Becket at Canterbury. For example, in 1177, Count Philip of Flanders and, in 1179, King Louis VII of France both made trips to Canterbury and were each met by Henry on these visits. Perhaps it was these meetings that inspired the king to build the keep at Dover as a resource for future visits of this kind.

Of course, it must be remembered that although Becket had at one time been a great ally of Henry II, he subsequently became a thorn in the side of the king in a clash between royal and church power, and had thereafter been killed in Canterbury Cathedral, almost certainly on Henry's say-so, on 29 December 1170. However, since then, Henry had been on a pilgrimage to Canterbury, in 1174, and made peace with his former antagonist. This fact is reflected on the second floor of the Dover keep, where there is a beautiful chapel dedicated to Becket's memory.

Henry certainly spared no cost at Dover. From the financial year 1179–80 to the end of his reign in 1189 he spent £5,991 – more than on any other castle in his realm and in fact equating to nearly two-thirds of the total combined amount (£9,263) he spent on all English castles.

▸ *The tower keep at Dover Castle, built in 1181-87 for Henry II by Maurice the Engineer stands resolute more than 900 years later. The 29m (95ft) walls were as much as 6.5m (21ft) thick at the base. A defensive wall with 14 towers was built at the same time.*

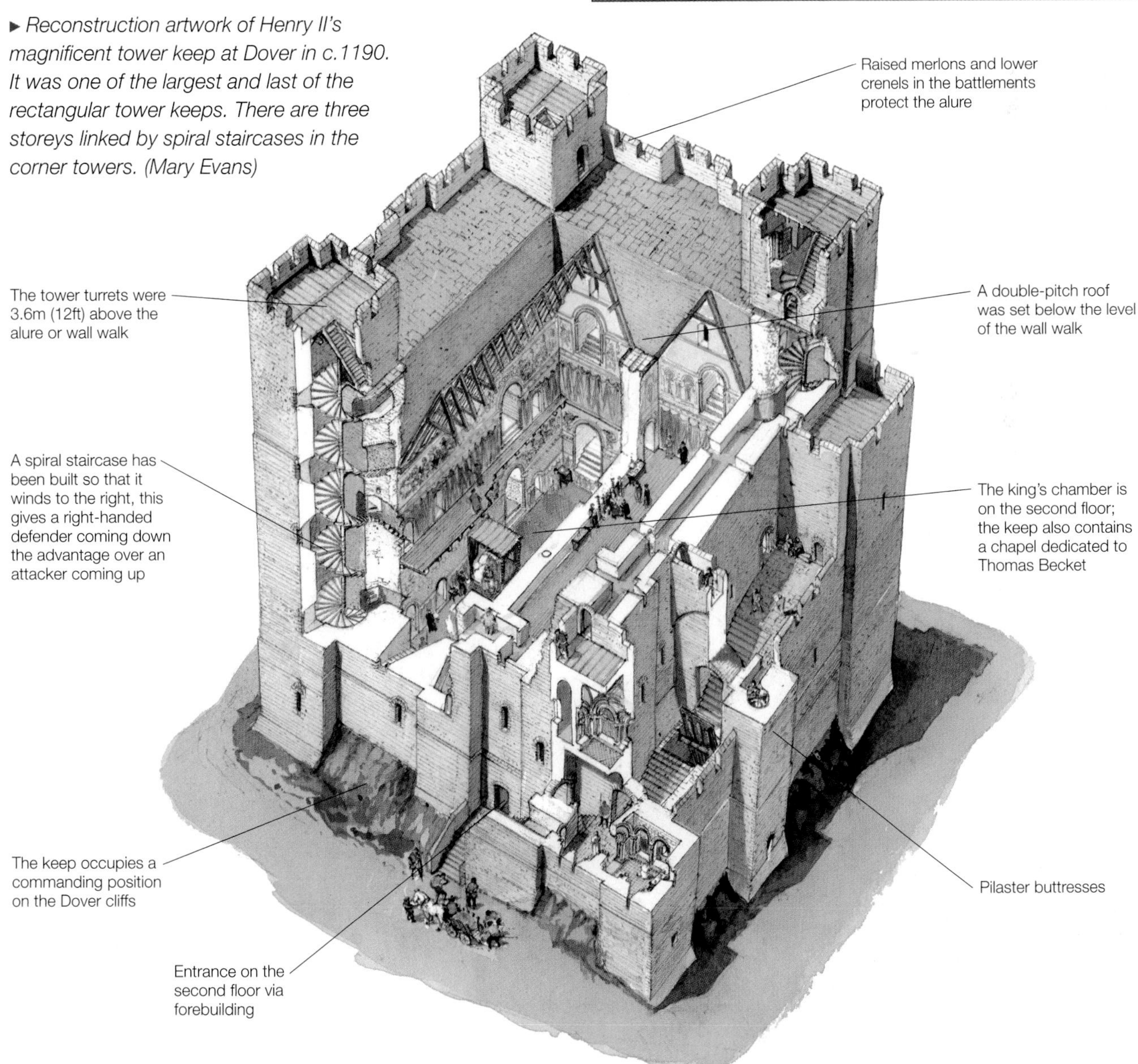

▸ *Reconstruction artwork of Henry II's magnificent tower keep at Dover in c.1190. It was one of the largest and last of the rectangular tower keeps. There are three storeys linked by spiral staircases in the corner towers. (Mary Evans)*

MOVING MATERIALS

A huge amount of material needs to be moved around the Guédelon site every day during building season. Most materials are carried by horse-drawn cart. The horses need to be calm in temperament and are trained to respond to the carters' voices. They also need to be capable of manoeuvring through tight spaces. Sometimes individual stones are moved in handcarts while small loads of rocks, mortar and lime are carried in handbaskets.

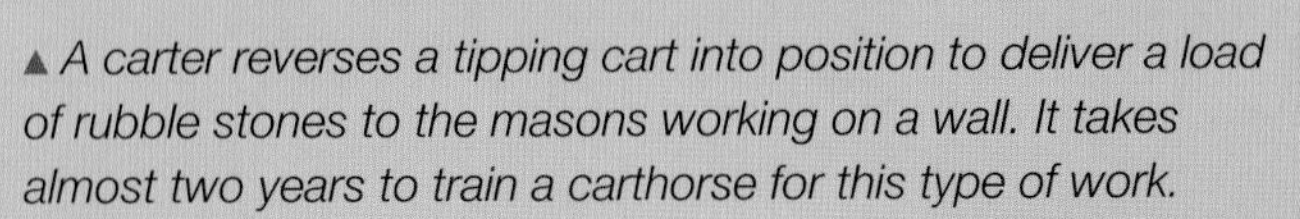

▲ *A carter reverses a tipping cart into position to deliver a load of rubble stones to the masons working on a wall. It takes almost two years to train a carthorse for this type of work.*

▲ *Two masons lower a dressed stone onto a handcart prior to wheeling it to the base of the castle walls.*

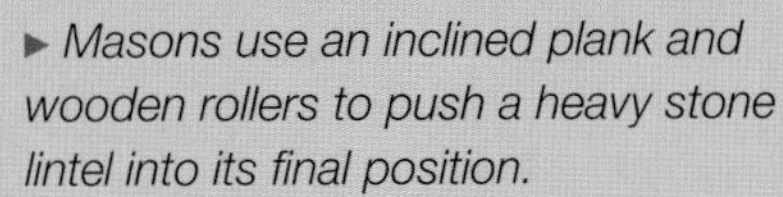

► *Masons use an inclined plank and wooden rollers to push a heavy stone lintel into its final position.*

▼ *Timber and long wooden beams can be hauled using the pole arch. Here the carpenters have transported a tie beam ready for hoisting onto the castle walls.*

► *Small loads can be carried around the site by hand. Four-handled wicker baskets are specially made in the basket makers' lodge and used to transport small stones for rubble, mortar and lime. The lime is very corrosive and the baskets need to be replaced frequently.*

ROUND AND POLYGONAL TOWER KEEPS

An alternative to the square or rectangular tower keep was the rather more graceful-looking cylindrical keep – as found at the once-imposing Château de Coucy in France, the great circular keep built by William Marshal at Pembroke Castle, and in the Great Tower of Guédelon. Elsewhere, for instance at Orford and Conisbrough castles, the circular keep was given buttressing towers to create a polygonal outline.

At Pembroke Castle, William Marshall built one of the earliest cylindrical keeps found in England and Wales during the period between becoming earl in 1199 and his death in 1219. Set on a plinth, it is 24m (80ft) tall and measures 16m (52ft) in diameter. Its entrance was on the first floor, accessed by stone steps, and within the keep there was a spiral staircase connecting the four storeys. At the top, putlog holes survive that would have supported a wooden fighting platform. Then, above this level is a domed roof that originally had a second layer of battlements from which soldiers could overlook those fighting on the wooden hoarding below.

The cylindrical tower keep at Coucy castle was dynamited during the First World War so cannot be seen today, but we know from historical accounts that its dimensions and design made it arguably the greatest cylindrical tower keep ever constructed. The circular donjon, built for Enguerrand III, Lord of Coucy, in *c.*1225, stood within an encasing wall and a ditch. It was more than 30m (100ft) in diameter, with walls 7.5m (25ft) thick at ground level, and was about 55m (180ft) tall. Its three storeys had magnificent rib vaults – a feature that also appears at Guédelon, where a superb cross-rib vault was built for the lord's chamber in the round Great Tower.

► *Orford Castle in Suffolk, built 1165–73, has a circular main keep with two attached rectangular turrets and a rectangular forebuilding. The central tower is 27m (90ft) tall. This remarkable building may have been the work of Ailnoth the Engineer.*

▼ *The majestic 16m (52ft)-diameter cylindrical keep (left) built by William Marshall at Pembroke Castle. Note the putlog holes around the top that would have supported wooden hoarding. Originally the keep had a domed roof. (Cadw)*

▼ *Coucy Castle – the greatest cylindrical tower keep ever constructed? There was a single chamber on each floor of the three-storey, 30m (100ft)-diameter circular donjon. It was destroyed in the First World War.*

► *The handsome cylindrical Great Tower rises at the northeast corner of the Guédelon courtyard. Its key role is to provide a lookout position and a final refuge in case of attack, but it also contains a fine second-floor residential chamber. Note the scarp – the sloping base of the tower.*

Each floor contained a large single chamber. In addition, the ground floor had a well, a fireplace, a latrine and a spiral staircase leading up to the higher levels. The first floor also contained a fireplace and latrine, and there was a postern gate that gave access to an alure around the top of the wall enclosing the ditch. The top floor contained a grand chamber and a mural gallery, along with recessed wooden balconies about 3m (10ft) above the main room.

THE CIRCULAR KEEP AT GUÉDELON

Philip II, on whose castle plans Guédelon is based, constructed a series of circular donjons in France – including those at Bourges, Chinon, Dourdan, Gisors and Rouen – as well as at the Louvre in Paris. The Great Tower at Guédelon has a round plan like these donjons, and like Coucy. It is accessed via a heavy wooden door from the courtyard and contains a cellar with a water cistern, and above it a shooting gallery on the ground floor, from which arrows and crossbow quarrels can be unleashed through arrow loops into the surrounding forest. A spiral mural staircase leads up to the lord's chamber on the first floor and from there to an octagonal room, with window seats, on the second floor. There will be defensive wooden hoarding fitted on the top of the tower once the building is finished.

One of the great feats achieved by master mason Florian Renucci and his teams of masons and carpenters at Guédelon was the planning, carving, construction and fitting of the cross-rib vault in the lord's chamber in the Great Tower. With six limestone ribs, it is the widest, tallest and most elaborate of the castle's vaults – 7m (23ft) high and 7m wide, it contains 100m^3 (3,500ft^3) of stone and mortar. The vault is crowned with a keystone decorated with a floral motif that was chosen by Florian Renucci, and is a copy of the carving found on a keystone at Dourdan Castle.

Building the cross-rib vaulting

In creating the lord's chamber and its cross-rib vault, the masons dressed the sandstone blocks for the facing walls and carved the corbels (the projecting load-supporting stones) and 84 voussoirs (the wedge-shaped blocks used for the ribs). They then built six arcs formerets – arches in the walls where the webbing in between the arches of the cross-rib descends to meet the walls. At this point the walls were 2.73m (almost 9ft) thick and needed to be very strong to

▲ *Building the cross-rib vault in the lord's chamber on the first floor of the Guédelon Great Tower. The walls have been built up, and the corbels and tas-de-charge have been fixed.*

▲ *The carpenters have positioned the wooden centring to support the stones of the vault while they are being positioned. A platform has also been constructed around the edges.*

▲ *The stone masons and carters worked together to transport the fragile keystone from the masons' lodge, raise it to the top of the tower and position it gently on the centring.*

▲ *The masons have built up the ribs in the vault by placing voussoirs simultaneously on each arm of the centring. The final voussoir stones are still to be inserted.*

support the vault's weight, so correspondingly vast amounts of mortar and rubble stones were therefore needed to make them. The masons hoisted the stones to the upper levels of the Great Tower where they were working using the double-wheel treadmill, which was fitted on the adjoining curtain wall. They needed to use the treadmill 12 times per day to keep the masons supplied.

In constructing an arch, the keystone is the final stone to be put in place at the top, but when building a rib vault, the opposite is true: the keystone is the first to be laid. At Guédelon, this was placed at the top of the wooden centring (framing that is used to support an arch or vault) that had been installed with great skill and care by the carpenters – particularly because the keystone, which took no less than one month to carve, was extremely delicate. Once in positon, the keystone was the guide for the building up of the ribs around the centring.

The carpenters made the centring needed to support the vault while it was under construction. For this cross-rib vault they adapted an earlier centring they had made for the construction of the rib vault on the ground floor chamber of the Great Tower, which had then been dismantled and stored in the carpenters' workshop. Now they rebuilt it in the workshop and enlarged it to make it suitable for the lord's chamber.

To install it, they then dismantled it again and hoisted the sections onto the tower before rebuilding the structure in situ. From inside the lord's chamber they built a putlog scaffold to support the centring. The scaffold combined vertical poles and angled braces supporting putlogs. Each of the six ribs bore a load of approximately 25 tonnes. At the base of each rib were the tas-de-charges, made up of a springer stone, a counter springer and the first two voussoirs. The springer stones are much longer than the voussoirs; and they are

▲ *Beneath the vault the masons have gently lowered the wooden centring – and proved that the ribs will hold. Now they are building the webbing with rubble stones and mortar.*

▲ *The finished cross-rib vault viewed from within the first-floor lord's chamber is a thing of beauty – and a tremendous achievement for master mason Florian Renucci and his team.*

▲ *The window seat in the lord's chamber in the Great Tower. Window seats enabled castle-dwellers to make the most of available light when reading or embroidering.*

deeply embedded in the rubble core, where they help distribute the load into the wall. The keystone and voussoirs were cut with abreuvoirs – or joggle joints – grooves that are filled with mortar and help the stones bond, which has the effect of preventing movement from side to side and so making the arch more secure.

Moving, hoisting and positioning the keystone was a fraught manoeuvre. Its floral motif, carefully carved over several weeks, was fragile and might easily be damaged by being knocked. The whole team worked together transporting the stone from the stonemasons' lodge, lifting using the treadmill winch and positioning it very carefully on the top of the centring, where it was the guide for the masons building up the stones in the ribs. After the keystone and voussoirs had been placed around the centring, the centring was lowered by gently removing the wooden wedges positioned at the base of the six branches of the centring.

Building the mural staircase

At the same time that the vaulting was being erected, another team of masons was at work building the vaulted mural stairway that leads to the second floor of the Great Tower and is located in the thickness of the wall. These mural staircases and passages could be very dark and gloomy, but became much brighter when the walls were limewashed – a matter of only a couple of hours' work. The contrast between before and after is quite startling.

Creating octagonal rooms

After building and installing the cross-rib vault in the lord's chamber, the masons began laying out the octagonal second-floor chamber in the Great Tower – the room above the cross-rib vault of the lord's chamber. To keep them supplied with building materials, the double-wheeled treadmill was mounted on the top level of the tower itself – a full 16m

◂ *Springer stones (bottom) are longer than voussoirs (top). They are carved (left) with joggle joints – grooves that are filled with mortar and help the stones bond.*

(more than 50ft) above the bottom of the dry ditch far below. They also finished the mural stairway and the vaulted corridor it led into outside the octagonal chamber – a space that was planned with a well-proportioned fireplace and two windows with windows seats.

POLYGONAL OUTLINE

The master mason responsible for the cylindrical keep at Conisbrough Castle made an impressive change to the basic design of the circular keep, laying out six semi-polygonal turrets around its circumference. Built by Henry II's illegitimate half-brother Hamelin in 1165–90 after his marriage in 1164 to Isabella, granddaughter and heiress of William de Warenne – the Norman lord who built Lewes Castle – the keep is 19m (62ft) in diameter and stands 28m (92ft) tall, with walls 4.5m (15ft) thick. The six turrets are solid up to roof level, except at the second floor where one of them contains a vaulted, hexagonal chapel. A bread oven and two water cisterns are at the top of the keep, together with a shelter and two observation posts: it was equipped to withstand a siege.

The keep was built on the northeast side of the inner bailey. Conisbrough had two baileys, its outer one, measuring 79 x 37m (260 x 120ft), connected by a drawbridge to the larger inner one of 88 x 62m (290 x 205ft). While military and archaeological historians praise its unusual design, they also note that the solid buttresses were ineffective in terms of defence – they were vulnerable to undermining and had no arrow slots through which crossbowmen and longbowmen could keep attackers at bay.

▴ *The mural staircase in the Great Tower, showing how lime rendering makes the available light spread to improve visibility.*

This polygonal keep would have been complete when King John visited Conisbrough Castle in 1201. At this point, the ground floor served as a basement, for access was via the first floor. There were two upper floors that contained – as in the Guédelon Great Tower – the lord's chamber and a large

▾ *Plans of the polygonal keep at Conisbroguh, floor by floor, from the entrance on the first-floor level to the rooftop and its battlemented wallwalk. Note the staircases in the walls.*

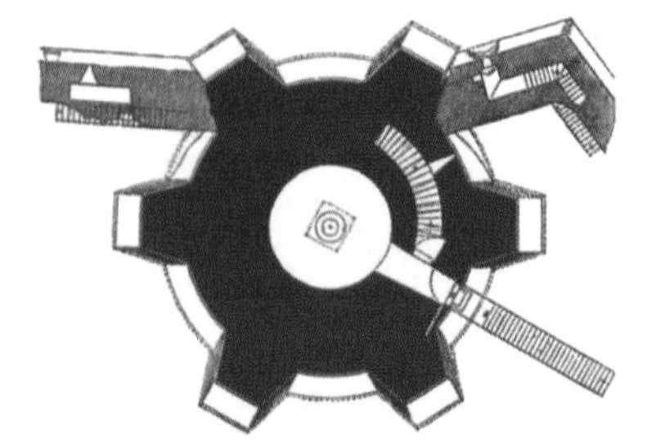

First floor

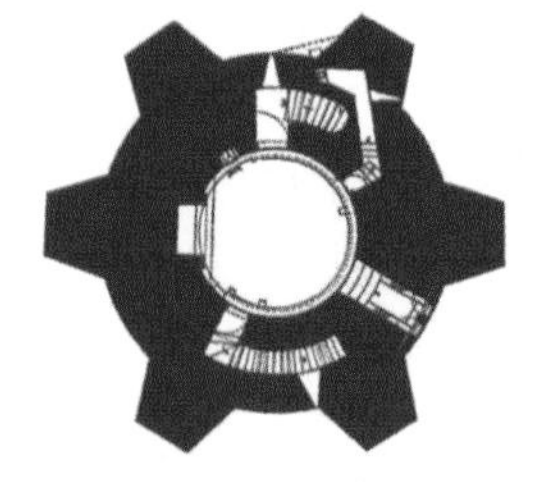

Second floor

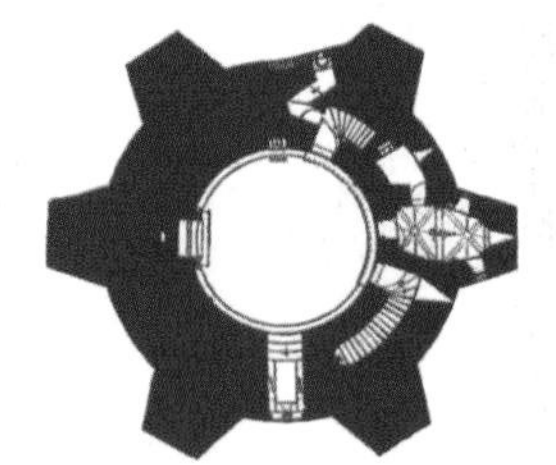

Third floor

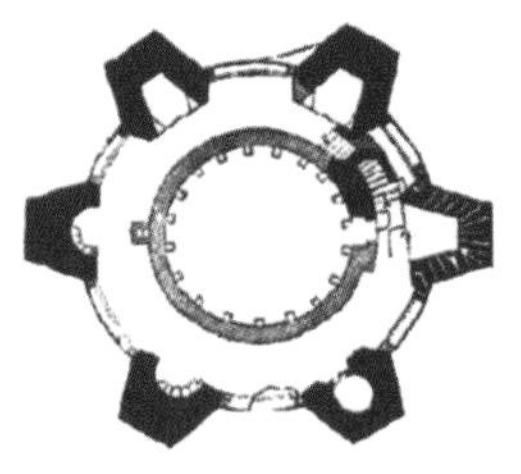

Roof

window with window seat. The window measured 1.42m x 56cm (4.7 x 1.8ft). In the 14th century, after a dispute, the castle was seized by King Edward II who visited in 1322 and spent a considerable amount repairing the structures at Conisbrough and at nearby Pontefract.

The near-contemporary keep at Orford Castle in Suffolk, built for Henry II in 1165–73, had a similar combination of a circular main keep with attached turrets – in this case, two rectangular turrets and a rectangular forebuilding. The second-floor accommodation – containing a large hall beneath a domed roof, private chamber and kitchen – was probably meant for the king himself; a similar, less grand set of rooms was laid out in the floor below, accessed by a staircase. The chapel was in the upper part of the forebuilding. The tower was 27m (89ft) tall. Like the keep at Conisbrough, Orford Castle keep does not have an effective design in terms of defence, since the rectangular turrets created blind spots for defenders, and corner chambers and staircases made it vulnerable. Some authorities have argued that it was intended as a politically symbolic design, meant to signify regal or imperial power.

▲ *The walls of Guédelon's Great Tower must support the thrust of the stone vaults. The walls become less thick on each level because there is less weight to support.*

▼ *The beautifully sited Conisbrough Castle. In the 19th century its remains so impressed author Sir Walter Scott that he used it as the setting for his celebrated novel* Ivanhoe.

6

PRIVATE ROOMS AND LIVING CHAMBERS

The castle's living quarters were typically focused on the great hall, in and around which the entire household may have lived. Sometimes, however, accommodation for guests, retainers and family was also found in the gatehouse, tower keep and other parts of the castle. At Guédelon, the North Range at the rear of the courtyard opposite the gatehouse contains a beautiful decorated antechamber giving on to a magnificent Great Hall. There is also accommodation in the corner towers of Guédelon's quadrangular layout, and the Great Tower at the courtyard's northeast corner.

PRIVATE ROOMS AND GUEST ACCOMMODATION

Living quarters beyond the great hall included chambers for the lord and family and the castle constable, as well as guest rooms for elite visitors. Of these, there were often private chambers reserved for the lord's wife and her ladies, perhaps decorated with floral and animal designs and fitted with window seats, sometimes overlooking and connected to secluded gardens.

Providing well-appointed accommodation for noble and royal visitors was a statement of power and status. At Warwick Castle, guest accommodation was very visibly provided in the imposing, machicolated Caesar's Tower and Guy's Tower, built in full view of the world on either side of the castle's gatehouse in the 14th century. Elsewhere, the king himself, Henry II, was happy to lavish money on the keep at Dover Castle in order to provide splendid rooms for greeting and accommodating royal and noble visitors.

▼ *The imposing Caesar's Tower at Warwick Castle, built c.1350. Its rooms have a stone vault on every storey. Note the machicolations and the two levels of parapets at the top.*

▲ *The view across the River Wye sees Chepstow Castle in its clifftop site. The castle was built to control a river crossing, and was originally called Striguil, Welsh for 'river bend'.*

CHEPSTOW CASTLE

At Chepstow Castle in Wales, Roger Bigod's master mason Ralf Gogun built fine residential quarters for lord and family on the north side of the lower bailey in 1278–85. These grand buildings – known as 'the Gloriette' – were made ready for a visit by King Edward I in December 1285. Roger Bigod also built Marten's Tower at the southeast corner of the Lower Bailey in *c.*1287-93.

The residential buildings, which occupied the entire north side of the lower bailey, contained two ground-floor halls. They were centred on two substantial halls – the west or greater one being much bigger and more magnificent than the east or lesser one. Each had its own buttery and pantry and its own private rooms. Because the ground sloped quite sharply to the east, the buttery and pantry of the east hall could stand directly beneath those of the west one, but still give directly on to the east hall. There was no kitchen, which must have been situated elsewhere in the bailey – either free standing or built against one of the curtain walls.

The walls were faced with purple freestone and the windows and doorways were all shaped to a point at the top. The west or greater hall was a splendid building, measuring 18 x 9m (58 x 29ft), and remains indicate that there were two large windows giving on to the courtyard, which were

► *The interior of Marten's Tower, in the Lower Bailey at Chepstow. It was renamed after Henry Marten, a lawyer who signed Charles I's death warrant, and who was imprisoned there after the restoration of the monarchy. (Alamy)*

originally decorated with high-quality floral carving. A three-storey chamber block adjoining the lower bailey gatehouse was accessible through a doorway from the east hall of the residential building. This chamber block contained a ground-floor room (probably for guards), which connected through a doorway to a prison within the gatehouse.

The two storeys above each contained a fine residential chamber, each with a latrine opening over the side of the cliff as well as two substantial windows, one in the south and one in the north walls. There was no internal stairway in this block and the rooms on the upper storeys were accessed via wooden stairways: the first floor from the courtyard and the second floor from a platform built outside the lesser hall.

► *The domestic block in the Lower Bailey of Chepstow Castle. The tower-like part is a porch that led into Roger Bigod's hall. (Cadw)*

▼ *Chepstow Castle: the interior of the larger of Roger Bigod's halls in the Lower Bailey – the wooden steps lead up to the earl's chamber or gloriette. Note the pointed arches on the doorways. (Cadw)*

◄ A colourful private chamber in the Château de Langeais, in the Loire Valley, gives an idea of what the private rooms of a medieval castle would have looked like, with its grand fireplace, bedstead and beautiful floor and wall decorations. The remains of a 10th-century stone keep built by the Count of Anjou are still standing on the site. (Getty)

Marshall's Tower

Also at Chepstow, the sadly much reduced remains of a tower in the southwest corner of the upper bailey indicate that there was a room there, which was possibly intended for the countess and her ladies. This tower, now known as Marshall's Tower, was built by William Marshall in the very early 13th century – certainly before his death in 1219. The large room, measuring 11 x 5.8m (36 x 19ft) was probably accessed by a wooden stairway from the courtyard and contained four windows, two facing west and two facing south. The windows are small externally because they were looking out beyond the castle and were therefore vulnerable, but all four were fitted internally with window seats. There are some remains of fine moulding around the windows and on the walls there are a few traces of plaster with a design in red paint. Some other castles also had private galleries,

EDUCATION AND EXPECTATIONS

For most of their first decade, the children of the castle were educated by the chaplain, and after the classes were finished were free to spend time with the lord's wife and her ladies in private chambers away from the hustle and bustle of castle life. At around the age of eight or nine, however, boys were commonly sent away to another castle or lordly residence to begin training as a squire, in preparation for eventual knighthood. Meanwhile, girls as young as eight, nine or ten were often betrothed to be married – and were normally married before they turned 14. In the meantime they, too, were frequently sent away to other households, where they learned how to conduct themselves among people of their class, as well as being trained in administering a household, cooking, sewing, embroidery and weaving.

► A French miniature of the 15th century shows a knight visiting a lady in a room full of colour and comfort. (Getty)

▸ *Inside the 'House of Colours' the artists have decorated the walls using their own mineral-based paints. As you quickly see when walking around the site, the golden-yellow ochre of the local earth is the dominant colour at Guédelon.*

cloister-like walkways and gardens that were used exclusively by the countess and her womenfolk.

In a room such as this, the ladies might sit over their embroidery, tell tales and share gossip of castle life; once the chaplain had released their children from their lessons, they might also spend time with them. Perhaps it was a place for contemplation and quiet withdrawal from the bustle of castle life, too. The quarters often overlooked gardens, a deer park or water (such as the mere at Kenilworth Castle) and were painted within with naturalistic scenes of plants and animals. This kind of room was colourfully and beautifully decorated – something that it easy to forget since medieval castles survive merely as bare stone blocks.

DECORATING GUÉDELON

At Guédelon, the castle builders took up the challenge of trying to recreate the kind of painted wall decoration that the residents of a castle of this type would have enjoyed. In the antechamber to the Great Hall in the Guédelon North Range, craftsmen prepared the walls and painted murals using paints made with ochre and hematite found on site. The designs in these murals were carefully researched and based on those found in Meauce Castle (Bourgogne) and Alluyes Castle (Eure-et-Loire), and the Church of St Peter in nearby Moutiers, which contains 13th-century murals. The on site artists chose not to represent animals or human figures but to concentrate instead on abstract and floral designs.

They also used a decorative style called 'stones and roses' – in which the wall is painted to look like masonry with the addition of tiny roses. This was among the most common designs used to decorate rooms in the middle years of the 13th century. A similar style using sunbursts in place of roses was used in Marshall's Tower at Chepstow Castle. The style in which the wall was painted, usually with red lines on a white background, to look like finished ashlar brickwork, was called 'fictive masonry'. In the chapel of Manorbier Castle in Pembrokeshire, Wales, painted rosettes were added to the

▾ *Floral motifs decorate a ceiling in the Château de Larroque-Toirac. The castle, on a clifftop above the Lot River in central southwestern France, was originally constructed in the 13th century and rebuilt in the 15th century. (Getty)*

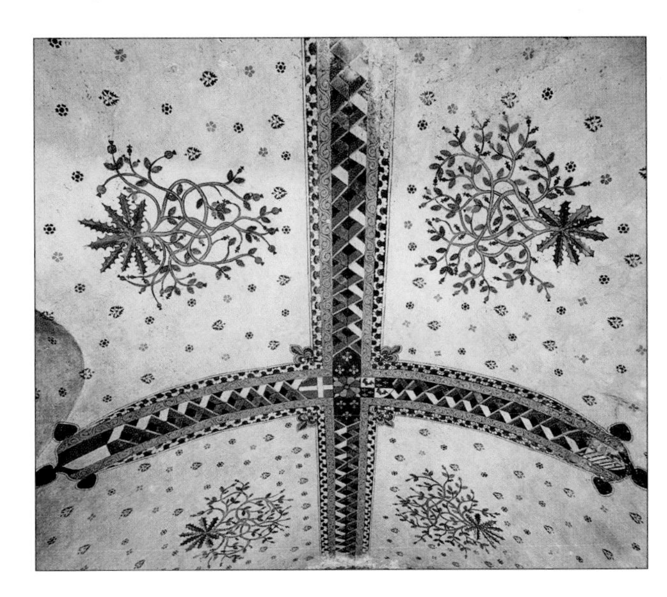

MAKING PAINTS FROM MINERAL PIGMENTS

The colour workshop is situated about 250m (yards) to the east of the eastern gatehouse at Guédelon. There, the women in charge of the 'House of Colours' use plant-based dyes to make coloured cloth and wools, and mineral pigments to mix a range of hues.

In order to create the latter, the women use the clays, stones and ochre-coloured earth found in abundance on the castle site to produce 12 colours. For instance, yellow ochre can be heated, which causes it to turn red and provide burnt-red ochre. Clay can produce beige colours – when heated, it turns a pinkish-beige colour, quarry sand gives orange colours; hematite, dark red. In the places where charcoal earth clamps have been positioned, the women gather burnt charcoal dust, with which they create dark grey and black. When they mix charcoal with lime, they produce bluey-grey tints. The earth itself can be processed to make a pigment that can be used to mix up paints. First, they wash it by mixing it with water, then they leave it to stand: the heavier grains sink to the bottom and separate from the watery solution that contains the finer particles. They set aside this water and allow it to evaporate naturally, leaving behind the useful pigment.

▼ Yellow ochre and burnt-red ochre. The finer the minerals are ground, the better the paint. These are mixed with water to make the paints used in decorating the castle.

▼ Abstract and floral designs decorate the lime-plastered, lime-washed walls in the antechamber. The designs are based on those in the nearby church in Moutiers.

▼ The four handsome windows on the upper storey of the North Range are all in the same style – a pointed-arch, two-light mullion design. They look out onto the courtyard and are large enough to let copious amounts of light into the hall.

painted ashlar design – the same style that was was used in the bishops' palace at nearby Lamphey. A complex and beautiful scheme was used by Ewenny Priory in the Vale of Glamorgan, Wales, where the painters used red lines to suggest masonry and then decorated the masonry 'blocks' they had created with alternating flowers and cinquefoils. The itinerant craftsmen that worked on such schemes in priories and abbeys were the same men who worked in castles – and used the same methods and designs there. We know of one of these painters in the Welsh castles – Stephen the Painter, who decorated a room in Rhuddlan Castle before Edward I stayed there in 1283. At Ewenny the painters also depicted architectural features such as 'columns' on the wall.

To create these designs, the painters first lime-rendered and limewashed the walls and then they or the master mason created the grid on the wall by using a string covered in coloured chalk and pulled straight. When the string was 'snapped' – that is, tweaked – it hit against the wall and left a coloured straight line for the painters to follow. They then either made a light incision into the surface or drew over the chalk lines in a thicker chalk grid before they started painting.

MEDIEVAL SKILLS: DECORATING

The onsite painters went to great pains to create authentic decorations on the interior walls of the castle. Before beginning the murals in the antechamber to the Great Hall in the North Range, they conducted a careful trial with the help of art historian and mural specialist Juliette Rollier, and heritage painter Marie-Paule Dubois. They used only paints made with mineral pigments found on site, ground and mixed by hand with local water. The castle team based their designs on careful study of existing murals, particularly those in the church of Saint-Pierre in Moutiers, and have been extending the skills they developed in decorating the Great Hall antechamber to other sites round Guédelon.

1 This lovely red-orange mineral pigment is derived from ochre found on site in the clay and the quarry, ground down by hand using a pestle and mortar. Medieval murals used locally produced colours, so it is appropriate that the 'House of Colours' uses only Guédelon materials in making its paints.

2 A painter first applies a coat of lime render – a mix of lime putty and quarry sand – to the wall with a trowel. There is a lot of evidence for lime renders being applied to both inner and outer walls of medieval castles. The wall in the background has been limewashed.

3 The artisans test colours and designs on the wall. The colours beneath numbers 1 and 2 represent different stages in the finish – *enduit chaud plus sable* ('lime render plus sand') or *badigeon blanc de chaux* ('lime whitewash'). The white surface is the base to which colours are applied.

4 After testing and trials, painters began painting the murals in the antechamber in summer 2012. The upper part of the wall is decorated with a style called 'stones and roses' – painted to look like masonry with the addition of tiny roses. This was a popular design in interior decoration in the mid-13th century.

▲ *The quatrefoil-topped window in the western gable end of the Great Hall looks out toward the Chapel Tower – still under construction at that stage.*

▲ *A rounded arch two-light window and window seats in the south-facing eaves wall of the Great Hall, looking out over the gatehouse and courtyard.*

At Guédelon, at first the team of decorators applied a scratch coat and then a render coat to the walls in order to achieve a perfectly flat finish. However, a closer study of medieval walls revealed that painters in the Middle Ages often applied just one thick coat of render to the stones, leaving a more undulating surface. The Guédelon painters have adapted their practices accordingly. The walls were then painted with limewash, producing a pure-white surface to paint on. The craftsmen and women then set to work making the first line drawings for the motifs and friezes.

WINDOWS AND WINDOW SEATS

Residential accommodation was made more comfortable by the provision of good light through large, sometimes glazed, windows, usually overlooking the inner parts of castle. Well-proportioned windows, of course, added beauty to a fine building; in themselves they were a mark of status. At Guédelon, four two-light windows carved from limestone are set in the southern facade of the North Range and another window with a sculpted quatrefoil element is in the western gable end. As in the ladies' chamber at Chepstow, each of the windows is fitted with a stone window seat to make the most of natural light for as long as possible when they were embroidering or reading.

In designing the windows, the master mason at Guédelon had to match the facade of other castles built *c.*1230-40, following the style established by Philip II. He chose to use pointed-arch two-light mullion windows with trefoil mouldings, based on the design at the castle of Crépy-en-Valois (Oise). This was sketched on site and then adapted to suit the dimensions at Guédelon. Locally sourced hard Donzy limestone was selected for the windows, which, because it was hard, would work well alongside the sandstone already being used in the castle. It would also not set off chemical changes that might cause damage. The banker masons quickly adapted to working the very different stone.

When making these windows, the banker masons dressed the limestone in their lodge, fitting all the elements together there to make sure no adjustments were needed before they were transported for fitting.

BUILDING TECHNIQUES: FITTING A TWO-LIGHT WINDOW

In a 13th-century castle, the style and number of windows were as much a matter of prestige as the beauty and colour of the interior decoration. Master mason Florian Renucci's great knowledge and careful research at the French castle of Crépy-en-Valois in Oise ensured that the four windows and the entire facade of the North Range have an authentic 13th-century look. Looking across the courtyard or from beyond the walls as you approach the castle, the locally sourced limestone of the windows looks beautiful against the stonework of the North Range. The first three windows open into the Great Hall, while the fourth gives into the adjoining chamber adorned with murals.

1 Before fitting the window, the masons performed a 'dry assembly' (without mortar) of the finished stones in the castle courtyard. Then they carefully dismantled the window and carried the stones one by one to the point of assembly on the upper floor of the North Range.

2 The windows in the Great Hall have a window seat so people can sit comfortably within to look out at the courtyard or make the most of the available light. At this point of the window's construction the stones that form the window seat are all in place. The mason checks they are absolutely level.

3 The masons build the wall around a two-light window on the eaves wall. Only the last voussoirs of the arch need to be fixed above the tympanum. The bright-white limestone will mellow over time.

4 One of the five completed two-light windows in the North Range. The question of whether the windows would have been glazed in a castle such as Guédelon is still being studied. Wooden shutters, or oiled parchment stretched across wooden frames, are also being considered.

DOMESTIC COMFORTS

Aside from providing a roof over the head and protection from both the elements and enemies without, the best and more comfortable noble accommodation was fitted with a latrine – and sometimes even with running water. Some rooms were also equipped with their own mural fireplaces for heating, and candlestick holders set in the walls, bringing both warmth and light into what could otherwise be a dark, chilly space.

Running water in a building was a true luxury in medieval times, but master masons had various ingenious ways of achieving this much sought-after amenity and piped water wasn't as rare as you may think. At Restormel Castle in Cornwall, for instance, water from a local spring was piped into the rooms built within the shell keep, which had been converted from its former motte-and-bailey incarnation in the 12th and13th centuries by Robert de Cardinham. Other castle buildings that featured piped water include the keeps at Newcastle-upon-Tyne and Dover, both designed by King Henry II's master mason, Maurice the Engineer. In both of these cases the water was piped by gravity, using water drawn on the second floor from an extended well shaft.

WELLS AND CISTERNS

In the vast majority of cases, the principal source of water in castles was the well. Situating this in the best position, often next to the kitchen, was a key part of castle planning. Early in the construction process, miners and earthworkers would set to work digging the well, lining the earth shaft they created with stone to prevent collapses, if necessary; when digging through rock, they did not need to line the shaft with stone – although the upper reaches were normally stone-lined regardless. This can be seen in the 18m (59ft)-deep rock-cut well at Rochester, the upper half of which had been lined.

The well in the courtyard at Guédelon is 7m (23ft) deep and topped with a curb stone 1.75m (5ft 9in) across and 22cm (9in) thick, weighing 1.5 tonnes. This was laboriously cut by the masons from a sizeable fissure-free bed of sandstone in the quarry that the master mason had been told about by the quarrymen who had discovered it.

Cisterns or water tanks were also used to collect and store rainwater for later use. In the keeps of Dover and Newcastle-upon-Tyne, for instance, cisterns were constructed beside the well. Elsewhere, cisterns were built on the roofs of the keeps, as at Orford and Conisbrough castles, or even as part of towers, as happened at Caernarfon Castle, where the Cistern Tower in the south curtain wall is so called because it contained a stone-lined tank that was used for collecting rainwater. At Guédelon, the castle builders built two cisterns: one in the chapel tower and one in the Great Tower. The one in the basement of the chapel tower is 3m (10ft) deep and is positioned beneath a domed roof containing a central aperture fitted with a forged grille.

▾ *The well was not always next to the kitchen. The one at Harlech Castle in Wales is set into the north inner curtain wall alongside what was once the bakehouse. (Cadw)*

▴ *The oculus of the water cistern in the basement of the Chapel Tower. The cistern is 3m (10ft) deep, with a domed roof. Water storage was of great strategic importance.*

BUILDING TECHNIQUES: INSTALLING A LATRINE

In the building seasons of 2008–10 the team at Guédelon designed and built a latrine in the lord's chamber on the first floor of the Great Tower. The latrine gives directly into the ditch to the east side of the castle.

1 In May 2008 the team is building up the wall of the lord's chamber, and the masons have laid out the narrow space that the latrine will occupy. The latrine will be built on sandstone corbels, which project out from the Great Tower's walls.

2 A year later, in July 2009, the walls are being built up either side of the latrine. In the interior, the stone base of the toilets been installed – it is here covered with a piece of wood. The conditions are cramped and drafty – for the opening gives directly into the ditch.

3 All the stonework on the protruding latrine shaft has been completed, and the masons remove the scaffolding around the latrine. Note the sandstone corbels, which support the latrine shaft.

4 By June 2010 the 'garderobe' is finished. Clothes are said to have been stored near the latrines as the ammonia fumes helped to kill off mites in the fabric. The whitewashed walls make the room lighter and the lime kills bacteria.

5 The finished latrine shaft. Note the relieving arch above the sloping roof. At the base of the shaft is the hole through which waste would have fallen into the ditch below. There is a small guttering spout at floor level

◄ *A reconstructed bathing room in Leeds Castle, Kent. The white curtain surrounds a wooden tub in which the king, queen or other noble guest at Leeds would sit on a stool. Servants would provide heated water in wooden buckets with which to wash, using homemade soap of wood ash, soda or animal fat. Leeds Castle was King Edward I's favourite residence.*

LATRINES

Toilets or latrines were also known as garderobes, from a French word originally meaning a wardrobe or a private space that by extension came to be used for the toilet. (The word garderobe was also used simply to mean a small room or cupboard.) Latrines were often fitted within the external walls and gave issue directly into the ditch or moat, the sea, or even over the edge of a cliff, as at the keep of Peveril Castle in Derbyshire, built 1176–77. Sometimes more than one latrine gave into a shaft like this; at the late 14th-century Bodiam Castle, for instance, 28 latrines gave directly into the moat that surrounds the castle. At Guédelon, meanwhile, a single latrine in the North Range gives directly into the dry ditch below.

Within the garderobe the sense of cleanliness was much improved when the latrine walls were limewashed. There was no such thing as toilet paper, of course; people used a fistful of hay or perhaps a piece of moss instead. Outside, the smell must have been very bad in the ditch; when the waste went into the moat, as at Bodiam, the waters were no more than an open sewer. The best hope was to position the latrines so they gave issue into a river or stream, the moving water of which could carry waste and smells away.

The latrines themselves could be very smelly, especially in hot weather. This was because, even if it gave into running water, the shaft itself would inevitably be dirty. Indeed, such was the scale of the problem that Henry III made a celebrated complaint about the smell issuing from his private latrine in the Tower of London, grumbling to the constable of the castle: 'the privy in the chamber of our wardrobe at London is situated in an undue and improper place, wherefore it smells badly' and demanding that another be built 'even though it should cost a hundred pounds'. It was the unhappy task of a junior member of the household to clean out both these shafts and the pit at the bottom, where there was one, with a bucket and spade.

An improvement was the development of a corbelled latrine shaft that was external to the castle wall and so better ventilated. Sometimes these were set in the angles between walls – for example, at the Château de Coucy, corbelled latrines were situated between the rounded towers and the curtain wall. In castles of the monastic orders, designed for large numbers, latrines were gathered together in a single building – a latrine tower, called dansk by the Teutonic Knights. A version of the communal latrine was also built at Conwy Castle, where a set of three latrines was put in a single-storey tower. Moreover, a set of 12 corbelled latrines was built in the town walls of Conwy for the use of royal staff in the 13th century. At Coity Castle, also in Wales, there were three levels of latrines with shafts emptying into a common basement in a latrine tower in the inner bailey. At Langley Castle (*c.* 1350) in Northumberland, three storeys of latrines were housed in one of the four corner towers, all of which were within a recess set beneath an arch and gave down long shafts into a ground-floor pit that was washed by a stream.

BATHING

Baths were taken in a wooden tub – perhaps in a private chamber or an area of the hall that could be curtained off. Typically, the lord would sit on a stool positioned in the tub. Water had to be drawn from the well, heated in the kitchens and carried to the lord's quarters in wooden buckets. Kings

▸ *The large mural fireplace in the Great Hall at Guédelon. Bright sunlight outside suggests this is a warm day but large logs are ready in the fireplace to warm the room should the temperature drop, even though the hall isn't finished. The size of the fireplace, the four windows and the overall dimensions of the space will make for an impressive, lordly room once the floor and wall decoration is in place.*

and the wealthiest nobles might import perfumed soaps made from olive oil in the Mediterranean region; otherwise, soaps were made in the castle estate from wood ash, soda and animal fat. However, even for the nobility, a bath was a rare event – King John of England is said to have bathed only once every two to three weeks.

▾ *An illustration depicting 14th-century author Christine de Pizan presenting a manuscript to Isabel of Bavaria. The image shows the colourful decorations of a castle room in the period, including wall motifs of fleur-de-lys. (Getty)*

LIGHTING AND HEATING

Heating in the medieval castle was provided by open fires, in the earliest days by an open hearth in the centre of the great hall. Smoke generally rose to the level of the roof, where a louvre allowed it out into the air, though in some designs, for example in the keep at Warkworth Castle, flues were fitted into the embrasures of windows. Later on in the period, in great towers or halls containing residential accommodation, master masons began to experiment with fitting fireplaces with flues in the walls leading to chimneys on the roof.

At Guédelon, the octagonal chamber that occupies the second floor of the Great Tower and the antechamber to the Great Hall in the North Range both have well-proportioned mural fireplaces. Sometimes these were fitted with a hood, which made it possible to bring the hearth further forwards into the room, and with curved backs – often lined with ceramic tiles – to bounce the heat back into the room as much as possible. Tiles were used because of the fact that they would absorb some of the heat and then radiate it back into the room, and because they wouldn't crack.

In some cases, master masons were able to make the most of sunlight as a natural source of heat. For example, the best residential chambers in the keep at Conisbrough Castle were aligned to catch the morning sunlight.

Windows, of course, also provided a key source of light during daylight hours, but at night candles made from tallow or wax were set in spiked iron candlesticks or on brackets fixed in the walls. Alternatives for interior lighting were wood torches or rushlights, which were made by twisting strands of rush and dipping them into grease or tallow before setting them alight.

ROOFING THE GUÉDELON NORTH RANGE

The North Range at Guédelon is situated directly facing the gatehouse across the courtyard. This means that in addition to looking beautiful it also immediately makes a statement about the level of comfort the lord was able to provide for his retinue and for visitors. Great care has been taken over its appearance, with the white limestone of the four two-light windows setting off the russet colouring of the stonework and the expanse of reddish, kiln-fired tiles across the roof.

Roofing the length of the North Range – covering both the Great Hall and the mural-decorated antechamber to its east – was always going to be a substantial challenge for the master mason and the carpenters. This is in part because when looking at the remains of medieval castles there is often little left to inform us about what the roof looked like and how it was constructed beyond the profile presented by the gable end of a building – and occasionally masonry marks and sockets. On the White Tower of the Tower of London and the keep at Rochester Castle, for example, we can see that there were two roofs – one either side of the cross wall that divided each building, each about 6m (20ft) in height and with a pitch of roughly 45 degrees – beyond this is conjecture.

At Guédelon, the initial nine trusses of the North Range roof were raised above the antechamber – the beautiful spacious room that is now adorned with floral murals. To do this, the carpenters fitted a temporary floor at the base of the rafters – the level of the top of the walls – by installing floorboards and using putlogs that were already in place in the walls. Then, once they had raised the first nine trusses, they were able to use this temporary flooring as a place to store the trusses they needed for the rest of the roof – the section over the Great Hall.

However, before they moved on, the carpenters first tiled this initial section of the roof, attaching more than 900 oak

▼ *The North Range in 2011, not long after the completion of its roof. The tiles at the right-hand end, which were put in place well in advance of the others, have weathered, while those at the left-hand end still have a newly fired look.*

▲ *The all-wood structure of the North Range pitched roof, viewed from below, during the process of tiling the Great Hall. The beautiful trusses look their best, lit from above and below.*

battens and laying some 6,000 tiles, which were produced by three firings of the kiln.

For the whole roof, the carpenters fitted 47 trusses in total. The first 33 were erected as described above, raised from flooring constructed at the base of the rafters, but for the final 14 trusses the carpenters needed to find a new technique. This was because they were blocked by the gable wall at the west end of the Great Hall from being able to raise the trusses as they had been doing elsewhere. The materials for these trusses were instead raised using the treadmill and reassembled on the temporary flooring, and the trusses themselves were then raised and ranged vertically against the ones that were already in place.

The head carpenter, Nicolas, had the idea of building a rail along which the carpenters could slide the last trusses and place them into position. The rail, which stood on two posts, was sunk into a hole that had been left in the masonry of the west gable wall for this use – an example of how the different castle-building teams, in this case the masons and carpenters, worked together under the direction of their masters and, overall, of the master mason, to build a castle. Using the rail not only meant it was easier to pull the trusses along and into position, but it was also much safer since it was now impossible for the trusses to fall over. The worker seated in the roof kicked the trusses along the rail and guided them with ropes. Carpenters below helped with long-handled forks. They were then carefully positioned one by one, moving away from the west gable end.

THE ROLE OF THE CARPENTERS

The carpenters at Guédelon have their own workshop about 200m (yards) southeast of the main gatehouse. Here, they make the castle's heavy wooden doors from solid oak panels; the centrings used to support the vaults while they are under construction; and the putlogs – the wooden timbers that support the scaffolding. In the castle, they are responsible for erecting, fitting and moving the scaffolding on the building works as they go up. In the medieval era, the carpenters would also have worked with the blacksmiths to construct and maintain trebuchets and other machines of war.

On the North Range at Guédelon, the carpenters constructed the massive framework of the roof, which consists of 47 trusses. The constituent timbers – king posts, rafters and tie beams – were all made and then assembled in the carpenter's lodge. Once the carpenters were sure the structure fitted together, they dismantled it – taking care to mark each segment – and then took the pieces to the North Range and reconstructed the roof in situ.

BUILDING TECHNIQUES: INSTALLING A TIMBER AND TILED PITCHED ROOF

The North Range was roofed and tiled over three seasons from 2008 to 2011. The design of the roof timbers is modelled on the roof timbers of the Parloir aux Bourgeois in Chartres. It is a common rafter roof made up of 47 trusses with curved angle braces. The principal trusses have king posts and tie beams. The framework required 150 oak trees, 13m (43ft) in length. They were first hewn and then moved to the tracing floor for the joints to be cut. By stepping into the shoes of medieval builders, and learning as they worked, Guédelon's carpenters have had to test theories as to how their counterparts in the Middle Ages would have resolved a number of technical issues.

1 In 2008, the first roof trusses were raised into position against the gable at the eastern end of the North Range. The first six are in position and the workers can be seen beyond the exterior scaffolding working on the temporary flooring they installed.

2 The initial section of the North Range roof, the part above the decorated antechamber at the building's east end, was completed and tiled before the rest of the structure was given its roof. In this picture from 2008, the windows can be seen in position, with the walls being built up around them.

3 The roof trusses and other timbers were crafted and put together in the carpenters' lodge, then disassembled and lifted piece by piece to the rooftop using the treadmill winch. Here a roof truss is being assembled in a horizontal layout across the rooftop before being raised into its final vertical position.

4 The carpenters complete the assembly of one of the roof trusses on the rooftop. One is drilling a hole using a large auger drill, the other is attaching one of the thick ropes used on the scaffolding to the truss. The other end of the rope is attached to the top end of the wall gable.

5 The operation is repeated – moving away from the gable at each turn. The majority of the workers are supporting the A-frame, while the two further forward are pulling on the ropes attached to the pulleys high above to bring the A-frame into a vertical position. At the sides, two workers are tasked with ensuring that the base of the frame is in the right position.

6 To slide the trusses into position along the specially built rail, the worker seated above kicks the truss away from himself along the rail toward the west end of the roof, while the team of carpenters below guide it along.

7 Once the truss is moving, the carpenters below are able to help it along using long-handled forks. Here they have moved the first truss to its final position. The truss is fitted into the corresponding joints on the wall plates.

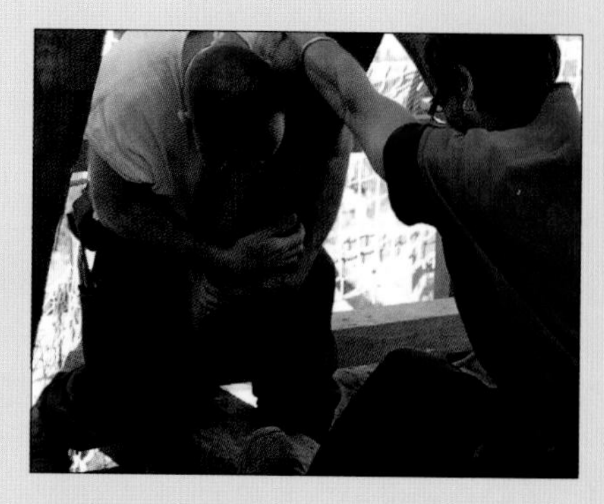

8 The tenon (projecting piece of wood) at one end of the rafter is fitted into the mortise (a cavity in the roof timber). Once this is done the carpenters fix a temporary board between two roof trusses to hold them in place.

9 The carpenters then position curved angle braces against the inside of each rafter. After doing this they check the distance between the roof trusses.

10 The first eight A-frames are in position. They have been covered with oak battens and a batch of clay tiles has been lifted to the rooftop.

11 The carpenters work along the roof nailing the oak battens in position. They can lean against the side of the sturdy roof structure while doing so.

12 The tilers fit the tiles to the oak battens. The tiles overlap by a good amount so that no rainwater can get into the rooms below. All the tiles have been handmade and fired in the kilns only a few hundred metres away in the Guédelon craft village.

13 In April 2011, high on the north-facing roof of the North Range the tilers fit the tiles into position. Tiles are stacked ready to be fitted into battens of the roof next to them. The roofed building centre-left is a former stonemasonry lodge.

7

THE GREAT HALL

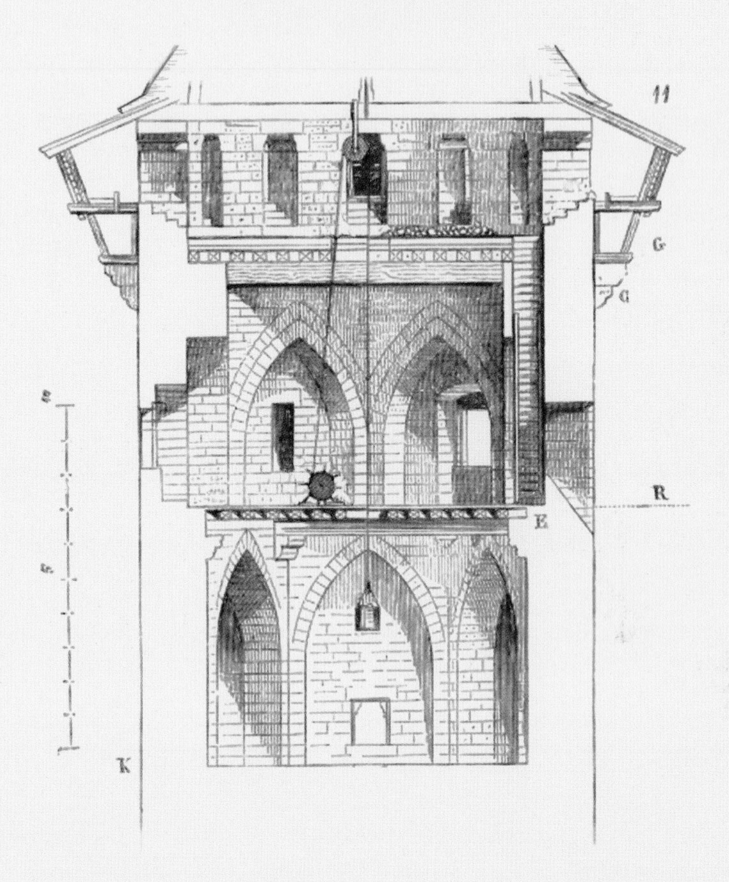

Like the castle as a whole, the Great Hall was a bold statement of feudal power. Its size and architectural features – including the number of windows and the intricacy and profusion of decorative embellishments – embodied the lord's wealth and importance. At Guédelon, the Great Hall occupies the main part of the upper storey in the North Range, directly opposite the entrance gateway and commanding the courtyard.

FOCUS OF CASTLE LIFE

In earlier castles of the medieval period, the entire household was centred on the great hall as the place where everybody – including the lord and his family – ate and slept together. Later, however, suites of rooms were installed that separated out the different ranks, providing a degree of privacy for the lord, his family and elite visitors, among others. Despite this segregation, though, the great hall remained key to castle life – a location for eating, greeting arrivals, settling legal matters and carrying out administration of the estate.

The great hall was intended to impress, not only by its size but also by the experience of being in it. Within the hall – perhaps bathed in sunlight entering through grand windows, and with a great central fire in an open hearth sending smoke up to the distant rafters – were found warmth, food and safety, provided and guaranteed by the lord's power. Under these conditions, the lord and his inner circle ate on a table on the raised dais, while others were seated at benches in the main part of the room. From his lofty position the lord could see everyone – and everyone could look up at him. Servants wearing the lord's livery – a visual reinforcement of his power – served the food.

Between mealtimes, the benches on which people sat were cleared away to the sides, creating a large open space. At the opposite end of the hall to the dais on which the lord dined there was often a wooden screen. This marked off a passage (the screen's passage) that gave into other nearby areas of the castle associated with providing for mealtimes, such as the kitchens, pantry and buttery.

In the early part of the medieval era, the lord and his family slept in the hall at the rear of the dais, usually behind a curtain that provided a modicum of privacy. Traditionally, other members of the household slumbered in the main part of the hall, on benches or on the rush-covered floor, which was sometime scattered with herbs. Later, the lord, his family and elite guests were provided with private chambers – one type was the solar, a room on the upper level of a two-storey hall, typically set back from the gallery. From this vantage point the lord and his lady could look down on those coming and going, eating and sleeping in the main hall.

The scale of the hall, together with its architectural features and decoration, was a bold statement of feudal power. Examples of ornate embellishments can be seen, for instance, in the Great Hall of Hedingham Castle, which contains Europe's biggest Norman arch as well as large windows with decorative carving, similar to those found in the larger of the two halls in Roger Bigod's residential block at Chepstow Castle. These added to the sense of grandeur. It was also quite common for the walls to be plastered and decorated, sometimes with a design that used red horizontal and vertical lines to imitate the effect of ashlar stones – as can be seen in fragments of plaster in the hall at Okehampton Castle in Devon as well as in Marten's Tower, another of the structures built by Roger Bigod, at Chepstow.

◄ *Fine dining, 12th-century style. The guest hall in the tower keep at Dover Castle has been refurbished to look as it would have done in the time of Henry II. Henry's tower was intended to be an expression of royal power, and was built and decorated on a grand scale. (Mary Evans)*

► *A reconstruction of the splendid Great Hall built within the shell keep at Restormel Castle in the late 13th century by Edmund of Cornwall. It was one of several fine buildings, reputedly fitted with piped water, ranged around a central courtyard. It stood between the kitchen and a second, smaller hall. The castle in Edmund's era was more palace than fortification. (Getty)*

CENTRE OF ADMINISTRATION

After Mass in the chapel and breakfast in the great hall, benches were cleared away and the lord and his steward would typically start work on the administration of the estate – logging rents or other payments, making decisions in local disputes, receiving visits from nobles. The steward – sometimes called a seneschal – would work alongside a clerk, or sometimes the chaplain, who would draw up documents and make administrative notes while also keeping detailed accounts. In some households there was one steward in charge of domestic matters in the castle and a second responsible for the wider estate. Beneath the steward worked the chamberlain, who controlled supplies for and managed the great hall.

An usher stood on duty at the entrance to the hall to control the admission, or not, of visitors; a key aspect of the lord's power was his inaccessibility. This facility for privacy was made possible by the same architectural features that provided security in time of war. For example, circles of defence in a concentric castle, with the lord's quarters in the most secure location, also guaranteed a degree of privacy in times of peace. In the world of the medieval castle, only the elite had the option of this luxury.

Ceremonies performed in the hall included knights paying homage to their lord and men of lower social orders receiving badges, livery or gifts. The lord might preside over local disputes or grant permission, for example, for a tenant knight to pass his holdings on to his son.

THE ROLE OF THE CHAMBERLAIN

The chamberlain managed the lord's household – and as part of this role was in charge of supplies for, and administration of, the great hall. The name comes from the fact that he was in charge of the lord's or king's inner chamber, and he played an important role in limiting access to lord or king. In the royal household, the king's chamberlain was a leading nobleman and over time the title became a honorary one. (Getty)

ENTERTAINING

The great hall's size, decorations and atmosphere made it the perfect setting for hosting noble guests at banquets and entertainments. Chivalric tournaments, in which scores of knights took part, incorporated lavish feasts accompanied by performances of music and poetry. At some, the lady of the house presided as queen of the tournament, as judge, prize giver and chivalric inspiration. There were special feasts in the castle for the 'tournament queen' and her ladies.

The hall was also the site of great banquets. Liveried servants delivered food, elaborately presented on large and costly dishes, to the high table, where it was carved before the lord as he sat beside his family and closest knights and associates. Each of them had their own wine glass. On lower tables, people ate from shared dishes called messes, taking the food with their hands and eating it on a trencher, a slab of stale bread that stood in for a plate. They drank ale or wine from a common jug.

Among the staff were the pantler, who was responsible for the pantry (from the French *pain*, bread), where food was kept; the butler or bottler, who was in charge of the buttery, where butts of wine and ale were stored; and the cook, who commanded a team of servants in the kitchen. Another key member of the domestic staff was the keeper of the wardrobe, responsible for the lord's robes and clothes. Feasts were sometimes accompanied by entertainment, notably poems and music. In England, minstrels would play traditional songs, often their own compositions, on the lute, recorder and shawm (a forerunner of the oboe), with percussion and fiddles accompanying. Beginning in southern France in the 11th century, poet-musicians named troubadours composed and performed songs honouring courtly love – a tradition that celebrated the chaste and noble passion of knights for the lady at court who inspired them to bravery in battle and in tournaments. The troubadours of southern France had their counterparts in *minnesanger* at German courts and *trouvères* in northern France.

In addition to being the subject of poems and music, chivalry also featured in art, and the walls of halls were sometimes decorated with murals depicting chivalric scenes – we know that the hall at Tamworth Castle, for instance, once bore scenes of Arthurian romance, including the exploits of Sir Lancelot.

▼ *While knights ride out to tournament, a feast within depicts many details of medieval dining: liveried servants, a chamberlain with his mace behind the lord, a rich tapestry in the background and expensive dining vessels. (Getty)*

▼ *A banquet to honour Charles IV, King of France, 1322-28. While the diners enjoy the feast, in the foreground floats a vision of a castle siege, with attackers newly disembarked from a boat and defenders fighting them off. (Getty)*

▲ *The Great Hall in Guédelon's North Range, decorated for a celebration. Places are laid on the long table and the sun lights the room through one of the hall's quatrefoil windows.*

TOURNAMENTS AND THE CULT OF CHIVALRY

Jousting tournaments, in which knights competed, often accompanied the feasting at castles and served both as a means of entertainment and, together with the epic chansons and romances, as a way of developing and maintaining the cult of chivalry – the celebration of knightly virtue. Some later castles had a tiltyard or lists in which tournaments were held. Other tournaments were held in open country or parkland – one was held by Edward I in Windsor Park near the castle in 1278.

In larger establishments the herald, who wore a tabard or surcoat bearing the lord's coat of arms, was in charge of the tournaments – announcing competitors and generally overseeing the competition. King Edward I held at least five 'Round Table' tournaments inspired by the tales of feats of high chivalry by King Arthur and the Knights of the Round Table – including one at Kenilworth Castle in 1279, one in 1284 at Nefyn Castle in Wales and one in 1302 at Falkirk Castle in Scotland. These and other tournaments were followed by feasting, with some of the lords in attendance at the Round Table events being dressed 'in character' as celebrated knights of the Arthurian tradition. At the feasts, Edward reportedly arranged for squires to run in to make interruptions announcing unrest in the kingdom and calling on those present to demonstrate their bravery. In response, the knights, who did not know that this was part of the entertainment, rose to pledge themselves to acts of bravery. Afterwards, the king held them to their promises and used the event as preparation for a real military campaign.

King Edward III was also a great enthusiast of the cult of chivalry and presided over scores of tournaments. One such event took place in 1344, when he hosted a feast and tournament at Windsor Castle at which 200 knights and squires were in attendance. On the second day of the event, he announced his intention of founding a chivalric brotherhood, even laying plans to build a round great hall (the only one ever proposed) in the upper bailey at the castle, though this came to nothing. Four years later, in the spring and summer of 1348, he celebrated victories at the Battle of Crécy and Neville Cross against the Scots (both in 1346) and success in the siege of Calais (1347) by holding tournaments at Reading, Westminster, Lichfield, Bury St Edmunds, Canterbury, Eltham and Windsor castles. At Windsor Castle he founded the chivalric brotherhood of the Order of the Garter, the 26 founding knights of which were veterans of the Battle of Crécy campaign and of many tournaments.

▼ *A miniature from the* Livre des tournois *of René d'Anjou (1465) shows two groups of knights ready for contest with the lords and ladies looking on from specially constructed grandstands. Feasting will come afterwards.*

CHIMNEYS AND FIREPLACES

There are three chimneystacks in the roof of the North Range at Guédelon: one rises from the kitchen, one from the mural-decorated chamber adjacent to the Great Hall and one from the Great Hall itself. As the room dedicated to dining, entertainment and other communal activities, the Great Hall needed to be well heated; building a large mural fireplace was a major undertaking there there in 2010–12.

▸ *Stonemasons build the chimney walls around the flue. The canvas cloth above them protects the masons from the direct sun and also prevents the mortar from drying too quickly.*

▴ *High up on the North Range roof, one of the masons, Philippe, uses a trowel to apply mortar to the final four stones before fixing the chimneystack's sandstone capstone. The masons have built the chimneystack as high as possible to improve the draw.*

1 In the Great Hall, the limestone jambs have been built on either side of the hearth in summer 2008. Limestone niches for storage have been built into the northern curtain wall.

2 The following year, inside the fireplace, a mason puts the finishing touches to the limestone relieving arch at the top of the hood. The arch will help to distribute the weight of the chimney stack.

3 The oak lintel has been fixed on the sculpted corbels. The masons will now build the stone hood. The depth of the hearth is modelled on fireplaces in Dourdan Castle.

THE ENDURANCE AND EVOLUTION OF THE GREAT HALL

Despite the growth in private accommodation and the building elsewhere in the castle of other chambers for receiving noble guests, the great hall remained of central importance throughout the medieval period. The administrative heart of the castle, its imposing size and shape as well as its symbolism ensured its enduring dominance, and as time went by its design remained remarkably unchanged – always rectangular in shape, typically with large windows and a raised dais at one end and usually with a central hearth.

The Great Hall at Chepstow, begun in 1067 by William FitzOsbern and completed by 1090, provides an imposing example from early in the medieval period, and measures externally an impressive 30 x 12m (100 x 40ft). This trend for constructing great halls carried on right through the medieval period, as is evidenced by the magnificent 14m (46ft) wide great hall at Kenilworth Castle, built by master mason Henry Spenser for John of Gaunt at the close of the 14th century, which features stone panels and traceried windows.

The Chepstow Great Hall is celebrated as one of the oldest surviving stone buildings in Britain, although the roof and ceilings no longer exist. The oblong structure originally held a sloping cellar basement (with headroom of 2.3m [7ft 6in] at the east end and nothing in the west) and two upper storeys. The hall was on the first floor. The dais on which the lord sat would have been at the west end of this hall, where there was also a private room for the lord and his guests: here, a succession of powerful lords held court – FitzOsbern, Marshal and Bigod. Guests entered via a grand porch. Later, two phases of rebuilding work in *c.*1225–45 and *c.*1275–1300 transformed the Great Tower into a three-storey building.

▼ *The Great Hall at Caerphilly Castle was remodelled in 1322–26 for Hugh le Despenser the Younger by Master Thomas de la Bataille and William Hurley. Chepstow's hall may have boasted similar features in its time. (Cadw)*

▲ *The great hall at Stokesay Castle, Shropshire, built for wool merchant Laurence of Ludlow at the end of the 13th century, still has its original wooden arches in the roof. (Alamy)*

Another contemporary and similarly impressive great hall was built at Durham Castle – for many years the palace of the Bishop of Durham – by Bishop Antony Bek. This replaced the existing great hall of the Norman castle on the site, though it was made longer to the south, had new windows and roof and featured a bishop's throne at each end. It was lengthened further in the mid-14th century by Bishop Hatfield and was the largest in England until it was shortened at the end of the 15th century by Bishop Richard Foxe. Trumpeters' galleries in the upper walls are believed to date to Bishop Hatfield's time: the trumpeters would mark the bishop's entrance at formal ceremonies and perform during banquets. Today, the hall, refashioned in the 19th century, retains its 15th-century dimensions: 30m (100ft) long and 14m (46ft) tall.

▼ *A wooden staircase of 1291 in Stokesay hall led to private apartments. The treads are original, hewn from whole tree trunks. Carpenters' marks match those on the ceiling. (Alamy)*

▼ *The majestic Great Hall in the keep at Hedingham Castle is over the first and second floors of the four-storey building. Note the recessed windows. (© Hedingham)*

▲ *The Great Hall at Penshurst Place near Tonbridge, Kent, was built with a central hearth in 1341. Sir John Pulteney, who had the fortified manor house built, was four times Lord Mayor of London. Poet Sir Philip Sidney was born at Penshurst Place in 1554. (Alamy)*

▼ *The Great Hall at Craigmillar Castle, Edinburgh has a huge stone fireplace c.1500 and originally had a fine wooden ceiling (now lost). The castle was built in the 14th century by the Preston family. Here, in 1566, the murder of Mary Queen of Scots' husband, Lord Darnley was planned. (Getty)*

In Wales, the dramatic Great Hall at Caerphilly Castle owes much of its splendour to its remodelling in the early 14th century. This work was done by Hugh le Despenser, who had married Eleanor de Clare, descendant of the Norman lord Gilbert de Clare who had built the castle from 1268 onwards. Hugh relied on Thomas de la Bataile and William Hurley to do the work, and they raised the roof and added splendid carved doors and windows to the hall.

Nor were great halls necessarily confined to castles during the period. Stokesay Castle, which is more a fortified manor house than a traditional castle, for instance, contains one of the best-preserved medieval great halls. Built by wool merchant Laurence of Ludlow in the 1280–90s, it measures 16.6 x 9.4m (55 x 31ft), and features its original wooden arches supporting the roof. At the lower end a wooden stair leads to the solar.

HEARTHS: THE HEART OF THE HALL

The central hearth remained popular throughout the great hall's period of dominance. A good surviving example of an intact one can be found in the 18m (60ft) tall great hall at Penshurst Place, a fortified manor house in Kent that was built in 1341 for London merchant Sir John de Pulteney.

The enduring appeal and use of these central hearths is in some ways somewhat surprising, since it must have created such a fug of smoke in the hall. Perhaps, however, the pall became associated with the grandeur and traditions of great

► *The Great Hall at Guédelon in 2011, looking west and showing the unfinished floor, the partially completed fireplace and chimney breast, and the elegant quatrefoil-topped window in the gable end. The horizontal beams are tie beams and the vertical posts are king posts. The joists, which will support the floor, are still exposed.*

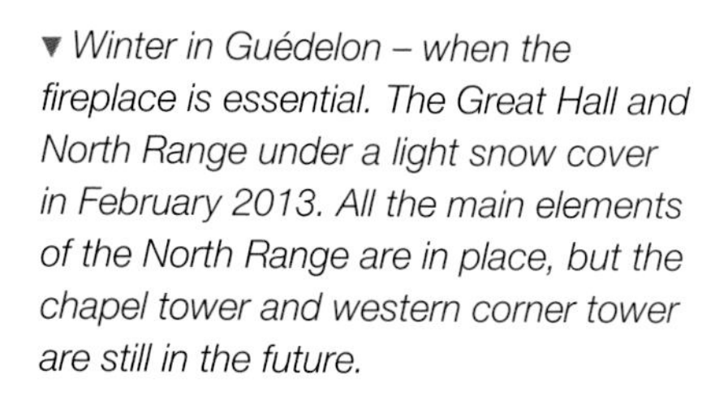

▼ *Winter in Guédelon – when the fireplace is essential. The Great Hall and North Range under a light snow cover in February 2013. All the main elements of the North Range are in place, but the chapel tower and western corner tower are still in the future.*

hall life and thus the lord and his retainers wanted to keep it. That said, some master masons did come up with some solutions in an attempt to solve the smoke problem. Master John Lewyn, for instance, used flues fitted in the top of the window embrasures in his keep at Warkworth Castle around 1390, and at Castle Bolton, *c.*1385. In this design, six flues (one above each of windows) drew smoke from the fireplace, out of the hall and into chimneys, which must have helped to clear the atmosphere.

In addition to these very common central hearths, some halls featured a mural fireplace in the wall at the rear of the dais, which would provide additional warmth for the lord and elite diners as they sat at their food and wine. In some cases, such as in the Great Hall at Kenilworth Castle, there seems not to have been a central hearth at all, for there were five fireplaces – one in each side wall and a triple one at the top end of the hall – which may well have provided sufficient heat and light.

At Guédelon, the masons opted to construct a hearth in the north (rear) wall of the Great Hall. Here, they lined the back wall of the hearth with tiles set in a herringbone pattern, providing a lining that is capable of resisting high

▲ *A mason affixes tiles in the rear of the Great Hall fireplace, creating a herringbone pattern. The use of tiles to protect the sandstone wall was a tried and tested method in the period.*

▲ *The Great Hall fireplace, fully tiled. The tilers have fitted floor tiles in front of the hearth as well as tiles in the fireplace.*

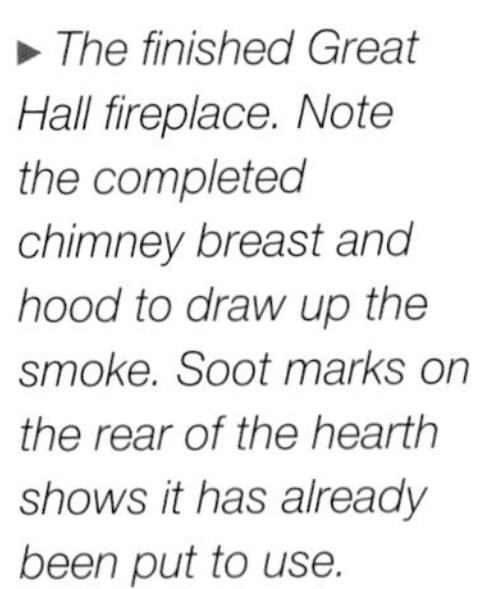

► *The finished Great Hall fireplace. Note the completed chimney breast and hood to draw up the smoke. Soot marks on the rear of the hearth shows it has already been put to use.*

temperatures and thus protects the sandstone wall of the fireplace. Moreover, the masons were keeping one eye on the future: it would be easier to repair or replace heat-damaged tiles than it would be to rebuild the section of sandstone wall if it were to become damaged by the fire. In addition to the tile lining, the masons also added a stone fireplace hood and the carpenters made and fitted an oak lintel.

CREATING CLAY TILES

The tiles in the Great Hall fireplace – like the floor and roof tiles – were made from clay extracted on the Guédelon site. At first the tilers dug the clay out from the ground, then pugged it (worked and mixed it to remove the air). They then mixed batches together, kneaded them until smooth, then used a wooden mould to form the tiles on top of a wooden bench, tamping down the clay and removing the surplus with a scraper to make a smooth surface. The tiles were then taken to the drying rack, where they were left to dry for several weeks before being stocked in the kiln for firing.

THE TILE-MAKING INDUSTRY

Making tiles for lining hearths, and for use elsewhere, was typically a family business, established close to a clay pit for raw materials, and a good supply of wood as fuel for the kiln. Where villages met both these criteria, they sometimes became specialist areas for tile making. In some places the lord owned the kiln – as he did other essential technology, such as the water mill – and levied a tax on its use.

In 13th-century France, strict regulations were introduced to govern the tile industry, specifying the quality of the clay used, the size of the tiles and the number of tiles that could be made in one firing – packing a kiln too full would adversely affect the quality of the tiles. Under these rules, bailiffs could seize tiles that were not made according to the regulations. This strict control was beneficial to castle builders since it meant that stewards and master masons could order supplies from any tile maker and be confident that the quality would be good.

MEDIEVAL SKILLS: MAKING AND FIRING TILES

In working out how tiles would have been made in a modest-sized French country castle like Guédelon, the tile makers studied archeological investigations – to learn about the types of clay used, the drying of moulded tiles, the shape of kilns and the methods for cooling tiles after firing. They also visited tile makers still using traditional methods. And they relied on trial and error. They were making adjustments, to practices and the kiln itself, for four working seasons.

1 After pugging and treating the clay, and picking out sticks and stones, it is kneaded like dough to lose air pockets.

2 The worked clay is then shaped with a wooden mould, the excess is then cut away to form a flat, evenly shaped tile.

3 Tiles in various shapes – square, star-shaped (as here) or other, are stored on the drying rack, for several days.

4 Before the firing an insulating layer of fired tiles are placed on top of the unfired tiles stacked in the kiln.

5 The tiler wears leather gloves and apron to withstand the searing heat needed in the kiln to fire the clay tiles.

6 The tiles are fired for 15 hours at a 1000 degrees celsius. About 3,000 tiles can made in one firing.

7 The kiln is left for several days before the tiles are cool enough to be taken out of the kiln.

8 The tiler inspects each tile as it comes out of the kiln to ensure that they have been fired satisfactorily.

9 The tiles are stacked ready for use. The roofers used 28,000 kiln-fired clay tiles to roof the North Range.

FLOORING IN MEDIEVAL CASTLES

Great halls presented a significant challenge for master masons and carpenters – their size made them difficult to fit with roofs and floors. The length of available timbers determined the width of rooms and roofs to a great extent: great towers were built with a crosswall, making it possible for each side to be floored and roofed independently. Halls were often floored using timber joists set within joist sockets in the masonry. The masons probably set the timbers in the sockets before completing the wall, and then built the wall around them. In some cases these timber joists were also supported centrally by a spine beam running at right angles.

In the impressively proportioned Scolland's Hall at Richmond Castle, there are surviving wall sockets along the side walls that were used to house the end of the timber joists and two square sockets, one in each end wall, that supported a cross beam. The cross-beam sockets are a little lower than side-wall sockets, indicating that the cross beam ran lengthwise, supported on posts, and the timber joists were set on top of it. Scolland's Hall, built in the 1060s, is 7.9m (26ft) wide and 23m (75ft) long. Similar sockets can be seen in the hall of the Great Tower at Chepstow, suggesting that there, too, a line of pillars down the centre of the room supported the main timbers. In some later castles, from the latter part of the 13th century onwards, the beams were further supported by braces and wall posts. Wall posts supporting the floor beams in the Eagle Tower (c.1283) in Caernarfon Castle rested on corbels.

The masons probably set the timbers in the sockets before completing the wall, and then built the wall around them. In some cases, these timber joists were also supported centrally by a spine beam running at right angles. For instance, at the impressively proportioned Scolland's Hall at Richmond Castle, North Yorkshire – built in the 1060s and measuring 7.9 x 23m (26 x 75ft) – there are surviving wall sockets along the side walls that were used to house the end of the timber joists, as well as two square sockets, one in each end wall, that

▲ *In the partially ruined hall of the Great Tower at Chepstow Castle in Wales, the sockets that secured the timber joists of the floor can be clearly seen along the wall. The hall probably dates from the 1060s. (Cadw)*

◄ *In Scolland's Hall at Richmond Castle in North Yorkshire, England, the socket for the main beam can be seen in the end wall below the first-floor window opening. This view of the hall, which also dates from around the 1060s, is from the east. (Alamy)*

supported a cross beam. The cross-beam sockets are a little lower than the side-wall ones, indicating that the cross beam ran lengthwise, supported on posts, and the joists were set on top of it. Similar sockets can be seen in the hall of the Great Tower at Chepstow, suggesting that there, too, a line of pillars supported the main timbers.

This is indicative of how closely the highly skilled carpenters and masons worked together through the building process in medieval castles. Timber elements were used from the foundations up, as we have seen. Their presence helped to make structures more secure when it took a good amount of time for the mortar to set.

LAYING THE FLOOR IN THE GREAT HALL

The floor of the Great Hall at Guédelon is supported by six oak purlins, each 7m (23ft) long, resting on corbels. There is no spine beam. Each beam weighed about 600kg (1,300lbs), had a cross section of 35cm² (3½in²) and needed to be raised 4.5m (15ft) above the ground to be fitted in place. This was a problem: the master mason and his team were concerned that this weight was at the very limit of what the treadmill winch could support, and in addition they were doubtful that the machinery could cope with lowering the beams precisely into position on the top of the wall at such a height. They therefore had to devise a different means of getting the purlins

► *The technique for lifting the very heavy purlins (main oak beams) used in the Great Hall floor. The team rolls the beam up a wooden ramp. No fewer than seven labourers are needed to manoeuvre the 600kg (1,300lb) beam.*

▼ *The masons left the walls partially finished so they slope upwards, and the labourers are able to roll the purlin gently up the incline. The huge beams were then stocked by the western gable while the front wall was built.*

► *Under the Great Hall floor tiles – in close up. A layer of tamped-down earth (left) on thin oak laths (right) has been laid between the joists. Mortar is later layered on top of the earth and then the tiles are placed in a neat pattern on the mortar.*

▲ *A member of the team uses an axe to square off the length of trunk.*

◄ *A woodcutter uses a sledgehammer to drive in wooden wedges into a length of oak. The oak splits.*

▼ *A pile of finished planks to be used for the roadway of the bridge that was built across the dry ditch.*

MEASUREMENTS

The units of measurement used on site varied from one castle to another in the Middle Ages. The master mason would define what an inch meant at a particular location and this would be displayed for all craftsmen to see. At Guédelon, the craftsmen use the following units, which date from the time of the Roman empire and were widely in use in the Middle Ages, often based on human proportions: the inch, foot, cubit and toise. The definition of an inch as 2.5cm was based on measurements taken at the nearby castle of Ratilly.

Inch = 2.5cm
Palm = 7.5cm (3in)
Hand = 12.5cm (5in)
Hand span = 20cm (8in)
Foot = 30cm (12in)
Cubit = an arm span = 44cm (18in)
Toise = 6ft = 180cm

into position. The solution they worked out was this: they built the walls of the North Range ground floor (the rooms beneath the Great Hall) so that they were higher at the western end than they were at the eastern end. A team of labourers were thus able to load one beam at a time on to the eastern end of the walls using a wooden ramp and then, working in pairs, roll it up the gentle slope along the top of the wall until it reached the western end.

The method worked, and the team managed to manoeuvre all six beams to the top of the wall in this way, storing them at the higher western end. They then built up the remaining sections of the wall so each end was level and were able to manoeuvre the beams and position each one precisely on its supporting corbel.

After installing the floor joists, the carpenters laid oak laths (thin strips of wood) between them. On top of this they put a layer of earth 20cm (8in) thick, and tamped it down to create a level surface. This was topped with a 5cm (2in) layer of mortar, on which the 4,000 kiln-fired floor tiles were laid, creating a beautifully level, tiled floor.

BUILDING TECHNIQUES: LAYING FLOOR TILES IN THE GREAT HALL

The laying of floor tiles in the upper floor of the North Range at Guédelon started in autumn 2012. On top of the oak laths laid between the joists a layer of earth was placed. Getting the earth into position was no mean feat. That year a special celebration was held for 'master builders' – those who had volunteered over the previous seasons. They formed a human chain to pass earth up from the courtyard to the first-floor room. They needed 6 tonnes of earth. The earth had to be tamped down – this, too, was a major job. Then the masons and tilers set to work, layering on a level or mortar and then laying out the kiln-fired terracotta tiles. The next year work began on tiling the Great Hall itself.

1 Here the layer of mortar on which the tiles are laid is visible. Some triangular tiles were fired to create straight edges at the end or sides of an area. The slight differentiation in colour is caused by different temperatures inside the kiln.

2 The tiler works on one area of the floor at a time. He taps lightly on top of the layer of tiles to make them settle into the mortar. In the foreground, a heavy two-handled wicker basket sits on the layer of earth and contains more tiles.

3 Lengths of string have been pulled across the room to help the tiler ensure he is laying in a neat, straight line. He works by the natural light falling through the large windows in the south wall of the Great Hall.

4 The floor will last longer and avoid damage if the surface is perfectly level. The finished tiled floor is a beautiful sight, an important part of the decor of medieval castles alongside whitewashed or painted walls and colourful hangings.

8

THE CHAPEL AND OTHER BUILDINGS

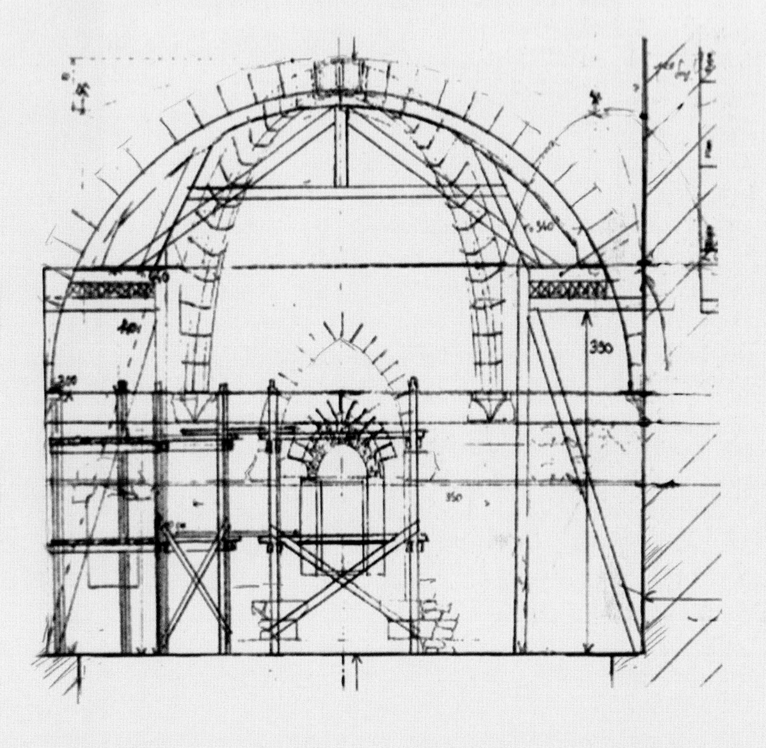

Functioning as the focal point of a wider community, castles always contained a centre for daily Christian worship and around them a range of working buildings. This is the case at Guédelon, too, where the site incorporates spaces for the masons, blacksmiths, basket weavers, woodworkers, carpenters and rope makers, kiln and a watermill. There is also the chapel, which occupies the second floor of the Chapel Tower.

◂ *The beautiful renovated chapel of Beaumaris Castle on Anglesey. (Cadw)*

CHAPELS AND VAULTED CEILINGS

Castles were simply not built without a chapel. In the earlier medieval period, this was often a small, modest chamber, but in later years a more substantial room, sometimes accompanied by a crypt to celebrate the lord's ancestors and embody the longevity of his power, became a status symbol. Vaulted ceilings – very beautiful to look at, hugely challenging to build – were found in castle chapels from the 11th century onwards.

In some castles the chapel was in the gatehouse. At Prudhoe Castle, Northumberland, a chapel was added to the 12th-century gatehouse in the 13th century. An apse was added to the east wall on the first floor, creating a small sanctuary with lancet windows and accessed through a pointed arch. In other castles the chapel was built in the keep or great tower. Several castles, like Guédelon, situated the chapel in one of the four corner towers in a quadrilangular layout. At Beaumaris Castle, for instance, the chapel was in the east wall of the inner ward, in one of the two D-shaped towers. Castles with a substantial keep, however, frequently placed the chapel in that structure's forebuilding – as in the rib-vaulted chapel at Newcastle keep (*c.*1168). At other times, the chapel was a freestanding building against one of the curtain walls, in the bailey, as at Harlech Castle, where the chapel stood against the south wall of the inner ward, or at Restormel Castle, where the chapel was set against the inner wall of the shell keep.

Chapels were sometimes situated in one of the highest rooms in the castle – at the top of a great tower or corner tower, so that nothing intervened between the place of worship and heaven. Often there was more than one chapel in a castle: a larger communal one for the whole castle community, complemented by a small chapel or oratory for the lord's private use, typically situated conveniently close to his private quarters in the keep, great tower or residential chamber block. At Dover Castle, where there is an originally Saxon church (St Mary in Castro) within the castle layout, the great tower or keep built for Henry II in 1179–88 contained a small royal chapel dedicated to Henry's former close friend turned bitter enemy, Thomas Becket. Like the Beaumaris chapel it is an example of a small place of worship dedicated to the king's use. Not long after his death, Becket was canonised by Pope Alexander III. At Conisbrough Castle, one of the six wedge-shaped buttresses around the circular tower housed a small, arched chapel on the third floor that gave directly on to the lord's chamber – a place for private devotions. In the royal lodgings at Conwy Castle, built in 1284–86 around a courtyard in the inner ward by Master James of St Georges for Edward I, the chapel was a small, chamber set in the walls' thickness in the north-east tower.

▲ *The royal chapel at Conwy Castle in Wales. Today it has modern stained glass telling the story of Edward I and the Welsh princes, fitted in the 13th-century glazing groove.*

▼ *At Beaumaris Castle a small castle chapel was built into one of the six towers of the inner curtain wall. The windows are visible. Note how narrow the outer ward is. (Cadw)*

CHAPLAIN AND ALMONER

The chapel was the chaplain's domain. Every day in the castle began with the saying of Mass, a task that was performed by the chaplain, and every meal was prefaced by him saying grace. His role also included being in charge of the lord's correspondence – he was typically one of the few literate people on site – and he engaged with the steward in record keeping and other written work necessary for the administration of the estates from the great hall. He was commonly in charge of the education of the lord's children, too, and the general spiritual needs of the castle's population.

Under his supervision was the almoner, who was responsible after every meal for collecting scraps of food and bread and distributing them to the poor. Sometimes these alms were passed on from the service rooms in and around the kitchen, or from outside the castle gates. The almoner's task was also to prevail upon the lord to maintain a good level of almsgiving, especially on the frequent saints' days, and to keep for the poor any robes, equipment or other possessions he might otherwise give to hangers-on.

▲ *A chaplain presides over a wedding in a 13th-century illustration. In addition to looking after the living, he would also say Masses for the souls of the dead. (Mary Evans)*

VAULTED CEILINGS IN EARLY CHAPELS

It was in chapels more than anywhere else in the castle that vaults were found in the 11th century. At the Tower of London, St John's Chapel in the White Tower, begun in 1078 by William I, is an early example of a chapel in a great tower. This was part of the original structure of the Tower and it is likely that it was intended for use by the royal family.

Notable today for its plainness, with simple, unmoulded arches supported on thick piers, the chapel was probably originally painted in bright colours. In 1240, Henry III added three stained-glass windows depicting the Virgin and Christ Child, as well as paintings of St John the Evangelist and St Edward the Confessor. It has a long and fascinating history – seemingly having been used to hold royal archives under Edward II, to imprison King John II of France in 1360, and for an all-night vigil by the Knights of the Bath in 1399, on the eve of the coronation of King Henry IV. Its altar and sanctuary were beneath an apse (a half-dome), while the nave was barrel vaulted and the side aisles had groin vaults.

St Nicholas' Chapel at Richmond Castle was built in the ground floor of the ruined Robin Hood Tower (the name probably dates to the Victorian era). and also had a barrel-vaulted ceiling, along with intriguing round windows. Dated to the late 11th century, it is one of the oldest surviving castle chapels in England. Remains of red paint are further evidence that the chapels of this period were decorated.

◄ *St John's Chapel in the White Tower of the Tower of London is one of England's oldest surviving chapels. It has unmoulded arches on sturdy piers, a barrel-vaulted nave, groin-vaulted side aisles and an apse over the altar.*

▲ *Guédelon's chapel has a rib vaulted roof, which was built over the 2014 and 2015 building seasons. The webbing has a coat of lime render.*

CHAPEL VIGIL: CHIVALRIC INDUCTION

In addition to being places of daily worship, castle chapels also played a key role in the induction of new knights to a chivalric order. In this ritual, the knight-elect would first take a bath, presumably to symbolise his being washed clean of sin in a reference to Christian baptism, before donning white garments and a red robe and being led to the chapel by more senior knights. In the chapel, the chaplain would bless the knight-elect's sword and then lay it on the altar, after which the knight-elect would keep vigil in the chapel for the night – as was undertaken by the Knights of the Bath in St John's Chapel prior to the coronation of King Henry IV. In the morning, after making confession and attending Mass, the knight-elect enjoyed breakfast with established knights, then was dressed by two of these, who put the spurs on his heels and equipped him with armour and helmet, as well as his sword, fresh from the altar. Finally, the lord or king put a girdle or belt on the knight-elect and struck him quite forcefully on the neck with his hand or sword – the accolade that allowed the new knight to join the chivalric brotherhood.

CHANTRY CHAPELS

In some castles lords established a chantry – a chapel staffed by a group of priests who were charged with the task of singing Masses for the well-being of the soul of the lord, his family, and his ancestors. At Bolton Castle, North Yorkshire, Richard le Scrope, 1st Baron Scrope of Bolton, had a license to establish a chantry within the castle in 1393. He had built the castle, using the celebrated master mason John Lewyn, in the late 1370s. Another college chapel within a castle was planned at Warkworth Castle in Northumberland, where remains suggest it would have extended in the form of a cross-shaped church across the bailey, making an inner courtyard between itself and the keep. The base was completed but the rest of the chapel was not built.

GUÉDELON'S CROSS-RIB VAULT

At Guédelon, master mason Florian Renucci and his team built a magnificent cross-rib vault on the ground floor of the chapel tower, the design of which was based on research and observations made at the 13th-century Château d'Yèvre-le-Châtel. The chamber was 3.8m (12ft 6in) in diameter, and the arch was to have a keystone, six ribs dressed in limestone, six corbels and 54 voussoirs, each 25cm (10in) wide.

The first task was for the carpenters to build in their lodge the centring that would support the arch while it was under construction. At the same time, the masons positioned the six corbels and the first three voussoirs at the base of each rib. After this, the carpenters and masons worked together to

▶ *The cross-rib vault in the basement of the Chapel Tower. The masons had built the first six corbels and three voussoirs at the base of each rib before positioning the centring.*

▲ *Five masons carefully move the keystone into position at the top of the centring. Note the joggle joints, which have been carved on the side.*

▲ *The masons put the final section of limestone into place. The keystone is already in position and these final ribs, which fit neatly against it, are called the counter-keystones. The centring is beneath them. They can be adjusted at the last minute if necessary.*

▲ *The limestone ribs are all in place. The centring can still be seen beneath. The masons have begun adding the webbing (the rubble infill between the ribs). Once they have finished the centring will be carefully removed from beneath the vault.*

position the centring very carefully, supporting it on moveable wooden wedges. The masons put the keystone in position at the top – contrary to what you might expect, this is not the last stone to be positioned but one of the first; the final stones would be the last six voussoirs (all known in this context as 'counter-keystones'), which can be manoeuvred and subtly adjusted at the last minute as required.

With the centring still in position, the masons worked on the webbing between the arches. The key moment was removing the wooden support to see if the arch would hold when it 'came under weight': had the extrados (the upper curve of the arch) been sufficiently weighted to hold? While the master mason, stonecutter and masons watched carefully from the outside top of the arch, looking to see whether there was any movement in the stonework, inside the chamber the carpenters partly removed the wedges beneath the centring to lower the wooden structure by a few centimetres. The arch held.

This was the first complex vault built at Guédelon and it was as much a moment of triumph for the modern workers involved as it must have been for their counterparts in the medieval period.

▲ *The lower elements in a ribs of the four-part chapel vault: the delicately carved, supporting corbel; the flat slab of the abacus; the springer stone; and the counter-springer above.*

QUADRIPARTITE VAULT

In the chapel itself, the team built a quadripartite vault (one with four ribs and therefore four parts), incorporating four beautifully sculpted corbels, four abacuses (flat slabs that form one of the elements of the column), four springer stones and counter-springer stones as well as 50 voussoirs and the keystone. Each sculpted corbel was carved by a different stonemason using designs that had been found on corbels at Dourdan Castle, and weighed about 150kg (330lb).

Mason Jean-Paul carved the keystone using a design of foliage inspired by a 13th-century carving in the Cluny Museum in Paris. Because of its weight and delicate floral carving, the keystone had to be handled with the utmost care as it was hoisted up the side of the chapel tower using the treadwheel winch and then moved into position in the chapel using wooden rollers.

The masons built three lancet windows in the outer walls of the tower and the chapel also held a Gothic tracery window containing 36 sculpted stones. Before beginning work on the stones for the window, the stonemasons laid out the designs on the tracing floor in the stonemasons' lodge. The beautiful window and fine carving of the corbels and keystone were appropriate for their function – as the castle's most sacred place, the chapel was typically the most highly decorated. Once complete, the walls were covered with lime mortar, made using lime created on site at Guédelon, and then with lime wash. Eventually they will be decorated with paintings.

In the wall to the right when facing the window they made the piscina, a recessed washing and storage area for vessels used in the Mass. They had originally intended for these vessels to be kept in a recess in the wall of the chapel but discovered, too late, that the walls were not thick enough to accommodate the recess.

◄ *The piscina in the wall of the chapel. A kind of washbasin, used by the priest to wash his hands and the chalices used in the Mass. Sometimes in ruined castles, a piscina is what proves to a historian that a particular room was a chapel.*

BUILDING TECHNIQUES: THE QUADRIPARTITE CHAPEL VAULT

Having constructed the monumental cross-rib vault on the ground floor of the chapel tower, the masons tried their hand at a four-part vault in the chapel itself – on the first floor of the tower. It is supported on four carved corbels and features a breathtaking swirl of foliage, captured in carved limestone by mason Jean-Paul, on its keystone.

1 Before setting up the centring, the masons completed the chapel's elegant lancet windows (see page 154).

2 The carved keystone has been lifted up to the first floor of the tower using the treadmill winch and is now very carefully moved by hand into position.

3 The men hold the keystone above the wooden centring as they manoeuvre it into position. The lifelike movement of the limestone foliage is clear to see.

4 Looking up from under the centring, the keystone can be seen safely in position, its delicate face downward. The relief on the faces of the workers is clear.

5 A bird's eye view of the keystone in place, with the top of two of the lancet windows visible and the stones being built up along the arms of the centring.

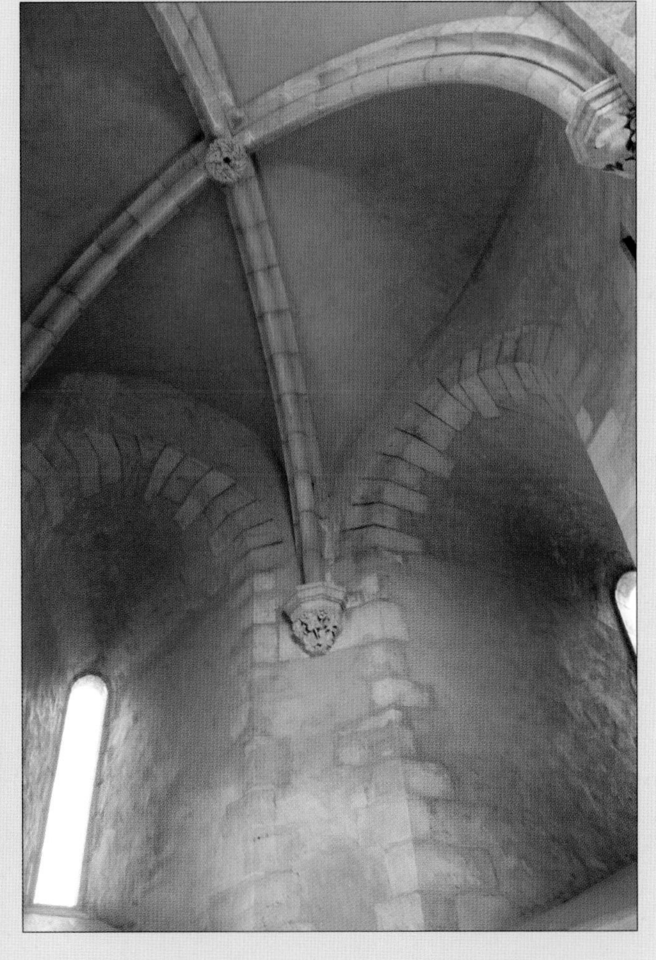

6 The finished vault. The carved corbels complement the keystone beautifully. The walls have been covered using lime mortar and lime wash to prepare them for later decoration.

BUILDING TECHNIQUES: A LANCET WINDOW

Before they could set to work on the vault in the chapel the masons had to complete the three lancet windows, each 2.1m (almost 7ft) high, in the outer walls of the chapel tower. Each window combined a pointed arch on the tower's inner wall, an embrasure (the window opening in the wall) with a conical vault and a chamfered pointed arch on the outer wall. They built the windows in the summer of 2015, and building a conical vault in the embrasure was another new challenge.

1 This is the pointed arch on the outer wall. At this stage, the wooden centring is still in position supporting the voussoirs. A double keystone has been fitted at the crown of the arch.

2 Four formers (wooden supports in the shape of the vault), on to which the masons will place wooden shuttering to build a structure to support the stones of the conical vault while it is under construction. The first limestone voussoirs are in place.

3 The first four limestone voussoirs are in place on each side of the wooden support. The masons are about to fit the shuttering, before they place the edge-bedded sandstone flagstones in position, on wooden shuttering.

4 There are six voussoirs on one side and five (not fully visible) on the other. Next, they will position the two counter-keystones. Note the wooden wedges, which will be removed when the formwork is taken down.

5 The window's pointed arch and conical vault is complete. The very top of the outer window is visible at the far end of the embrasure. Slanting shadows indicate the approaching end of another day on the Guédelon site.

6 The finished window, viewed from the outside, its white limestone contrasting with the sandy-coloured stone of the wall. Note the putlog scaffolding, erected so that the masons can work from the outside as well as inside.

WALL WALK FROM THE CHAPEL TOWER

In raising the Chapel Tower, the stonemasons constructed the spiral staircase that leads to the upper storeys at the same time as they built the outer walls. While the Chapel Tower was going up, the masons and carpenters cooperated on fabricating a covered wooden walkway along the curtain wall that connects the Chapel Tower to the western curtain wall. As they made the upper reaches of the curtain wall, the masons positioned three limestone corbels to support the roof of the covered wall walk. Lower down, they had left putlog holes to hold the supports for the gallery floor and in these the carpenters now inserted putlogs, before positioning the floorboards and a guardrail above. They then fixed the top plate and placed the rafters on top. Finally, the roof was fitted with shakes. The walkway skirts around the chapel tower, so that any sentries parading around the battlements would not need to pass through the chapel on their rounds.

The building of the wooden walkway is another reminder of the important role played by carpenters and by wooden structures in medieval castles. The first castles were entirely or almost entirely made of wood, but even after the move to stone structures there were many important and permanent wooden built elements such as this walkway. At Guédelon other timber-framed structures are planned for construction against the inner walls if the courtyard. The mint, in which Guédelon's own coins are made, is one of these.

▼ *The wooden walkway between the Chapel Tower and the western corner tower. Note the putlog supports below, and the stone corbels in the wall above, that support the rafters. The sloping roof of the lower storey is in the foreground.*

CASTLE AND VILLAGE

Guédelon is a typical modest rural castle of the 13th century that would have been home to about 30 people. Around the four walls of the castle is a sprawling village of craft lodges including those of the carpenters, stone masons, tilemakers, ropemakers and basket-weavers – as well as the kitchen gardens, the House of Colour for paints and dyes and, far away in the trees, the water mill.

◀ *The vegetable garden seen from the Great Tower. Guédelon's gardeners are experimenting with growing plants which 13th-century builders would have eaten: onions, radishes and parsnips.*

▶ *A basket maker weaves a wicker basket in her workshop to the north of the castle. Baskets woven from flexible branches of willow or hazel are used to store produce from the garden.*

▲ *The hydraulic water mill would have been an important source of revenue for a medieval lord and also meant an improvement in the peasant's living conditions.*

► *Three blacksmiths forging the metal spindle, part of the mechanism which will make the millstones spin.*

▼ *The new lodge for the carpenters and woodsmen was finished by 2016. There are two working areas – the larger building contains a covered floor on which they can lay out and perform trial assemblies of centrings and other wooden structures needed in the castle-building. The second, smaller building is the new lodge – conveniently close to the forest for the woodcutters.*

ANCILLARY BUILDINGS AND STAFF

A range of additional buildings for the craftspeople, herdsmen, mill workers and others who supported the castle typically grew up around the castle walls or within the outer bailey. Some castles, such Conwy or Caernarfon in Wales, provided protection for quite considerable adjacent planned settlements set within formidable town walls. At Guédelon, these types of buildings cluster in the shady woodland around the main castle site.

At Caernarfon in north Wales, King Edward I set out to create a new capital for the region alongside his castle. This he duly did in 1283–92, at a cost of approximately £3,500, building town walls some 734m (2,408ft) long and featuring two gatehouses and eight defensive towers. At the same time, between 1283 and 1287, town walls were built under his orders in Conwy that measured 1,300m (1,400 yards) in length and included three gatehouses and 21 towers. Here, the work of building the walls and castle cost the then extraordinary amount of £15,000.

These were planned towns, thought to have been inspired by the bastides established in France in this period, such as Aigues-Mortes in southern France. In them, new communities were established to exist alongside the castle, service its needs and be protected by it if necessary; the walled town and castle together were a statement of royal power, a way of settling an area.

Where settlements were not planned, they often grew up around castles anyway, initially to house those constructing the castle, then those who worked in and around the fortifications or otherwise made their living from the castle. Another common occurrence was that the lord or king built a castle on his demesne in the vicinity of an existing settlement.

▲ *Winter in a French village of the early 15th century – bee hives, a sheep pen, a hand cart, and a pitched wooden house are all echoed in the collection of buildings that surround Guédelon's castle. (Getty)*

◄ *The house of a spinner at Guédelon,as it would have been in the 13th century. Baskets of wool wait to be carded and spun into yarn on the wheel. Sleeping quarters are above the work area.*

LIFE ON THE DEMESNE

Under the feudal system, those living on the lord's estate were freemen or villeins – only the freemen were at liberty to leave, and could sell their land or manage it as they pleased; the villeins or serfs were at the mercy of the lord. Freemen living on the estate included the blacksmith, the cobbler who made shoes, the miller who ground people's flour, and the thatchers who thatched the roofs of the cottages. Serfs were typically ploughmen and herdsmen, making their living from the land. They needed the lord's permission, and had to pay a fee if, for example, they wanted to sell their stock or their cottage or even marry off their daughters.

In a medieval village a blacksmith's forge was a special place. Experts say that blacksmiths were seen as having magical, even supernatural, powers because they could somehow - mysteriously - make metal from rock. Blacksmiths were believed to have made a deal with the devil. But there were many stories of them coming off better, outwitting the devil; they could do a job for the devil (say, shoeing his horses) and be rewarded, but would not pay the ultimate price of forfeiting their soul – as people normally did in such tales. Folk tradition held that a blacksmith – like a king or queen – had the power to heal a person by touching them. There are stories of sick children or those with bad illnesses being taken to the forge and placed on the anvil, where the blacksmith would pretend to beat the illness out of them.

▼ *The medieval vegetable garden in the peaceful surroundings of the Guédelon forest lies around 30m (100ft) east of the eastern curtain wall. The farmers grow root vegetables, potherbs such as cabbages and lettuce, and legumes such as peas and beans as well as several aromatic plants.*

In a typical settlement, the people lived in one-room cottages with clay or wattle-and-daub walls and hard earth floors, sharing their eating and sleeping space with their animals and livestock as necessary. There was sometimes also a small area of kitchen garden outside. The fire was on an open hearth and its smoke escaped through the windows, which were not glazed, or at the eaves or through gaps in the thatch. They mostly used wooden or earthenware pots for cooking, although some had an iron pan, and ate at a trestle table sitting on wooden stools. They slept in the same place on mattresses stuffed with straw or flock; any belongings they needed to tidy away were put in a wooden chest. They ate soups or stews made with corn, beans or meal and occasionally a piece of bacon or salted pork, and had cheese and hard bread washed down with ale. The women created home-made clothes for all from wool or linen, washing them in the village stream, perhaps using wooden paddles made by their menfolk.

In the Middle Ages, labourers on a castle site, those working on crafts in adjacent villages and those tilling the land or keeping animals would typically be busy more or less from sunrise to sunset. Their working day would be an average of eight hours a day in autumn and winter and 12 hours a day from Easter through the summer months to the end of September. Those actually at work on building the castle would work only in the summer months. There was a weekend – Sunday was a day of rest, and on Saturday, as well as on the eve of feast days, work stopped around 3pm.

The feast days of the religious years made life more manageable.There were around 90 of these, on which no work was done – they were treated like a Sunday. On average, therefore, people worked 200 days a year.

◂ *The woodturner makes items for domestic use such as bowls, pestles and mortars, goblets, and plates. Here he hollows the interior of a bowl on a pole lathe in his lodge at the edge of the forest. The earliest illustration of a pole lathe is found on a 13th-century manuscript.*

▾ *The woodturner hammers a mandril in to a block of bowl-shaped wood ready for turning. Richard the Lionheart ordered 20,000 turned wooden bowls for his coronation.*

ESSENTIAL SERVICES

The people who made a living from the castle included the bowyer who made bows, the fletcher who made arrows, and the maker of crossbows and bolts. The carpenters worked on fabricating and maintaining machines of war such as the trebuchet, along with many other things. These men and various other craftspeople might have their workshops within the castle boundaries or in the settlements around the fortress on the lord's estate.

At Guédelon, a neat settlement of crafts lodges and other associated buildings has grown up in the beautiful woodland around the castle. Among these are the kiln, water mill and lime kiln. In the medieval period it was quite common for the feudal lord to establish such features and then charge his tenants a levy for using them. He had, after all, had to cover the expense of building a watermill on his land or having a kiln constructed in the first place.

Wood turners

The wood turner is one of the many craftspeople typically found on site, and is responsible for crafting cooking utensils (such as bowls, pestle and mortars, and porringers) and wooden tableware (such as dishes and goblets), as well as tool handles and pulleys for the construction site. This is no mean feat. When making a bowl, for example, the wood

▸ *The huge tracing floor in the new lodge was levelled, then covered with finely sieved sand and lime plaster to create a perfectly flat working surface.*

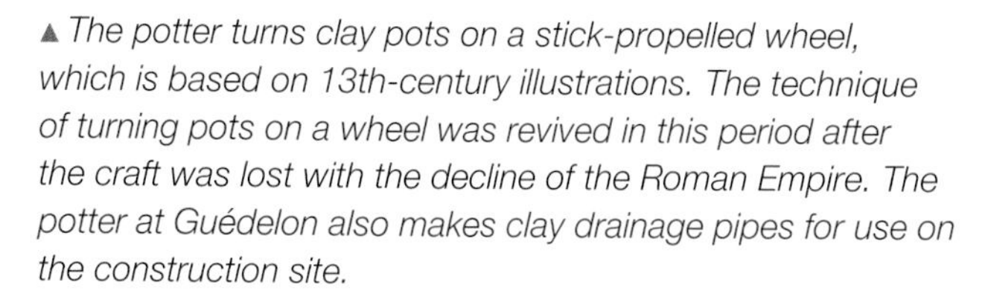

▲ *The potter turns clay pots on a stick-propelled wheel, which is based on 13th-century illustrations. The technique of turning pots on a wheel was revived in this period after the craft was lost with the decline of the Roman Empire. The potter at Guédelon also makes clay drainage pipes for use on the construction site.*

turner first axes out a bowl blank, then hammers a mandrill into its centre, which enables him to fix the bowl on a pole lathe between two metal spikes. A rope, wrapped around the mandrill and tied to a springy pole and a pedal on the ground, makes it possible to turn the piece of wood. With his hook tools, the turner thus first shapes the outside of the bowl, then hollows the interior. At Guédelon, he works mainly in birch, alder, beech, wild cherry and sycamore.

Specialist workshops

Craft lodges at Guédelon include one for the masons, one for the blacksmiths and a combined one for the woodsmen and carpenter-joiners. This latter combined workshop, situated about 100m (325ft) east of the eastern curtain wall, was fitted with a tracing floor large enough for laying out and putting together the wooden parts necessary for building work – for example the roof timbers and hoarding of the Great Tower.

Lime kiln

The craftspeople at Guédelon built and started using a lime kiln to make their own lime putty. To make the kiln, they cooperated with archaeologists at Inrap (the French National

▲ *Like the lime kiln, the tile kiln is built into the ground to the south of the castle. One of the tile makers needs to protect his head and face as he works wood into the fire to raise the temperature high enough. He also wears gloves, a thick apron and sturdy boots.*

▼ *Turned clay pots stacked in the longitudinal kiln in Guédelon forest. The kiln was built with the help and advice of archaeologists; the vault itself is constructed with interlocking clay pots specially made for this purpose.*

◀ *The basket makers work in dappled shade close to their lodge, just to the north of the castle. The base of the Great Tower can be seen behind them. Baskets on the ground wait to have sturdy handles attached to them.*

Institute for Preventative Archaeology) as with the water mill – basing its design on those of medieval kilns found in excavations. To make lime putty, they filled the kiln with small pieces of limestone from the stonemasons' lodge and fired them for four days and three nights continuously. They then left the kiln to cool for several days before taking quick lime out of the kiln and slaking it in wooden tubs filled with water. Immersed in water, the stones swelled, split and turn white – producing lime putty. The initial firing of the lime kiln produced 1,700 litres (about 375 gallons) of lime putty, which the workers stored in airtight containers for later use.

Basket-makers' Lodge and House of Colours

One of the craftswomen's workshops at Guédelon is the basket-makers' lodge, situated at the foot of the Great Tower about 10m (30ft) north of the castle walls on the former site of

▼ *At the House of Colours the lengths of wool are coloured with dyes made from plants grown on site. The dyer uses wild plants like nettles, mosses, tree barks and ferns to make earthy yellows and greens.*

▼ *Smoke from the stove in the house of colours drifts into the forest. The dyer uses specially cultivated 'tinctorial plants' such as madder, pastel, rhubarb root and mignonette to make brighter reds blues and yellows.*

▲ *The dyer hangs out woollen scarves to dry in her workshop. She has used onion skins to produce this bright yellow colour.*

the carpentry workshop. Here, the basket makers weave four-handled willow baskets that are used by the mortar makers and other workers to carry mortar around the site.

At the start of the project, the mortar makers used wooden troughs and buckets, but they found these containers to be very heavy when full of mortar. A solution was required. This was provided when the Guédelon team examined illustrations on medieval manuscripts, which gave them the idea of using much lighter baskets woven in willow for carrying sand and mortar. Fresh wet mortar is, however, highly corrosive, so the bottoms of the baskets are quickly damaged. The basket makers are thus kept busy repairing old baskets just as much as making new ones. They also work with willow and hazel shoots to make beehives, nesting boxes for birds, cases to protect clay gourds and window shutters for the workshops on site.

The House of Colours where earth pigments for use in making paint and plant dyes are produced. It stands some 30m (100ft) east of the eastern wall of the castle and contains a massive stove, the smoke from exits via a flue of unfired bricks built on the southern gable of the building.

Castle Laundry

Typically, villagers on the demesne got by washing their clothes in a stream or lake, but in some castles there was a room set aside for cleaning the castle inhabitants' linens and garments. The laundress was in charge of this process. The water used came from the well or a nearby source of running water – but not the moat, especially if latrines and the waste-water spouts emptied into it. The water was heated and a cleaning agent – maybe lye soap – was added, then the clothes were soaked, and moved around and beaten with wooden paddles.

MAKESHIFT STRUCTURES

Some of the craftsmen and women don't have a lodge and instead work as they make their way around the site. The carpenters can put up a makeshift structure to provide shelter for the mortar makers, for example, who tend to work close to where the mortar is needed. In recent months a wooden structure has also been built in the area where the gatehouse will be raised in the southern curtain wall.

▶ *The carpenters have built a makeshift shelter against the summer sun for the mortar makers. The mortar makers have spread out Guédelon quarry sand on the ground ready for mixing with lime and water. Hand- and horse-drawn carts wait ready for moving materials. Beyond, a wooden hut stands roughly close to where the gatehouse will be built.*

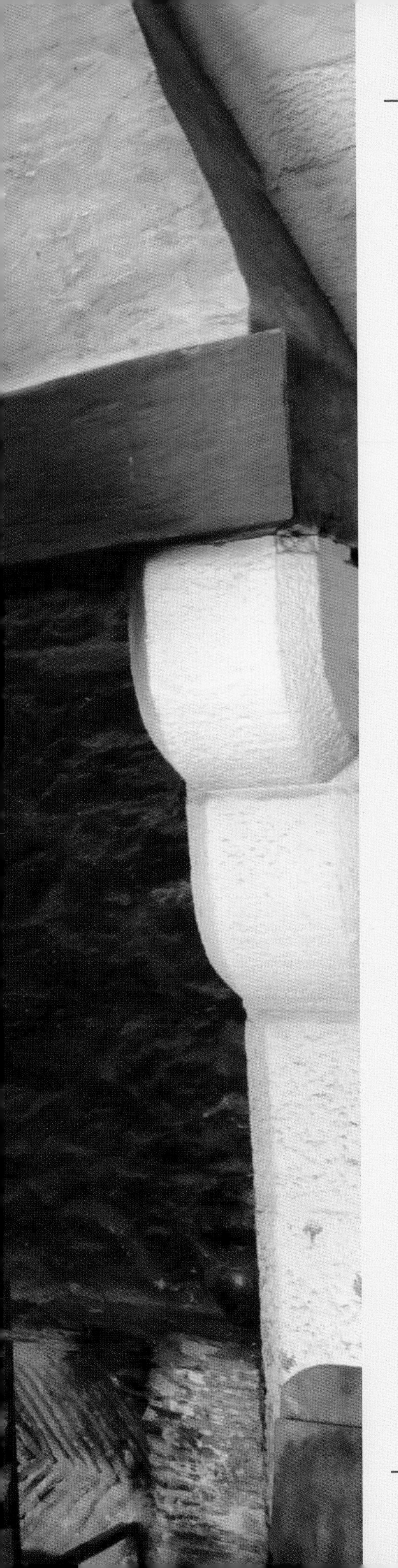

9

THE KITCHEN AND GARDENS

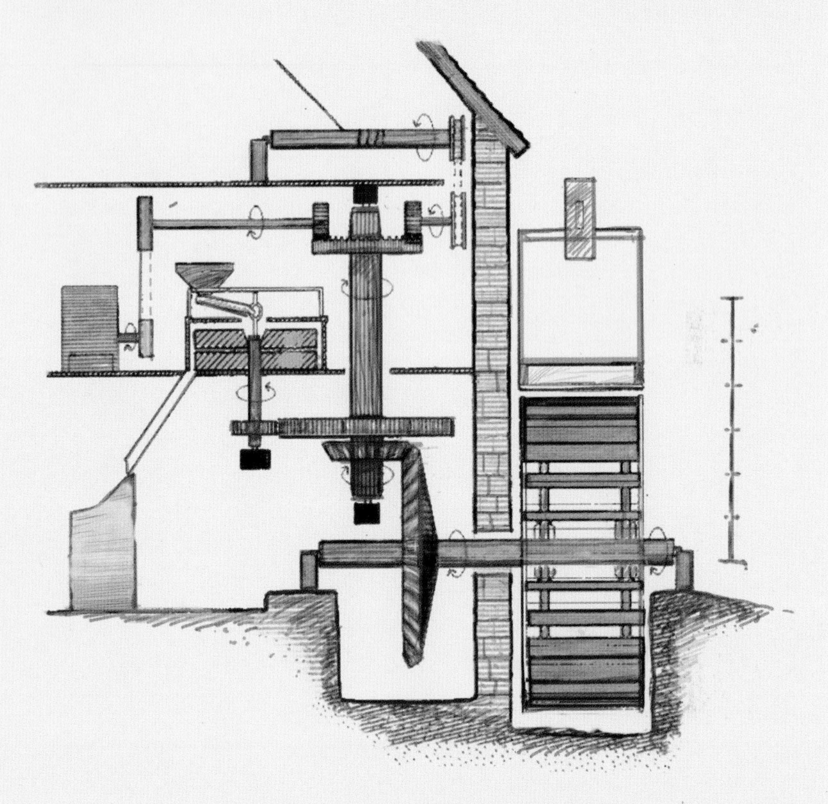

The cook and workers in the kitchen had to feed a large and hungry castle population. In a typical 13th-century castle the kitchen was linked to the great hall by a passage and situated close to a buttery and a pantry, and the task of supplying it with ingredients was huge. Because castles were designed to withstand siege, it was necessary too include gardens, food stores and areas for keeping poultry and livestock. Outside the walls there was usually a water mill, built at the lord's expense and then used, at a price, by the whole community.

SUPPLYING FOOD

Castles and their inhabitants drew on food grown on the lord's demesne beyond the castle walls as well as on the produce of the kitchen gardens and animals kept within the fortified settlement. To make flour, needed for the bread that was such a staple food for everyone, many castles had hand-operated mills or relied on windmills in the vicinity.

A typical kitchen garden in a medieval castle grew root vegetables such as carrots, parsnips, alexanders (similar to asparagus), burdock and skirrets (a vegetable not much grown in the modern era, which has sweet-tasting, bright-white roots). In addition, there would be plenty of legumes such as beans, lentils and peas, as well as lettuce, beets, cabbages and watercress. Several aromatic plants were grown with these. Many of these traditional crops are grown in the garden at Guédelon.

Other foods typically grown included pumpkins, leeks, spinach and onions. Herbs such as rosemary, fennel, mint, sage, borage, parsley, purslayne and garlic were used in salads. These herbs were also scattered on the rush flooring in the great hall to keep smells and pests and insects at bay.

The kitchen garden at Guédelon is situated alongside the House of Colours, about 30m (100ft) beyond the eastern wall, and grows many fruits and vegetables for use in the kitchen.

ANIMALS

A typical castle farmed pigs, poultry, pigeons, geese, goats and even cattle inside or around its walls. The cattle were hungry eaters and in winter had to be fed from stores of straw, so typically the numbers would be kept down to a level just sufficient for breeding in the new spring. What cows there

► *The Guédelon gardeners are cultivating a typical 13th-century kitchen garden, including skirrets and alexanders, and experimenting with medieval watering equipment!*

▼ *Foods typically used in a castle kitchen, including nuts and sees, berries and green vegetables. Note the wooden and wicker containers. (Alamy)*

▼ *In hot weather the pigs love to roll and sleep in the mud. In November pigs were released into the forest to be fattened up on acorns and beechnuts, this was called the pannage.*

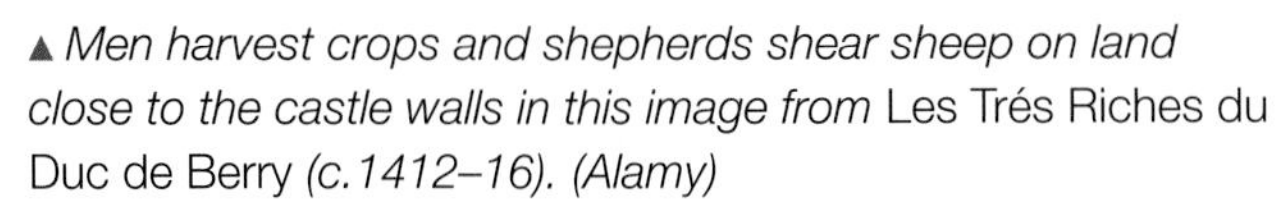

▲ *Men harvest crops and shepherds shear sheep on land close to the castle walls in this image from* Les Trés Riches du Duc de Berry *(c.1412–16). (Alamy)*

were provided milk for making butter and cheese, but the latter was also made from ewes' or goats' milk. There might also be pheasant, partridges and woodcock on the castle grounds, which would provide meat in the autumn.

Pigs were domestic animals who were free to go into and out of the thatched cottages inhabited by those who lived in settlements near and around the castle. On the castle grounds itself there was usually a pigpen in one of the baileys.

ANIMAL PARTS

Other animal parts were put to use – as far as possible, nothing was wasted. Sheep were sheared for their wool, which was a valuable item of trade in many places – notably in England. The hides (skins) of cattle, sheep and goats were used to make leather. Tanners bought cow hides to treat them in their tannery; fellmongers treated the skins of smaller animals, especially sheep. The cow hides often came with horns and hooves attached and tanners generally discarded the hooves and cores of the horns –archaeologists finding these remains know that a tannery was active there. The outer part of the horns were worked by horners. Leather was used to make sheaths and scabbards, harnesses, bottles, gloves and shoes, fine saddles and even some types of armour.

▲ *Sheep graze peacefully beside the Great Tower at Guédelon. Ouessant sheep, named after the isle from which they originate, are a primitive breed close to medieval sheep.*

The pigs would eat whatever they could get hold of, and in hot weather would roll and sleep in the mud; the dried mud on their skin protected them from lice and parasites. In times of peace they were set free in the autumn forest to fatten themselves up by eating beechnuts and acorns.

▼ *Geese are also kept at Guédelon and are free to roam around the crafts village outside the castle walls.*

▲ *The storeroom at Guédelon is on the ground floor of the North Range, adjacent to the kitchen. The walls have been lime washed and part of the floor has been tiled.*

◄ *A storeroom needed high windows and a secure door to prevent pilfering. The carpenters used wooden wedges to hold the door in position while they fitted the iron hinges, which were inserted into grooves they had chiselled on the front and back of the door. The door was held together with braided Guédelon rope while it was finished.*

STORE ROOMS

Supplies were carefully stored in the pantry, buttery and other rooms accessible from the kitchen. Fresh meat, whether farmed or hunted, was often salted to last the winter. The castle stores might also contain salted fish – known as stockfish. Fresh fruit or vegetables that would keep for months, such as apples and onions, were carefully wrapped and kept out of direct light for later use.

A secure storeroom was as essential to the economy of the castle and demesne as the work of the steward. Here, the lord kept not only supplies to feed castle residents but also products from the demesne provided under the feudal system as a kind of tax, such as sacks of flour or grain.

A little while after construction, the storeroom alongside the kitchen in the North Range ground floor at Guédelon was paved and limewashed – modifications that made it look much brighter and seem cleaner. Shelves and barrels were fitted and an oak grain chest, based on 13th-century designs, was carved by the carpenters from a single tree trunk. They then made a wooden lid for it and the blacksmiths made a lock to secure it. The carpenters and blacksmiths also worked together to make lockable wooden doors for the storeroom entrance, the gable wall and the kitchen gable wall.

The castle also imported more exotic supplies not available locally, such as spices, wines or shellfish. Spices were rare and very expensive because they had to be transported from overseas – reputedly an ounce of pepper cost a day's wages for a labourer. Merchants also provided other foods such as raisins, figs and fruits not available locally. The only sweetener aside from fruit was honey, collected from bees kept in hives often mounted on the castle walls. These hives were made of straw or from willow or reeds by the basket makers, who set up their stall in the bailey or, as at Guédelon, just outside the castle walls.

▲ *A hand quern, as used in the kitchen at Guédelon before the water mill was built. Several medieval castles had querns of this type to use in performing 'the daily grind'.*

WHEAT PROCESSING

At Guédelon, before the construction of the watermill the kitchens were fitted with a hand-operated quern, or flour mill. Consisting of two millstones (a runner and a bedstone) seated on a wooden support, the quern was operated by the baker using a pole fixed in the wooden frame. The baker placed the wheat between the stones, then rotated the pole to move the runner stone against the bedstone. After much hard work, the wheat would be ground into coarse, wholemeal flour.

Using a quern in this manner was common practice in medieval times. The castle needed to be self-sufficient in case it was cut off from supplies made at offsite watermills by war or when under siege, so having at least one milling facility within the castle precinct made perfect sense. Records show that Chester Castle had five hand-operated querns in 1301–02, and both Scarborough and Carmarthen castles also had onsite querns. Meanwhile, at Nottingham and Pembroke castles there were horse-operated mills, and at Windsor Castle under Henry III there were four querns. These supplemented the conventional watermills in the Windsor Great Park outside the castle.

Occasionally, watermills were part of the castle's defended area. At Beaumaris Castle there was a watermill beside the dock, both defended by the castle. At Caerphilly Castle, a defended watermill was part of the dam around the defences.

▼ *A carpenter hollows out a trunk to make a chest for the storeroom. He works with a double-headed axe at the interior of the trunk at the edge of the forest, near the carpenters' and woodsmen's lodge.*

▼ *The trunk is in position on the neatly tiled storeroom floor. The carpenters still have to fit the lid they have made for it. Storage containers for foodstuffs needed to be designed so to keep mice and rats at bay as much as possible.*

GUÉDELON'S WATERMILL

At Guédelon, the watermill was constructed with the help of archaeologists from Inrap to ensure it was as authentic as possible. The building was carefully researched and its design based on remains of 11th- and 12th-century watermills found at Thervay in Jura, eastern France. However, unfortunately the remains were incomplete and the carpenters, stonemasons and blacksmiths had to work together to establish how the missing elements must have been made and how the complete structure would have worked.

The hardest part of setting up a mill was putting together the wheel mechanism. To do this the workers at Guédelon made an axle, a rhynd (a support for the runner stone), teeth, a trundle wheel, a lantern gear and paddles. They then assembled the mechanism in situ followed by a considerable process of experimentation. One problem was that they found the running water made the wheel turn too fast or too slowly, or the grindstone was not properly calibrated. The aim was to produce a working mill that produced real ground flour.

1 One of the carpenters hollows out an oak for the mill race – the section that directs running water to the paddle wheel – making small blows with a specialised axe.

2 The paddles were fitted to the wheel while it was horizontal, then moved into a vertical position in the mill race.

3 A carpenter tests the mechanism of the trundle wheel and lantern pinion.

4 A mason dresses the stone for the millstone. It is made of a piece of specially selected limestone.

5 When the sluice is opened water is released into the mill race, which turns the paddles and rotates the wheel.

IN THE KITCHEN: PREPARING FOOD

The castle kitchen typically featured a large hearth and chimney with a facility for spit roasting, cooking over the fire in pots, a bread oven and access to a well or cistern for water. There was also a drain for sluicing out waste water – perhaps, as at Guédelon, issuing via a spout in the outer wall directly into the dry ditch or moat.

Early in the medieval period – even as late as 1200 or so, kitchens and store rooms were free-standing buildings in the bailey often built close to the great hall, or cooking was done on a hearth in the centre of the hall. Later in the period, as fire safety was improved, kitchens were built into the lower storeys of the great hall, linked by a passage that led from an area at the rear shielded by a screen.

At Hen Domen Castle in Wales archaeologists have found fragments of cooking pots in the centre of the area that they believe was the hall, which suggests that cooking was carried out on a hearth at its centre, as was done in the halls of Viking and Anglo Saxon lords. The hall might have been a timber building, but we can't know for sure since only traces of it remain today. At Weoley Castle, now in Birmingham, there are more visible remnants of a 13th-century oak kitchen that survived better than most because the waterlogged site helped preserve the lower walls. It measured 12.5 x 7m (40 x 23ft) and dated to *c.*1260 at the latest, and had a large stone fireplace used for cooking.

▼ In spite of some modern furniture, the kitchen at Chateau de Pierreclos, a castle close to Guédelon and built in the 14th century, is remarkably authentic and would have been similarly equipped. (Alamy)

KITCHEN FIREPLACE

When a castle kitchen was built of stone it had a substantial fireplace with a chimney. This enabled the cook to provide for large numbers of people by roasting sizeable animals or pieces of meat – a big boar, for example – on a spit. This could cause issues in terms of starting and maintaining a good fire: the wider and more open a fireplace, the harder it can be to get a draw on the fire.

There is evidence that this was a problem for which master masons sought solutions. At Carlisle Castle gatehouse – built in 1378 by master mason John Lewyn – for example, an

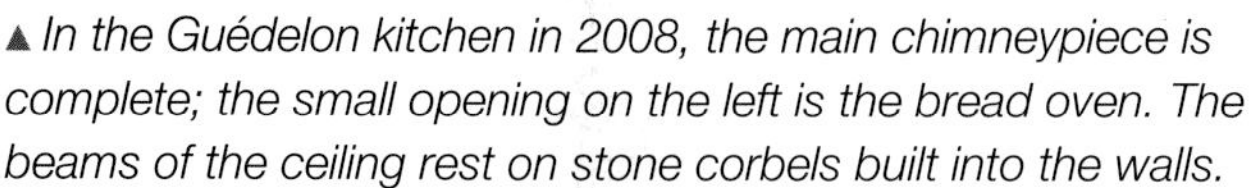

▲ *In the Guédelon kitchen in 2008, the main chimneypiece is complete; the small opening on the left is the bread oven. The beams of the ceiling rest on stone corbels built into the walls.*

▲ *Produce of the Guédelon kitchen garden has been harvested ready to be taken to the kitchen. The basket contains beets, leeks, carrots, chick peas and pot herbs.*

open-and-close aperture in the back of one of the kitchen fireplaces seems to have been used to address this difficulty; the cook could open the aperture to create a draught if one was needed to draw the fire.

For the kitchen fireplace at Guédelon the masons built a brick chimney stack that rose to the roof of the North Range, and the carpenters constructed a massive lintel for the fireplace in the kitchen. Guédelon's cooks are able to roast chickens on the spit, simmer soups and stews in iron pots, bake bread in the bread oven located in the back of the fireplace, and create medieval cakes and sweet or savoury tarts baked in ceramic dishes.

Initially, due to the size of the fireplace, the cook and baker encountered the same problem of insufficient draught from the fire almost certainly experienced by their medieval counterparts. They solved it by adding an extra piece of wood under the lintel and also raising the height of the hearth with unfired blocks of clay.

Ovens

Bread ovens were often cut into the back of the fireplace, as at Guédelon. They were flat-bottomed with a domed upper part and a small opening to the front. The baker lit a fire inside the bread oven to get the temperature to the right level; the smoke could rise up the main fireplace chimney. The baker could then scrape out the embers into the main fireplace as desired, and would slide the bread in and out on a long-handled wooden shovel.

► *The fireplace and bread oven under construction at Guédelon as the walls of the kitchen are built. When in use the kitchen fire is lit in the right part of the fireplace and a separate fire lit at the back of the bread oven. The smoke from both goes up the chimney.*

◂ *The Guédelon baker at work, preparing loaves and rolls. The fire has already been lit behind him, and when the oven is at the right temperature he will scrape out the embers before using a long-handled wooden paddle to place the loaves directly on to the oven floor.*

This worked well in theory but, as the baker found at Guédelon, it was very easy to make the oven too hot and burn the bread, and the right method was only discovered by trial and error. The oven could also be a fire hazard and in some castles was constructed in its own room for this very reason. We know from accounts dating to 1250 that Montgomery Castle, for example, had a separate kitchen and bakehouse, for the accounts detail costs associated with repairing the two rooms and installing a new oven in the bakehouse.

▾ *Chickens cooking on the metal spit before the fire in the Guédelon kitchen. The spit is turned using the handle on the right side. The layers of hooks on the stand make it possible to lower or raise the skewered meat. Basting juices are kept warm in the frying pan and applied with a sprig of rosemary.*

KITCHEN STAFF AND EQUIPMENT

The cook was in charge of a team of kitchen staff. Scullions were those at the bottom of the pile, condemned to carry out the most menial tasks in the kitchen, such as cleaning pots and dishes, sluicing down work surfaces or drawing water from the well if necessary. In smaller castles the cook might have to make do with a handful of helpers. But in grand noble or royal households, the kitchen included specialists for different tasks such as roasting meats, making sauces, watching the simmering pots, and making bread and pies. Others worked at grinding spices with a mortar and pestle, making breadcrumbs, churning butter and so on.

Other aspects of provisioning the great hall at mealtimes had their own hierarchy of staff: the butler was in charge of the buttery, where wine and ale was kept in bottles and large butts or barrels, and was responsible for ensuring a good supply for the lord's high table. The pantler, meanwhile, was in charge of the pantry – where bread was kept; the name came from the French for bread, *pain*. Fresh and cured meats were stored in the larder.

Equipment in medieval kitchens was basic, and there was usually not much of it. Standard items included a large cast iron pot or cauldron and a smaller cooking pot, which were set on or hung above the fire. There was also as a spit, often supported on a freestanding frame, for roasting meat over the fire, together with spoons for measuring, beating and stirring, and shears or scissors for cutting. An inventory of the equipment in the kitchen at Chepstow Castle included just one spit and three cauldrons.

At Guédelon, chicken and pork is cooked on a metal spit in front of the fire. In medieval castles, there was often a specialist in charge of the spit – in some kitchens, this was

► *A reconstruction of the kitchen in the Great Tower of Dover Castle as it looked in the reign of Henry II (1154-89). Note the mortar and pestle and terracotta crockery, the fire pit and three-legged cooking pots. (Mary Evans)*

the job of the 'spit boys'. They had to work in extreme temperatures very close to the fire and deal with blistering caused by handling the hot metal of the spit handle.

As now, decent illumination and cleanliness were key in food-preparation areas, and whitewashing the walls helped with both these requirements. At Guédelon, too, the kitchen was whitewashed and paving tiles were laid on the floor so that it could easily be kept clean.

WATER SUPPLY

The cook and kitchen workers needed water for washing vegetables and cooking, and also for sluicing away waste. To meet this demand, a well was often situated near the kitchen. At Bodiam Castle, for instance, there was a well in the basement of a tower next door to the kitchen that could only be accessed from that room, indicating it was solely used for cooking purposes. At Harlech Castle, however, the well was in the north inner curtain wall next to the bakehouse and main chapel, while at Chester Castle, a system of lead pipes connected the well, which was in the outer bailey, with a cistern that supplied the kitchen on the Great Hall's east side.

In the Guédelon kitchen, there is a floor-level drain for washing that directs used water out into the ditch behind the castle. A similar set-up existed in many medieval castle kitchens, for example at Warkworth, where the drain led to a spout that guides the water to fall at a distance from the wall.

BREWERS AND VINTNERS

A castle's brewer was in charge of making huge quantities of beer and ales. He brewed ale on site in the brewhouse using hops, barley, wheat, malt and grain: the ale did not last well, so he had to work all the time, not just seasonally, in order to meet requirements. Sometimes beers and ale would also be purchased locally if demand was greater than usual. Depending on where the castle was, wine might also be made seasonally on the demesne, using locally grown grapes. The vintner was in charge. This would be the case, of course, in Italy or France, and certainly in Burgundy, where Guédelon is situated. Further north, wine was imported from other countries, and transported to the castle in butts or barrels. The butler, in charge of the buttery, looked after bottles and barrels of wine once it was on site. (Getty)

FEEDING THE CASTLE

The food prepared and served in the castle hall varied a great deal from day to day – from simple everyday roasts to elaborate multi-course feasts that featured rare and expensive ingredients. Of course, not every resident of the castle had access to such delicacies, although on feast days sometimes even those at the lowest end of the hall could eat well. Often, however, for the lower orders, rations were more meagre, with the best foods reserved for the nobility.

A TYPICAL DAY

For most people, the main meal of the day was taken at 10.00 or 11.00 in the morning. Before that, on rising, people might simply have a drink of ale and perhaps eat a piece of bread; the lord, his family and associates sometimes would stretch to a glass of wine and some meat served with bread.

The main meal in the castle was more likely to include meat for all – perhaps bacon, pork, mutton or beef. In early Spring, when fresh game wasn't yet available and the winter butchering was months ago, only salted meat and fish might be left in the larder. This is when spices such as pepper, nutmeg, ginger and cloves would be relied on; though expensive, they were often necessary to mask the flavour of less-than-fresh meat. A third meal, supper, was served in the evening but was much lighter than the main dinner, consisting of pigeon pie, perhaps, or a light dish of fish such as sturgeon. Lighter, that is, unless the lord was entertaining guests or hosting a banquet.

▲ *Skinning the boar. Retainers would get to work dealing with animals killed by the lord and his followers on the hunt. This miniature is from a 14th-century French manuscript. (Getty)*

CASTLE FOOD AND DRINK

The main part of any meal for the higher classes would be based around meat and fish, although there would also be vegetable dishes and desserts. The meat itself, depending on type, cut and age, was generally stewed, grilled or spit roasted, although sometimes it was minced and served with herbs, breadcrumbs and milk in a kind of meat patty. People were happy to eat birds such as gulls or starlings, herons and peacocks. If a hunting trip had been a success, there would be venison or wild boar, while other wild meat such as hare, rabbit and game birds would be supplied by castle staff, hunted with the help of hunting dogs trained to flush out or fetch quarry. Fish was often on the menu, always on Fridays and in Lent when the Church decreed that meat could not be served. Fish might come from the moat, local streams or

▼ *Salted fish, such as eels, salmon, bream and trout, was served when fresh fish was not available, especially in inland areas. Fish was often cooked in ale and salted water or fried.*

► *An* arboulastre *(herb tart) from the Guédelon kitchen, a medieval savoury tart made with eggs and seasonal herbs including fresh mint. Mint is both an aid to digestion and helps keep breath fresh.*

rivers, and some castles kept fishponds. Salted herring or stockfish were served when fresh fish was not available.

To drink, there would be wine and beer, depending on status. The finest wines would be reserved for the nobles, who had their own wine glass or goblet, but lower down the hall the lower classes would be served beer, which they often had to drink from a shared jug. Water from the river, moat or elsewhere was generally not safe to drink, and so even children drank beer, which after the brewing process would be free of contamination, and was much weaker than the stronger beers we have today. Children may have also occasionally been given milk to drink – but historians believe milk was usually reserved for making butter and cheese, which was essentially a way of preserving it, as milk in these times was seasonal.

SEATING AND STATUS

A few of the highest-ranking diners had chairs but most people sat on benches; the English word banquet is derived from Old French for 'little bench'. Everyone dined on trestle tables; the lord and highest-ranking nobles on a raised dais and the lower orders in the main body of the hall. Salt, which was rare and highly valued, was placed in the centre of the high table; there was none available for the lower orders – this is the origin of the traditional English reference to being 'above or below the salt' when discussing social rank.

On the high table, sliced meat was served by liveried servants on a silver platter to the lord and his family and guests. In the lower hall, people typically helped themselves from a shared dish called a mess and often ate off slabs of bread called trenchers, although sometimes the bread was instead placed in a bowl and covered with stew or soup, or had meat paste spread on it. People ate sliced meat with their fingers – they often had no implements beyond a knife, which they would provide themselves.

Table manners were important, especially at the high table, and manuals were issued advising people how to behave politely. The 15th-century French *Les Contenances de la Table* ('Table Ways') instructed people to wipe their mouth before drinking from the shared jug and said they should avoid scratching themselves or picking their teeth at table, among other words of advice.

▲ *The involvement in the hunt of many members of the medieval court, including ladies, is clear from this 15th-century Flemish tapestry. It is one of four tapestries that once hung in Hardwick Hall, owned by the Countess of Shrewsbury, better known as 'Bess of Hardwick'.*

TO THE HUNT

Sometimes the lord and his entourage would devote the whole day to hunting, riding out with horses and dogs (and a falcon) to hunt deer and wild boar in the forests. This served not only as entertainment and exercise for all concerned – honing all of the participants' skills in the process, and training the young men in horse riding and skills needed for the battlefield – but it also helped to boost the castle's meat supply and enabled the lord to take stock of the condition of the estate and the creatures on it. When out hunting, the party, which would typically include the ladies of the castle and various grooms and retainers, would take food with them from the castle kitchens for a midday meal. This might consist of cold meats and pastries, washed down with wine, and handed out by servants.

FEAST AT GLOUCESTER CASTLE

Feasts were often extremely elaborate and enormously expensive affairs, consisting of multiple courses and a staggering quantity of food. For example, Henry III, at one such event in 1246 – held in one of his favourite residences, the now-demolished Gloucester Castle – ordered more than 1,000 hares, rabbits and partridges, 5,000 chickens, 10,000 eels, 90 boars, more than 30 peacocks and 36 swans.

AFTERWORD

Work continues apace at Guédelon Castle, 20 years after building work began in May 1997 and 19 years after it was first opened to the public. This time span is considerably longer than a typical medieval castle would have taken to build. Experts estimate that a 13th-century castle of the size and status of Guédelon would probably have taken 12–15 years to complete; The Louvre – a larger, royal castle – took just 10 years to build, while King Richard I of England oversaw the building of his majestic Château-Gaillard in an extraordinary 12–18 months. The Guédelon team will take longer than their medieval counterparts because, unlike on a royal construction site, there are not thousands of workers; very often they are reviving almost forgotten techniques and, most importantly, at least half of their time is devoted to explaining their work to the visiting public.

At the end of each season Guédelon looks more and more like a finished castle. The most noticeable developments during the building season of 2017, during which this book was written, have been in the rise of the gatehouse and the interior of the western corner tower. The dimensions of the gatehouse have been scaled down compared to the original plan, which was deemed too ostentatious. The new plan is closer to the scale and size of the type of gatehouse that would have been built by a modest, low-ranking lord such as the fictitious Lord of Guédelon. Instead of protruding into the courtyard, the inner walls of the gatehouse run directly from the east to west corner towers, creating a less imposing edifice and cutting overall building costs.

Before a team of masons began work on the gatehouse's twin towers they needed to prepare the ground, as this area of the castle enceinte had been left untouched for more than 15 years. Over the years rainwater had inevitably soaked into the masonry – potentially washing away some of the mortar. To check that the base of the towers was still solid and did not contain hollows or 'galleries', the masons spent some time pouring buckets of water onto the ground around the tower bases. If the water soaked away too quickly it suggested there were galleries, and they poured liquid mortar in to consolidate the masonry and ensure it would be able to support the weight of the gatehouse.

Through much of the season the double-drummed treadwheel winch was in position between the two towers of the gatehouse keeping the masons well supplied with building materials. On either side of the main gate the masons began

▼ *The east and west towers of the gatehouse have been steadily rising through the 2017 season. Work has also been progressing on the pigeon-loft tower in the western corner.*

◄ *A worker unloads building materials from the double-drummed treadwheel winch for use in the eastern gatehouse tower.*

► *On the spacious tracing floor in their lodge, the carpenter-joiners prepare the roof timbers for the chapel tower roof.*

constructing chambers in the towers that will eventually be fitted out as shooting galleries – rooms from which bowmen could operate. In the western tower of the gatehouse three of the four planned arrow loops have been built. The inner walls of the tower are now 1.8m (6ft) high.

PORTCULLIS

In the eastern gatehouse tower the masons are constructing a spiral staircase, and this year have built up the jambs of the door to a height of 1m (3ft) and fixed the first two steps. This staircase will lead to an upper chamber from which the mechanism for the portcullis will be operated. Inside the gatehouse passage the first grooved stones in which the portcullis will slide have been fixed. In the 2018 season, the huge arch linking the east and west towers of the gatehouse will be constructed, and three flanking arrow loops will be built in the eastern tower.

PIGEON-LOFT TOWER

Another team of masons has been hard at work in the western corner tower. Here they have built two barrel-vaulted corridors, two arrow loops, two windows and a staircase formed of stone steps embedded in the wall. This tower is the one earmarked to be the pigeon-loft tower, and in the 2018 season the uppermost chamber will be given a wooden ceiling and be fitted with nesting boxes for the comfort of its future residents. Two doors will be added to allow people to walk through the pigeon-loft from the western wall to the southern curtain wall.

CHAPEL TOWER ROOF

Meanwhile the carpenters have been working on hewing the 265 pieces needed to assemble the pepper pot roof timbers of the Chapel Tower. All the hewing has been finished, and now the many joints have to be cut in the different planes. The curved wall plates are currently assembled on the tracing floor in the carpenter-joiners' and woodsmen's lodge. Around the middle of the 2018 season, the roof timbers will be transported and hoisted onto the tower using specially adapted lifting machinery, before being assembled in situ.

The tile makers have been producing and firing the many hundreds of trapezoidal roof tiles that will be used to roof the chapel tower.

WHAT LIES AHEAD FOR GUÉDELON CASTLE?

There are another 10, 12 or even 15 years of construction ahead, but the team of master-builders don't intend to limit their ambitions to the castle walls. Plans are already underway to build a medieval town of the type that would have been built under the protection of a castle. Inside the castle itself, the walls will be painted, some windows glazed and wooden shutters fitted.

Having built up an unprecedented level of expertise and insight into medieval construction and craft techniques, the project will continue to be a fascinating example of living archaeology; by running and maintaining it, the Guédelon team will no doubt continue to uncover invaluable practical information about 13th-century castle life.

► *A mason works on an arch in the pigeon-loft tower. The wooden support is still in place beneath the arch. The chapel tower is visible in the background.*

GLOSSARY

Almoner Member of the lord's household with responsibility for his giving of alms to the poor.
Alure *See* wall walk.
Apse Usually vaulted, semicircular projecting area of building
Arcade Series of arches borne on columns or piers.
Arrow loop Slit in wall through which bowmen and crossbowmen fired arrows and bolts when defending the castle.
Ashlar Square-edged dressed masonry, laid in horizontal courses.
Bailey Defended castle courtyard; in a motte-and-bailey castle, the area – enclosed by a ditch and palisade – around the central motte or mound on which stood the castle's main tower that housed the lord and was the castle's ultimate refuge.
Banker mason A mason who shapes stone for construction.
Barbican Outer fortification intended to provide protection for the castle gateway.
Barrel vault Arched vault between two walls.
Bartizan Overhanging turret added for defence or ornament, usually at a corner where two walls met and, when built for defensive purposes, enabling castle defenders to get a clear view in two directions.
Bastion Typically angular projection from curtain wall designed to give defenders a good angle of fire.
Batter Splayed base added to a curtain wall to strengthen the castle's defences by making the wall harder to scale or otherwise assault.
Battlements Crenellated top of curtain wall, with crenels (gaps) and merlons (raised defensive sections). Behind the battlements, sentries and bowmen/crossbowmen patrolled the wall walk.
Belfry Mobile wooden siege tower that could be moved right up to the castle walls during an attack.
Berm Strip of ground between the castle ditch and its curtain wall.
Blind arcade Series of arches without openings, used as decoration on a solid wall.
Boss Central stone, often decorated, in a vault. *See also* keystone.
Buttery Service room associated with the great hall, generally accessed via a screens passage, and used to store wine and ale in butts and bottles. *See also* pantry
Buttress Masonry support built to make a wall stronger or work against the lateral force exerted by a roof or vault.
Centring Timber frame used to support vaults and arches while they are being built, then removed once the structures are complete and self-supporting.
Chamber Private residential room in the castle, contrasted to the public space of the great hall.
Cistern Water-storage tank.
Constable Official in charge of running and defending the castle when its lord was absent.
Corbel Stone projecting from a wall to support a timber structure (such as a roof, floor or hoarding) or a stone archaeological element.
Crenels Lower sections of a parapet – the gaps between the merlons along the battlements – through which bowmen and crossbowmen fired. Also known as an embrasure, *see also* merlon.
Cruck Curved timbers cut from a single tree that when placed together form an inward-curving arch that rises from the ground to the roof level in order to support a building's wall and roof.
Curtain wall Outer defensive wall enclosing castle grounds.
Demesne Part of the lord's landholding that was farmed on his account personally, and not leased out to others.
Donjon Tower stronghold in Anglo-Norman castle (from French *donjon*, and Latin *dominium*, 'lordship'). Similar to 'tower keep'.
Drum tower Rounded tower projecting from a curtain wall.
Embrasure Splayed opening in a wall for an arrow loop or window; also an alternative term for crenel.
Enceinte Enclosing fortified wall around a town or castle.
Fictive masonry Lines painted on a wall to imitate those of ashlar stonework.
Forebuilding Projection from the front of the keep housing the entrance.
Gable Triangular section of wall at the end of a building between two sloping areas of roofing.
Garderobe Alternative name for latrine.
Groin vault A type of vault constructed from intersecting barrel vaults; the edge (arris) where the two vaults meet is called the groin.
Hall keep Lower-lying form of tower keep.
Hammer-beam roof Timber roof in which hammer beams (horizontal elements that project from the base of the structure) support the weight.
Hoardings Wooden structures at the top of castle walls or wall towers that provided a fighting platform for defensive bowmen and crossbowman and guards; sometimes kept permanently in position and sometimes removable so they could be fitted only in times of war.
Keep Alternate name for great tower or donjon.
Keystone Central stone in a vault or arch that locks the others in position. *See also* boss.
Latrine Privy or toilet.
Levelling course Horizonal line of dressed stone in a stretch of rough walling, used by masons to check that the masonry is level.
Lintel Horizontal element spanning an opening such as a window or door that generally carries the weight above the opening.
Machicolation Stone projection at the top of a curtain wall with a slotted floor through which arrows could be fired and missiles dropped. The same word was used for slots in the

roof of the gateway passage through which guards could attack incomers attempting to break into the castle.

Mangonel Stone-throwing siege engine. *See also* trebuchet.

Marshal Official in lord's household in charge of the horses and soldiers.

Merlon Raised section of the parapet on the battlements. The merlons provided cover for bowmen, crossbowmen and other soldiers on the walkway around the top of defensive curtain wall; they fired through the gaps (corbels).

Mortise Timber socket into which a tenon (another piece of timber) is fitted.

Motte Man-made mound or natural hill; central feature of Anglo-Norman 'motte-and-bailey' castle. A tower, often built of wood, housed the lord's accommodation and was the refuge if the castle came under attack.

Mural tower Tower built into the curtain wall.

Murder holes Alternative name for a type of machicolation in the roof above the entrance in a gatehouse, used for firing down upon or dropping missiles on soldiers attempting to storm the gatehouse; could also be used for pouring water to douse fires set by attackers.

Outwork Outer fortification, built beyond main castle walls.

Padstone Stone supporting a timber post.

Palisade Wooden fence or barrier set into the earth, sometimes made of individual stakes.

Pantry Service room associated with the great hall, generally accessed via the screens passage, and used to store bread. *See also* buttery.

Parapet Raised stone wall, part of the battlements. When crenellated it has crenels and merlons in its top part.

Pier Vertical supporting element in an arch.

Piscina Basin in a chapel, to the side of the altar, for washing the chalice, paten, ciborium and other vessels used in celebrating Mass.

Plinth Projecting part at the base of a wall.

Portcullis Wooden grille, often encased in metal and with sharp points in its lower part, used as an additional barrier in the castle gateway. It ran in grooves at the sides of the gateway and was raised and lowered by chain using a winch device situated above the opening in the gatehouse guardroom. The portcullis was a formidable weapon when dropped suddenly to attack/deter invaders.

Postern gate Rear entrance/exit to castle. Usually small and suitable only for those on foot.

Quoins Dressed corner stones.

Ravelin Triangular fortified outwork.

Rendering Plaster on wall, typically limewashed.

Revetment Timber or stone wall on the side of a ditch.

Rib Arch that supports a vault.

Rib vault A type of vault in which ribs (stone arches) carry the weight of the structure.

Romanesque Refers to 11–12th-century architecture; in England also known as Norman.

Sally port Alternative name for postern or rear gate.

Scarp Edge of the earth platform on which the castle is constructed; the sloping inner edge of the dry ditch.

Screens passage Passageway leading off the rear of the great hall, hidden from view by a screen, and connecting to food and drink storage and preparation areas – the buttery, pantry and kitchen.

Shaft Column that is part of a window surround or door jamb.

Shell keep Masonry wall enclosing the flat top of a motte (mound), typically raised to replace the motte palisade in a motte-and-bailey castle.

Solar Early form of private chamber in a castle, used by the lord and family, typically off the upper floor in the great hall and giving on to a gallery.

Talus Splayed base to a wall, taller than a batter.

Tas-de-charge French term, for which there is no equivalent in English, given to the lower courses of ribs of a Gothic vault.

Tiltyard Long enclosed area used by knights and squires to practise jousting.

Tracery Patterned wood or stonework in a window.

Trebuchet Stone-throwing siege engine that uses counterpoise weights to generate force.

Vault Arched roof made of stone.

Voussoir Stone wedge that is part of an arch.

Wall walk Walkway/fighting platform along the inner part at the top of a curtain wall, behind and protected by battlements – used by sentries and bowmen/crossbowmen. Also known as an alure.

Ward Alternative name for a bailey – a castle courtyard.

Wattle and daub Combination of a wooden lattice (wattle) and clay or earth (daub) used to fill in wall panels in a building erected with a timber frame.

Webbing Infill of masonry or rubble in a vault.

WHO'S WHO

Edward I, King of England, reigned 1272–1307
Fought in the Ninth Crusade (1271–72) while Prince Edward, crushed Welsh and Scottish rebellions, commissioned building of Flint, Aberystwyth, Rhuddlan, Harlech, Conwy, Caernarfon and Beaumaris castles.

Henry II, King of England, reigned 1154–89
His clash with Archbishop Thomas Becket led to Becket's death in 1170. Significant building work on castles at Arundel, Bamburgh, Dover, Hastings, Kenilworth, Newcastle-upon-Tyne, Orford and Windsor.

John Lewyn active 1370s–90s
Master mason based in northern England, served Durham Priory and the Bishop of Durham, then worked for the Crown in the north of England. Carried out important building work at Castle Bolton in Yorkshire, Carlisle Castle gatehouse in Cumberland, Roxburgh Castle in the Scottish Borders and the Great Tower at Warkworth Castle in Northumberland.

Master James of St Georges, *c.*1230–1309
Master mason, from 1285 Master of the Royal Works in Wales. Worked on Flint, Rhuddlan, Conway, Harlech, Caernarfon and Beaumaris castles, and at Linlithgow and Stirling castles in Scotland in 1302–04. He was born in Savoy and his name is thought to have come the castle he designed near Lyon, France, that of Saint-Georges-d'Espéranche.

Maurice the Engineer, flourished 1174–87
Master mason/engineer to King Henry II. Carried out significant work at Newcastle-upon-Tyne and Dover castles.

Philip II, King of France, reigned 1180–1223
Extended French territory at the expense of the English Crown and was named 'Augustus' by the French chronicler Rigord. Built the Louvre in Paris and many castles in standardised 'Philippien' style modelled on this Paris fortress.

Richard I, King of England, reigned 1189–99
Lauded as a great warrior and military leader and nicknamed 'Lionheart', Richard was closely involved in the design and construction of his castle at Gaillard in 1196–98.

William I, King of England, reigned 1066–87
Duke of Normandy who led the Norman invasion in England in 1066. Founded castles at Pevensey, Hastings, Dover and Wallingford and the Tower of London, among others.

William Marshall, 1st Earl of Pembroke, 1146–1219
English statesman, celebrated by Stephen Langton, Archbishop of Canterbury, as 'the greatest knight that ever lived'. He rose from relatively humble origins largely through success in fighting tournaments in France, and served Henry II and Richard I. Undertook important building work at Pembroke and Chepstow castles.

INDEX

ACKNOWLEDGEMENTS

Unless otherwise stated images are provided and reproduced with the permission of Guedelon. Images marked (Cadw) are reproduced with the kind permission of the Cadw Photographic Library (Welsh Castles) © Crown copyright (2017). Thanks to Hedingham Castle for the photos on page 99 and to David Anstiss page 94br. Additional images are provided by Shutterstock, Getty, Alamy and Mary Evans.

Guédelon welcomes visitors from March to October each year. Advice on how to get there can be found at www.guedelon.fr, where you can also sign up for newsletters.
Guédelon, D955, 89520 Treigny, France
Tel : + 33 (0)3 86 45 69 15
Standard : 03 86 45 66 66

Artworks by Simon Smith,
Design by Nigel Partridge

First published in February 2018

British Library Cataloguing in Publication Data
A catalogue record for this book is available from the British Library.

ISBN 978 1 78521 147 8

Library of Congress catalog card no. 2017949635
Published by Haynes Publishing, Sparkford, Yeovil, Somerset BA22 7JJ, UK
Tel: 01963 440635
Int. tel: +44 1963 440635
Website: www.haynes.com

Haynes North America Inc.
861 Lawrence Drive, Newbury Park, California 91320, USA

Printed and bound in Malaysia

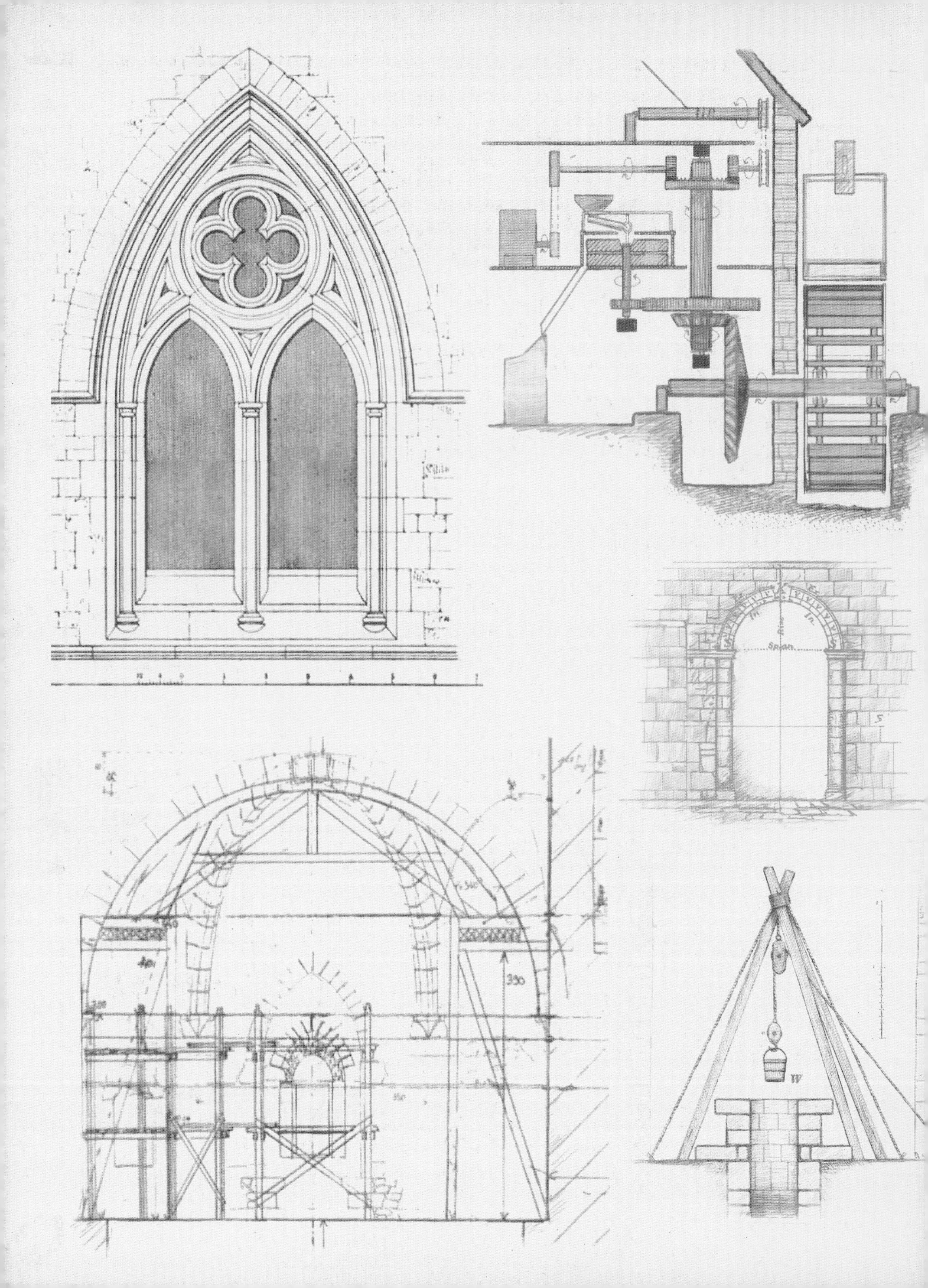

Span
Rise
350
W